BETTER TOGETHER

BETTER TOGETHER

Bishop David Sheppard
and
Archbishop Derek Worlock

Hodder & Stoughton
LONDON SYDNEY AUCKLAND TORONTO

ILLUSTRATION CREDITS

Front cover *Liverpool Daily Post & Echo;* **Back cover** *Sue Williams;* **Page 1** *(both) Catholic Pictorial;* **Page 2** *(above) Liverpool Daily Post & Echo, (below) Catholic Pictorial;* **Page 3** *(all) Catholic Pictorial;* **Page 4** *(above) Mercury Press Agency, (below) Liverpool Daily Post & Echo;* **Page 5** *Liverpool Daily Post & Echo;* **Page 6** *(both) Liverpool Daily Post & Echo;* **Page 7** *(above) L'Osservatore Romano, (below) Liverpool Daily Post & Echo;* **Page 8** *(both) Liverpool Daily Post & Echo;* **Page 9** *(both) Bob Wilkes;* **Page 10** *Catholic Pictorial;* **Page 11** *(above) Liverpool Daily Post & Echo, (below) Colin Thomas and Terry Mealey;* **Page 12** *(above) Geoff Roberts, (below) Liverpool Daily Post & Echo;* **Page 13** *(both) Terry Mealey;* **Page 14** *(above) Catholic Pictorial, (below) Open Eye;* **Page 15** *(both) Open Eye;* **Page 16** *(above) Open Eye, (below) Sue Williams.*

British Library Cataloguing in Publication Data

Sheppard, David
   Better together.
   1. Liverpool (Merseyside) – Social
   conditions – 20th century   2. Liverpool
   (Merseyside) – Social conditions –
   Religious aspects – Christianity
   I. Title   II. Worlock, Derek
   261.8'3   BT738

ISBN 0 340 41848 6

BETTER TOGETHER

CONTENTS

INTRODUCTION

When we arrived in Liverpool within months of one another in the mid-1970s, people assumed that we were strangers. So separate were we expected to be in background and in office that we frequently found ourselves introduced as if we were meeting for the first time. In fact we had known each other slightly when serving in the East End of London more than ten years earlier. We shared many of the same interests, which presumably had played some part in our appointments to Liverpool with its social problems and vibrant traditions. From the time of our arrival together, it was plain that we must give high priority to trying to help replace a diminished but residual sectarianism of old religious bitterness with a positive partnership in Christian mission.

This book is about how we have tried to respond together to the challenge which faced us then and to a great extent faces us still. We do not, of course, pretend to have made major progress in solving the economic problems of Merseyside, nor the even more intractable difficulties standing in the way of Christian unity. We believe that the unity and renewal of the Church are inextricably bound up with the unity and renewal of the human community. Our story is about discovering and working out deep convictions that in both church life and in the wider community of today's society we act better together.

The lessons we offer our readers have not been learnt in the serenity of a lecture room or on an ecclesiastical commission. Though a two-fold theme runs throughout the book, it is neither a handbook of economics and social theory, nor a theological compendium. Much of the experience recorded is personal but we have not attempted a joint autobiography. Our story is set in the context of one particular city with its confusing history of division. The lessons we have learnt have been hammered out in the sometimes white-hot forge of a post-industrial city going through years of momentous and painful change.

In setting about our task we have been helped by several important factors. Although we are of different traditions and readily, if regretfully, acknowledge certain doctrinal differences which divide us, we are conscious of our overwhelming allegiance to Christ. We have developed an increasing understanding of what we share through our faith and baptism, and of the mission which flows from the task that Christ left to all his followers. In our concern for our neighbour we have found immense community needs to which there are no specific denominational answers, but in which there has been much to do together. We have drawn real inspiration from the spirit of those we have been called to serve, and found great support from those who have worked with us. Another particular strength has been the fact that we enjoy each other's friendship and trust.

After working some years together we came to recognise that, with the collaboration of our Free Church brethren, we were being called to help make the Christian voice heard nationally, as well as locally. People expressed surprise that such a partnership should exist in Liverpool, and began to speak of the 'Mersey Miracle'. Our efforts to respond to the calls made on us from many parts of Britain told us that the possibly unique social situation in Liverpool had provided us with a unique experience of working together – for Christ and for the city. We began to wonder whether this too was something we should share on a wider basis.

Once we had conceived the idea, it took us two years to plan this book and it has taken us almost as long to write it. We lacked neither motivation nor encouragement. Our problem has been to find the time and determine the method. Many authors go away for some time to write a book. That was out of the question for us. The method presented an even greater challenge. The straightforward answer might have been for us as individuals to write alternate chapters, or even two halves of each chapter. That would have given us the side-by-side approach. Yet the emphasis of the book was to be 'together'. Even if we were able to settle on a method to produce a joint 'pen' for the whole text, how far were we able to write with a single viewpoint? How great a restriction would the use of 'we' prove to be? We now share many anecdotes and experiences, but some upon which we needed to draw applied to only one of us.

We decided to allow ourselves at the beginning of the book one chapter apiece in which to set down the very different traditions and circumstances which were the background to our coming to Liverpool. Thereafter we have written together of Liverpool as we have found it over the years. There follow eight chapters, written jointly, about various aspects of our life and work together; and a final chapter in which we have suggested, in the light of our experience, certain lessons to be kept in mind in seeking a way forward. Because of the built-in restrictions of the method to which we have already referred, we decided to include some paragraphs in indented italicised print in which one of us could make a particular point or tell a personal story. This has enabled us as individuals to introduce our own examples, reminiscences or clarifications, and on occasion to set out points about which we wish to make plain our differing opinions or beliefs. It has seemed as important for us to explain our differences frankly and honestly as it has been to reveal the immense range of beliefs which we share.

It has sometimes seemed a laborious process to produce a joint text. Having worked out the general plan of the book, we developed the following process for each chapter: firstly, we have met together for several hours to agree the content of the chapter; secondly, one of us has written a first rough draft, fleshing out the agreed points; thirdly, the other has then had the freedom to reorganise and re-write a second draft, adding his own reflections; fourthly, that draft passes back to the first person so that he may amend, delete or add to it; fifthly, the corrected draft passes back to the other person, for acceptance or further correction if necessary. We have sometimes interchanged our roles as to who has done what. It has been a long process, but we know no other way of writing together. We hope that it will prove to have been 'better together', though the title, explained in chapter nine, has a broader context than the process of joint authorship.

We are very grateful to many lay people and clergy who have kept us informed and have advised us over the years, particularly during the preparation and writing of this book. Especially we would mention those who have read the text at various stages and offered their comments and criticisms: Grace Sheppard, Bishop Alan Clark, Canon Eric James, Miss Pat Jones, Mgr Vincent Nichols, Mr Alfred Stocks and Mrs Mary Tanner. Those closest to us have supported and encouraged us through many months of extra demands brought about by the writing of this book. In addition to Grace Sheppard, our Chaplains Mark Boyling and John Furnival willingly bore these added burdens. With Father Paul Thompson, they also sifted through many photographs and commissioned others. Most of all, our thanks are due to Mrs Jean Jones, who typed one draft after another and patiently brought the text together. Finally, we make grateful acknowledgement to *The New*

Jerusalem Bible, from which as a general rule scriptural texts have been drawn.

In endeavouring to share this complex story of Christian partnership in a hurt city, we earnestly hope that two factors may be plain: our devotion to Christ and his gospel, and our commitment to the service of Liverpool and its people.

Liverpool
September 1987

1 THE ROMAN ROAD

by Derek Worlock

My father and my mother were both converts to the Roman Catholic faith. It was a hard decision for them, as it was reached during their seven years' engagement to be married. At that stage my father was a journalist. He subsequently entered politics. My mother's father, who was a stockbroker, regarded journalism as a doubtful profession with uncertain prospects. So his approval was withheld. I am surprised that this deterred my mother, who had great spirit and at the time was an active worker in the promotion of women's suffrage. She insisted later that she was a suffragist rather than a militant suffragette; but she had the courage to sell her organisation's newspaper outside the House of Commons and crossed swords with the police as well as with certain Members of Parliament whom she described as 'no gentlemen'.

For a long time my mother, who regarded herself as a High Church Anglican, had felt drawn to the Roman Catholic Church. But not so long as my father, who had been sent to Keble College at Oxford with a view to ordination, to which he had not felt able to proceed. Had he decided otherwise and been ordained in the Church of England, he would not have been the first in his family. Some years ago a kindly genealogist sent me a partial family tree, covering three centuries on my father's side. This record reveals the names of no less than twelve ancestors in holy orders, the earliest being the Reverend John Baylies, who was a military chaplain at the battle of Dettingen in 1743.

Perhaps it was the approach of the First World War which led my parents to their decision to be married. But first they decided to seek admission to the Roman Catholic Church. They took themselves off to fashionable Farm Street in Mayfair, where the same Jesuit dealt separately with their enquiries and instruction without divulging to either the other's spiritual progress. Eventually, as was the custom at the time, he baptised them conditionally and they were married in the Catholic Church in St John's Wood in June 1914.

Their second son, I was born with my twin sister during the post-war baby boom which followed the Armistice and the return of the nation's menfolk from France. We were born in the flats opposite Lord's cricket ground. (Any connection between this and the co-author of this book is coincidental.) My sister and I were small at birth, so my mother insisted that the local curate baptise us at the earliest opportunity. He was summoned to our home where, according to my parents, we were baptised in a rose-bowl. The priest later insisted that he had used a pudding-basin. Despite subsequent debate, no one has ever cast doubt on the fact that my baptism was valid and that the water actually flowed.

I must be one of the few people who can never remember any time in my life when I did not wish to be a priest, or indeed when it was not understood by others that I had so declared my intention. It was alleged by my parents that I first expressed this desire when I was three years of age. I have no recollection of this, nor can I have had the least idea what it meant. None the less my earliest memories are in the setting of my family's acceptance of my eventual ordination and of the standard of behaviour expected of me in the meantime. How to set about achieving this desire was unknown to all of us.

My earliest schooling was at non-Catholic establishments. When in 1930 we left London to live in Winchester, I was sent as a boarder to a preparatory school at which I was the only Roman Catholic pupil. I was just ten at the time and my understanding of my faith was limited. My mother had prepared me for my first confession and Holy Communion. I had been confirmed at the age of seven. But, for the integrity of my faith, I was 'excused' attendance at all Scripture and Religious Knowledge classes. In recognition of freedom of conscience I was not required to attend the school chapel or morning prayers in the school library. I spent many a lonely hour in the corridor outside whatever was in progress, increasingly doubtful of the nature of my privilege. But I recall the hurt from the taunts of the other boys that I was a 'foreigner' or an untouchable. In those days there were even fewer sensitivities among small boys than there are today.

By the grace of God and a certain innate cussedness my sense of vocation survived. The need to resist any requirement to conform was an important element in the faith of English Catholics. It was part of our inherited pride in the sacrifices of martyrs from previous centuries. Conscious as we were of our Englishness, we lived a very separate religious life. Even to be present at a funeral or wedding in a non-Catholic church required ecclesiastical sanction. Due care had to be exercised not even to give the impression of joining in the recitation of 'Protestant' prayers and hymn-singing. The observance of Friday abstinence became the public proclamation of faith by 'fish on Fridays' and was almost as important as not falling into the trap of adding 'For thine is the Kingdom, etc.' to the Lord's Prayer.

These separate ways did not make for ease of relationships at my prep school in Winchester. The headmaster was good about what was regarded as my religious diet on Fridays. On Sundays I was allowed out to Mass in the local Catholic church. If there were measles or mumps in the town, my father would collect me by car and take me to the chapel at Tichborne House some eight miles away. We always enjoyed this as he told me that slipping into the chapel by the side door made him think of the martyrs and penal days.

I had no real sense of persecution but I was careful not to be caught off my guard. This led to my only experience of corporal punishment. Challenged by another boy who, after a history lesson on the Reformation, informed me that the pope was a rude word (of which I did not know the precise meaning), I stoutly defended the papal honour in the only way known to a schoolboy. As we were locked in fisticuffs, the headmaster entered the classroom. We were quickly separated, taken to his study and both beaten as a sign that there was to be no religious discrimination in the school.

When the time came for me to go to public school a new difficulty arose. Catholic friends advised my parents that there were special colleges where boys seeking training for the priesthood were educated, but acceptance by the bishop of the local diocese was a prerequisite. Enquiry revealed that the then Bishop of Portsmouth, Timothy Cotter, originally from County Cork, normally drew his priests from Ireland or from those with Irish parentage. We were advised that the unsuitability of my background made it useless to apply. It was only after a series of false starts, which would have involved my entering a religious order, that my mother finally approached the bishop who had confirmed me in London, where he was an auxiliary bishop of Westminster. Difficulties disappeared overnight. On the strength of a medical and my last term's school report, I became a junior seminarist for the Archdiocese of Westminster. In January 1934 I entered St Edmund's College near Ware in Hertfordshire. I was still thirteen years of age.

Now the sense of 'separateness' took a new form. The college was divided into three houses. Two were for those called 'lay boys' and the third for those who even at that early age were being prepared for priesthood. We attended the same classes and played the same games but lived in a separate part of the building and followed a different regime. Close contact between 'church boys' and 'lay boys' was discouraged. But the nearly five years I spent in the school were happy at the time as well as in retrospect. The separation proved of little eventual consequence. Less than twenty per cent of the junior seminarists reached the priesthood. Some decided that the life was not for them. Others had it decided for them. Most made excellent laymen, though half my class at St Edmund's failed to survive the Second World War. For us to be nineteen in 1939 was the same as being eighteen in 1914.

Even though the seminary in which I was prepared for priesthood was scarcely *hortus conclusus* (an enclosed garden), it was clearly recognised that separation from the 'world' was an important element in our academic and spiritual training. Pastoral experience would come soon enough in practice. Vacations were regarded as a testing-time rather than for relaxation. Canon Law was a guide to the Church's discipline. Moral theology ranked next in importance to dogmatic theology. In the four-year course on church history our lecturer played with the fascinating question of what would have happened in this country if the Spanish Armada had landed. At some stage I learnt about the Councils of the Church but I have to admit that I have no recollection of being taught ecumenism as such. It was wartime and we were allowed to be enthusiastic about the efforts of Cardinal Hinsley at Westminster, Archbishop Temple at Lambeth and Bishop George Bell of Chichester to promote, through the 'Sword of the Spirit', a united Christian front in face of the evils of Nazism; but this had little connection with the various penalties we learnt were to be incurred through *communicatio in sacris* (prohibited participation in religious rites).

Before ordination we were advised that these six years of academic learning were designed merely to prepare us for future study and thought. In retrospect one appreciates their connection with the spirit and practice of apologetics which was an essential part of the priest's equipment. As a small boy I had been told off for always having an answer. Now I learnt the vital importance of knowing the Church's answer on every question, and above all of winning the argument, even if it meant demolishing your adversary (in the nicest possible way) in the process. Undoubtedly this was a reflection of the defensive attitude of a minority community, but we were enormously proud of those public speakers, like Frank Sheed and Fr Vincent McNabb OP, who could hold forth at Speakers' Corner in Hyde Park, expert in their witness and in their ability to answer questions of any kind and to destroy unwary hecklers.

In fact at St Edmund's we were generally fortunate in our lecturers and in those who helped our spiritual development throughout such a long course. We learnt from our fellow students the value of community, but we were taught to be self-sufficient and adaptable. The six-year withdrawal (rather than separation) from the world constituted in itself a considerable test. In my case most of it coincided with the Second World War, and this made it more difficult to sustain. As theological students, we were classified as having reserved occupations and not subject to call-up. This arrangement had been made by the Churches so that we might replace in the parishes those who had gone to be chaplains to the Forces. Not many of us were given the 'white feather' treatment. When relatives and friends were killed, the pressure at least to postpone one's training was acute. Curiously enough, in this difficult situation I was most encouraged by my only brother who soon afterwards was lost at sea.

The separation from the world was formalised with the reception of the tonsure. The shaving of the head had from early centuries been seen as something which set cleric or monk apart from the world. For me the preliminaries had greater significance. Since I was under the age of twenty-one and was to be admitted as a cleric for Westminster, the written consent of the bishop of my home diocese was required. Dr Timothy Cotter ran true to form, declining to sign the document as he did not believe that a native of his diocese with my background was capable of having a vocation. Eventually my parish priest from Winchester, who by then was Bishop Cotter's auxiliary, pleaded my cause and the old bishop reluctantly agreed. The document reached the seminary on the day when my year-group was due for tonsure. It was immediately after the ceremony that we learnt that Bishop Cotter had died suddenly that morning. But the die was cast and I had joined the Archdiocese of Westminster.

The sequel can be told at this stage. My parish priest, Bishop John Henry King, succeeded Bishop Cotter and invited me to return to the diocese of Portsmouth, saying that I would be 'safe' with him. I declined not only because Westminster had befriended me but on the score that even he could not guarantee what his successor might do to me. John Henry King lived to a great age and it was I who was appointed his successor at Portsmouth exactly twenty-five years after Bishop Cotter had signed me away. Not for nothing was I subsequently called in certain circles 'Bishop Cotter's last will and testament'.

I was ordained to the priesthood in Westminster Cathedral in June 1944, just a few days before D-Day. Prior to ordination I had been seriously ill and was told by a specialist that I would never be able to do a full day's work again. I could be a curate in a country parish where an elderly parish priest might require some help. This report was duly sent to Archbishop's House at Westminster where presumably it was lost. I was appointed third curate at the busy parish of Our Lady of Victories in High Street, Kensington. I arrived with the first of the flying bombs and we were under frequent bombardment for several months. I administered the sacrament of anointing over fifty times before I had a case of natural death. A few days after my arrival, I was with the elderly parish priest when we heard the engine of an approaching flying bomb switch off. He hung out of the window to see it. Hearing the rush of air, I flung him to the ground and fell on top of him before the window crashed in on the pair of us. We were untouched, but nearly fifty civilians were killed outside the presbytery. Our church had already been destroyed.

When a bomb fell I would make my way to the scene, often to be greeted by Civil Defence workers calling out, as they dug out a body, 'Here, Padre, here's one of yours.' Identification was frequently impossible but I was expected conditionally to absolve and if possible to anoint. Often I would come across the then vicar of Holy Trinity, Brompton, who would turn his hand to sweeping up glass and rubble in the street. He once told me that he envied my sacramental role but with his broom he was humbly trying to serve the community. It is hard to believe that such a contrast would exist today.

Within a year of my ordination my medical record was finally lost and I was appointed private secretary to the Archbishop of Westminster. Bernard Griffin was only forty-five when he was appointed to succeed Cardinal Hinsley. With the war still in progress communication with Rome was difficult, yet he was given clear indication that he should beware of doctrinal entanglement with the inter-Church initiatives of his predecessor. The 'Sword of the Spirit', which had been founded by Hinsley, and the Anglican 'Religion and Life' movement had already run into difficulties. Coexistence rather than collaboration was the order of the day. For the ten years after the war the gap between the Roman Catholic Church and the other Churches in Britain tended to increase. The post-war years were for Catholics a time of emergence from the catacombs, a period of expansion and of growing self-confidence. But justification for this was not acknowledged by other authorities, civil or ecclesiastical.

When Archbishop Griffin was appointed a cardinal in 1946, the same honour was conferred on the Archbishops of Sydney and Toronto. As the three commonwealth cardinals, they came back from Rome to London, where I had the greatest difficulty in securing an audience for them at Buckingham Palace. When they asked that at the end of the audience they might present their principal aides travelling with them, I received a message from the Private Secretary that my 'suggestion was most improper'. Some time later we made history by negotiating with the Home Office that representatives of the Roman Catholic Church might be received with the official 'Privileged Bodies' to present a loyal address to the King on the betrothal of his daughter, now the Queen. We were to be admitted after the others on condition that there was no breach of the Ecclesiastical Titles Act by reference to any diocesan territorial jurisdiction. The four metropolitan archbishops led the delegation, which was deliberately made up of Catholics prominent in the government, political parties, trade unions and the services, including several holders of the Victoria Cross. The patriotic point was taken, but there was near disaster at the end. Cardinal Griffin, as agreed, introduced 'Archbishop Richard Downey'. 'Oh yes,' said King George VI smiling, 'you are the Archbishop of Liverpool, aren't you?' (Consternation in court.)

The relationship with Lambeth was no easier. The famous joint letters to *The Times*, which during the war had dealt with national crises and which had been signed by the Archbishop of Canterbury, Cardinal Hinsley, the Moderator of the Free Churches and the Chief Rabbi, soon came to an end. There were several reasons for this. No consultation took place before drafting. A prepared text would be received from Archbishop Fisher with a request for signature. Cardinal Griffin was not alone in resenting this. The whole project eventually foundered on unwillingness to correct a double negative and, more significantly, over the order of precedence of the signatories. Thereafter contact between the archbishop and the cardinal was restricted to an occasional encounter at an official reception. With the exception of Bishop Bell, with whom there were useful joint initiatives about the refugees in Germany, the Churches went their separate ways.

There was almost no collaboration, for example, regarding the immense amount of post-war social legislation, nor was help sought or given as religious persecution grew in Eastern Europe.

These difficulties and differences arose mainly from the failure to recognise what we would now regard as essential Christian bonds. In this respect feelings were probably mutual. I recall a long correspondence in *The Times* in early 1950 on 'Catholicism Today'. This culminated in a leading article which found it necessary to observe: 'Roman Catholics are not in fact committed, as is widely believed, to the doctrine that all non-Catholics are damned.' A few weeks later my cardinal archbishop felt it necessary to make matters plain in a pastoral letter: 'We Catholics believe', he wrote, 'that our Church is the one, true Church founded by Jesus Christ whose Vicar on earth, His Holiness the pope, speaks with an infallible voice when defining doctrines. We cannot, therefore, hold that other denominations are equally true. We should be untrue to ourselves and dishonest to those who are seeking the truth were we to pretend that they are.' Then, in case the issue of Rome and reunion needed further clarification, he added: 'To us in this country reunion can only mean the resumption of that unity which was destroyed at the time of the Protestant Reformation. A call for reunion means an invitation to all non-Catholics to join the one, true Church. It means, in other words, submission to the Holy See.'

In practice the sharpest differences seemed to arise over moral issues. As the official Roman Catholic spokesman to the press, I did not always find it easy to produce the requisite instant wisdom on all subjects. If Roman Catholics were judged by others to classify all moral stances as absolutely right or absolutely wrong, the 'others' were certainly considered by Catholics as substituting expediency and compromise for principle. There seemed to be no meeting-point, no common ground. But issues of national interest and loyalty still proved the flash-point. For the Queen's coronation in 1953 a papal legate was dispatched from Rome. But lest he appear to condone or participate in Protestant religious worship, he sat in a specially constructed box opposite the entrance to the Abbey while the coronation rite proceeded inside. At least the previous evening, Mass had been offered for the Queen in every Catholic church throughout the country. This was a considerable advance on what had occurred the previous year on the death of George VI, for whom as a nominal 'heretic' we had not been allowed to pray in public.

During the months immediately after the coronation, Westminster Abbey was closed to the public so that the customary interior arrangement might be restored. This meant that on 13 October, the feast of St Edward, visitors were denied access to the saint's shrine. It happened that all our bishops were meeting at Westminster that day. So I telephoned the dean to ask if after dark they might be admitted privately to the Abbey. To this Doctor Don kindly agreed, saying that a side door would be left open so that we might enter unattended. It was a moving moment when all of us trooped silently into the Abbey and went to the shrine to pray for 'Reunion' – all, that is, except one of the bishops who walked slowly around the sanctuary singing *Kyrie Eleison* in the belief that it might have been the first time since the Reformation that those blessed words had been heard within the Abbey walls.

Prayers can produce unexpected results. Next morning, at a meeting of the Convocation of Canterbury, Archbishop Fisher commended an anonymous tract published that day entitled 'Infallible Fallacies'. He described the booklet as containing 'a reply, brief but effective, courteous, quickly read and cheap, to some of the arguments of Roman Catholic propaganda'. The press bombardment on my phone was immediate and difficult to withstand, the more so as my mother had died during the night. I gave the task of a considered answer to the well-known Jesuit apologist, Father Joseph Christie SJ, who replied with a pamphlet entitled 'Anglicans Anonymous'. Honours even: but scarcely a victory for ecumenical charity.

An interesting attempt at a breakthrough was made by Canon John Collins, acting for Sir Stafford Cripps, who convened an inter-denominational meeting in the Albert Hall in connection with 'Christian Action' and to give himself the chance to tell the Churches their responsibilities in social justice. John Collins always claimed to understand our conscientious difficulties which he kindly described as 'consistent'. But we were in trouble again when a further meeting in the Albert Hall was called during the vacancy following the death of Cardinal Griffin in 1956. This time Doctor Fisher insisted that the Lord's Prayer be said by those present and aloud. This meant that there could be no ducking the 'which' or 'who' controversy and the problematical doxology, at that time not used by Catholics.

I was therefore dispatched to Lambeth by the senior archbishop, William Godfrey of Liverpool, who was to succeed to Westminster a few weeks later. Geoffrey Fisher, still very much the headmaster, stood in front of his study fire, blinking at me as I explained our predicament and asked that the Our Father be said in silence: thereby conscientious differences might be observed. At last he exploded, saying that this request from Archbishop Godfrey was monstrous. 'Haven't you Romans lived in this country long enough', he demanded of me, 'to know that we are the Establishment and you must toe the line?' I rose and asked him to withdraw. 'What did I say?' he responded. I explained the implications of his remark but there was no gainsaying him. He led me to the top of that formidable staircase at Lambeth Palace and, as I descended with as much dignity as I could muster, I heard him calling after me, 'Aggression. It's Roman aggression.'

Such an unhappy recollection serves to emphasise the marvel of the enlightenment and change which were almost upon us. In October 1958 Angelo Roncalli was elected to the papacy as John XXIII and the process of throwing open the windows began. In the following January he announced his intention of calling an ecumenical Council of the Church, and in June he followed it up with an encyclical letter on 'Truth, Unity and Peace, in the spirit of love'. This was new language, not least in the section dealing with unity of faith. After emphasising that the unity of the Church was the desire of its divine founder, he went on to argue that truth is one and contrary truths cannot coexist. The next passage was historic:

But there are many points which the Church leaves to the discussion of theologians, in that there is no absolute certainty about them, and, as an eminent English writer John Henry Newman remarked, such controversies do not disrupt the Church's unity, rather they contribute greatly to a deeper and better understanding of her dogmas. These very differences shed in effect a new light on the Church's teaching, and pave the way to the attainment of unity. There is a saying attributed to various services and structures expressed in different words, but it is none the less true and unassailable. It runs: 'Unity in essentials, freedom in uncertainties, in all things charity'.

(*Ad Petri Cathedram*, 49, 50)

Struggle as I might to keep pace with such developments, I was totally unprepared for the announcement that at the end of the year Archbishop Fisher was to visit Rome in order to meet the new Pope, the first such encounter since the Reformation. Though the emphasis was on a courtesy call, it was a courtesy which opened the way for immense developments. It is said that when they met, Pope John spoke about St Gregory the Great and St Augustine's mission to Canterbury. Archbishop Fisher, delighted with the warmth of the reception by the Pope, spoke of future unity in terms of a commonwealth of Churches. It was at least an interesting first meeting. Equally interesting was the subsequent Parliamentary debate, revealing a surprising degree of support for ecumenism and an end to bigotry.

The first announcement of Vatican II as an ecumenical Council led to some confusion. My instructions were to emphasise that this meant a general Council of the Church, whereas the media insisted that it was about Church unity. While many bishops throughout the world had their own particular hobby-horses to ride, it was soon evident that the main focus would be on the nature of the Church. The relationships between Christians would therefore inevitably be on the agenda. The Holy See established a Secretariat for the Promotion of Christian Unity and the Archbishops of Canterbury and York appointed a personal representative to the Vatican. As secretary to Cardinal Godfrey, I went back and forth to Rome from 1960 to 1962 for preparatory meetings. It was agreed that I would also serve as secretary to the English-speaking bishops and later, as the Council began, I was appointed an expert consultant on the laity's role, which had increasingly become my interest. But the long hard meetings of the Central Preparatory Commission revealed the radical differences of approach to the Council and the foreseeable contest between the cardinals of the Roman curia and their 'country-cousin' bishops from outside the Eternal City. It says much for the faith and perseverance of Pope John that the Council opened in October 1962.

This is not the place for a full account of the Second Vatican Council, which was certainly one of the greatest formative influences in my life. Its opening ceremony in St Peter's was for me an ecumenical disaster. Not merely were there no places for those of us required to carry the long silken trains of our eminent lords and masters, but we were quickly banished from the nearby space to which we had been moved to make way for the observers from the other Christian bodies. It ceased to be amusing after the first four hours standing in the passage. But we soon settled down to the longest in-service training course yet devised by the Church. The Council was spread over four annual sessions, each of nearly three months' duration. Between sessions I flew back and forth between London and Rome for my duties with commissions drafting Council documents, notably those on the Lay Apostolate and on The Church in the World Today. It was in the sub-committee writing the chapters on family life and on the socio-economic order that I first became friendly with a young Polish archbishop, Karol Wojtyla, now Pope John Paul II.

Cardinal Godfrey survived only the first session. He died in January 1963 after a long battle against cancer. He was happy to accept the will of the Church but was anxious about the changes which were foreshadowed. Soon after his funeral a Requiem Mass was arranged in Rome and I was duly summoned to be present. Afterwards Pope John sent for me and questioned me closely about the Cardinal's death. They had long been close friends but his interest seemed more than the demand of friendship. At last he was satisfied and turned to me with open arms. 'And now, dear Monsignor Strega,' he asked, remembering that Godfrey had once told him that Worlock meant a male witch, 'what will happen to you?' His concern was touching and I knelt for a blessing. He hauled me to my feet again and with a great bear-hug embraced me. I was quite choked and backed out of his room in the approved style. A minute later his secretary came chasing after me. 'The Holy Father says,' he blurted out, 'Tell that young man that when I embrace someone I mean it.' It was the last time I saw Pope John. He died the following June, also of cancer. Who can forget how the world kept vigil by television that Pentecost, during the final agony of an old man who in less than five years had changed the face and direction of the Church?

In September 1963, just before the second session of the Council, Archbishop Heenan of Liverpool was appointed to Westminster. So I began with my third archbishop – the red hat-trick, as it was called when he was made a cardinal shortly afterwards. But I had served nearly nineteen years at Archbishop's House and I felt justified in pleading to go to work in an East End parish. The following March I had my way and was appointed to lead a new team of priests to enliven Stepney. I was made Dean and Parish Priest of St Mary and St Michael's, Commercial Road, and arrived suitably enough on St Patrick's Day. Shortly beforehand I was invited by Archbishop Ramsey to dinner at Lambeth Palace, a nice act of reconciliation. That night the Archbishop's Chaplain, John Andrew, made the suggestion that I should meet a young parson who had just gone to work in Canning Town. So a few days later David Sheppard and I met for the first time at lunch. I regret to say that I can remember no more than an expressed willingness to make contact again after I had settled in.

If at my age I am allowed a happiest time in my life, it must be the following eighteen months at Stepney. The care of souls for the first time, the warmth of parish family life, the cheerful solidarity of East End dockers, a vast church which on occasion we could fill, a new presbytery and schools to replace those destroyed in the war, a kindly bank manager not too concerned about our vast parish debt and, best of all, a team of five priests of my own choice, all enthused at the prospect of working, living and praying together; and all this at a time when new and exciting developments were taking place in the liturgy and life of the Church – I was indeed a happy man. I was instructed by the Cardinal to experiment. I needed no encouragement to put into practice some of the things we were discussing at the same time in the Council in Rome. We had some seven thousand baptised Catholics in the parish. In eighteen months Mass attendance rose from nine hundred to two thousand.

Ecumenical relations in Stepney were varied. At monthly meetings of local clergy there were always a number of apologies for absence, often because two clerics of the same denomination would not meet. The Methodist was in particular demand by all of us because he alone was practised in the new art of public spontaneous prayer. The Presbyterian taught us that the care of the sick and needy did not have to be restricted to 'your own'. We also had a very High Church Anglo-Catholic neighbour who flew the Papal Flag (to the chagrin of our parishioners) and rang his bell to coincide with the consecration of the Mass in our church. The rector of Stepney was more formidable. He was the Rev. Edwyn Young, who gradually overcame his surprise when I turned up alongside him at civic occasions. One day I suggested that we walk home together. After a while he asked if I was aware that we were under observation from most nearby windows. Should we go our separate ways? Rather anxiously he accepted my reply that we should walk together in the middle of the street. Brave days. Soon afterwards he was appointed rector of the Parish Church of Liverpool. At his farewell reception I rashly gave him a papal medal which I had received from Pope John. 'Take this,' I said, 'you may need it up there.'

It was an enriching experience to commute between a family group discussion in a Stepney docker's flat and a high-powered commission meeting in the council chambers of the Vatican. There it was soon plain that the document on the Church (*Lumen Gentium*) was to be the platform upon which all Conciliar teaching would rest. Pope John had originally told us to start with a consideration of the liturgy, believing that if we understood how we worshipped we would understand the nature of the Church. But before we could consider the unity of the Church, it was necessary to establish the unity of the human family. Suddenly we began to hear more and more about 'the people of God'. Critical to the whole issue was an understanding of baptism and of the bond existing between baptised Christians. The basic concept of the Church was of a people holding different ministries and tasks, but with shared dignity and responsibility for the mission entrusted by Christ to his followers. When this was allied to the notion of baptism, it opened up a new approach to the promotion of Christian unity. Through baptism, it was argued, Catholic Christians are formed in the likeness of Christ, drawn into his redemptive life and mission, and – here was the breakthrough – 'joined in many ways to the baptised who are honoured by the name of Christian, but who do not profess the Catholic faith in its entirety or who have not preserved unity or communion under the successor of Peter' (*Dogmatic Constitution on the Church*, n. 15).

The Decree on Ecumenism which was to follow, treats first of 'the one Church of Christ', or simply 'the Church', before going on to deal with the Catholic Church, the differences between Christian Churches and ecclesial communities, and the points about which dialogue (the vogue word of the moment) must be encouraged. Again it was emphasised that baptism constituted the bond of unity among all those who through it are reborn and truly incorporated into Christ. The restoration of unity must henceforth be the concern of the whole Church, clergy and laity alike. As I wondered about the views of my dead parents, there was the assurance that 'every renewal of the Church essentially consists in an increase of fidelity to her own calling' (*Decree on Ecumenism*, n. 6). All this may seem trite now, so widely is it accepted, but I do not forget the exhilaration nor the spontaneous applause when during the debate on this subject in St Peter's, Cardinal Heenan rose to say in the name of our bishops from England and Wales: 'We promise our separated brethren that we shall cordially promote the ecumenical dialogue. We readily declare our intention of doing everything short of denying our faith, to bring about the union of Christians.'

It is significant that the term 'separated brethren', quite acceptable at that time, soon gave way to 'fellow Christians'. The observers from the other Churches, including John Moorman, the Bishop of Ripon, and Brother Roger Schutz of Taizé, had become a regular part of the Council scene and were increasingly consulted in the work of the commissions. Their seats in St Peter's were immediately opposite those for the experts (*periti*) where I sat each morning for the assembly. I do not know if they witnessed my discomfiture on the morning of Saturday 9 October 1965, during the final session of the Council, when I was summoned from my vantage point to where Cardinal Heenan was sitting, gesticulating to me across the chamber, the fingers and thumb of one hand held aloft. I was quick off the mark and walked across to give him five copies of the intervention he had delivered. 'No, you fathead,' he said briskly, 'meet me over there in five minutes.' He pointed to a chapel near the Sacristy. So it was that a few moments later he handed me a large envelope, containing my nomination by Pope Paul VI as Bishop of Portsmouth.

For the next two months I lived in three worlds. The drafting demands of the Council in its final stages were considerable. Now for the first time I was given a vote. This was satisfying, especially when one's own drafts were under consideration. But to vote I was moved aloft to an upper tribune for the most junior bishops, where significantly I could see and hear much less than before. I had also to placate my team of priests at Stepney who, remembering their commitment to me for five years, felt let down by my premature removal. Meantime the diocese of Portsmouth wondered when, if ever, they would see their new bishop and what he would do to them after the long benign reign of John Henry King, who had died the previous March. One of the earliest telephone calls was from the Chancellor of the diocese, anxious to complete a ceremonial booklet for my consecration as a bishop on my return. 'You must have a coat of arms and a motto', he insisted, 'by tomorrow morning at the latest.' It all seemed rather remote. But I chose a fleur de lis and a balance for St Mary and St Michael, and the blazing sun for St Edmund, patron of my new diocese. For the motto I chose *Caritas Christi eluceat* (Let the charity of Christ shine forth). It was taken from the documentation which we were debating in Council that day, the Decree on the Pastoral Office of Bishops, the paragraph dealing with their relations with 'separated brethren'.

I was consecrated by Cardinal Heenan in St John's Cathedral, Portsmouth, on 21 December 1965. I am still working out the meaning of the telegram I received from the Jesuit Archbishop Roberts: 'May the spirit of St Thomas uphold you.' But while others spoke of doubts, I was anxious to give the way, the truth and the life to my priests as a sign of the direction we would follow. To most of them the Second Vatican Council was no more than something which had conveniently taken all the bishops abroad for the best part of four years. What consequences had now to be faced? For the consecration ceremony I had carefully chosen hymn tunes which would be known also to non-Catholics. Would I insist on 'Protestant hymns' in the future? The Pope had given the bishops a plain gold ring at the end of the Council. Jewels seemed to have gone with the passing of the so-called 'triumphalist Church'. So I chose an episcopal cross of plain wood. Had I joined the Little Singers? Having been called 'Monsignor' since I was twenty-nine, I was now being addressed simply as 'Father' by the younger clergy. Where would it end? At a meeting with all the priests I was asked to state my priorities. 'We are going to do the lot,' I said, sounding more confident than I felt. 'If it comes to legislation to implement the Council, we will follow each decree. I will not choose. You will not choose. In a time of change the greatest test of orthodoxy is to follow Peter.' (Point scored by the new bishop.)

Divine providence was good in giving me such a span in the beautiful country of my upbringing, where generally priests and people gave me support and a welcome back to the scene of my earlier rejection. Most of the older priests were of Irish origin, if not actually Irish-born. It took some time to reassure them that I was not bent on revenge for what had happened to me at the hands of Bishop Cotter. Once I had visited their homes in Ireland and they discovered that I had often stayed with President de Valera, all was well. Anxiety was removed and almost without exception they gave me the same loyalty as they had given my aged predecessor. Just to start with, age was a difficulty. To succeed a bishop who had been in his eighties, and had a long white beard to prove it, was not easy for one only slightly more than half that age. Schoolchildren were surprised to find me clean-shaven and able to hear what they said without their shouting. I asked one small boy in the Isle of Wight what my predecessor had looked like. He thought for a moment and said: 'Just like God the Father, only older.' His memory was rightly revered.

The initiatives of Pope John and Archbishop Fisher had been marked by cautious courtesy and many of the post-Conciliar moves bore the same mark. By this time the Week of Prayer for Christian Unity had become established as the occasion of a meeting on neutral ground, often a town hall, where an Anglican, a Free Churchman and a Roman Catholic made speeches of general agreement, in that they carefully avoided any point which might give offence. Another nice touch was the encouragement of priests by Cardinal Heenan to invite local ministers (with spouses) to tea on the feast of the conversion of St Paul. But it was not too long before special annual services were devised, which were ecumenical only in the sense that the local incumbent invited his neighbours to be present and eventually to take part. The third stage was when each Church invited the others to its own form of worship, so that the 'getting to know you' process revealed you as you really were, rather than providing a special ecumenical cocktail. It was all very polite. Some years passed before trust had developed sufficiently that all the ministers concerned could actually meet in advance to plan together the form of service best suited to the occasion and the traditions represented.

With so many other developments in the cause of renewal, it was not surprising that ecumenism remained an annual event rather than an aspect of joint endeavour. The Roman Catholics of Hampshire and Berkshire comprised just five-and-a-half per cent of the total population, so that taking the initiative was not easy. Quite early on we succeeded in arranging throughout the City of Portsmouth that during the week before the Unity Octave trios of Anglican, Catholic and Free Church laity visited each household in the city, presenting a list of all available religious services, and saying together, 'We represent the Christians of Portsmouth.' That was a great moment. The venture was marred only slightly by the story of the angry householder who closed the door saying, 'No, thank you. We're Roman Catholics,' only to find the letter-box opening so that one of those outside might reply, 'Then come out and meet your parish priest.'

It was a relationship which grew steadily over the ten years. There were difficulties, but only once did I encounter protest banners and these remained at a respectful distance across the street. More delicate was the occasion when the Anglican bishop's daughter wished to marry a Catholic young man and it had to be in a Catholic church. We produced what became known as the 'Portsmouth solution', whereby the marriage rite and promises took place in the Catholic church in the morning and the full celebration took place in the bride's church that afternoon, with her father presiding. It was far from perfect but it helped to pave the way for the possibility of granting permission for the Catholic to be married in the rite of another Christian Church.

More hilarious was the setback when a group of Catholic enthusiasts took their reluctant priest to attend Evensong in the local Anglican church. The vicar was touched and secretly arranged to take his entire confirmation class to evening Mass at the Catholic church the following Sunday. Unknown to him it was the Sunday when the congregation is counted carefully as the basis on which the parish is assessed so much per head, as a tax towards the central funds of the diocese. To the priest the presence of the vicar was scant consolation for his having to fork out £1 for each member of the confirmation class.

The first time I preached in Winchester Cathedral, on a Good Friday, I thought much of my parents buried in the nearby cemetery. How would they have reacted? Some weeks later I went to preach in the parish church of the village in which we had lived outside Winchester. In all those years I had never entered the village church. Apart from one other villager, we were the only Roman Catholics and used to attend Mass five miles away. That night, as I entered Easton, the bells of the village church rang out and it seemed that all the village, including now seventeen Catholics, were there. At that precious moment I knew that my parents would have been with me. It was astonishing how often, preaching in a town church, with all denominations present, people would ·reach out to me and say, 'This is how it should be.' A foretaste of the future?

In the early 1970s, with the help of John Phillips, the Anglican Bishop, we began to organise conferences for all the clergy to study the doctrinal issues spotlighted in the reports of the Anglican/ Roman Catholic International Commission. Presuppositions about each other's beliefs proved as difficult as the different use of accepted terminology. The pace of progress and understanding was gathering, but it was to be a long road. In 1967 an Ecumenical Directory had been issued by Rome. This included a section on 'The validity of baptism conferred by ministers of Churches and ecclesial communities separated from the Roman Catholic Church'. Baptism was hailed as the sacramental bond of unity, the foundation of communion among all Christians. Various safeguards were mentioned and local Churches were invited to discuss their practice in baptising. In October 1970 the Roman Catholic Bishops of England and Wales duly informed the British Council of Churches of its desire to recognise the validity of the baptism of all the Churches eligible for membership of the BCC. A new era in Christian partnership had begun.

In February 1976 the letter informing me of the Pope's decision to transfer me from Portsmouth to the Archdiocese of Liverpool fell like a bombshell on my breakfast table. As a successor to the ailing Archbishop George Andrew Beck, the priests of the Archdiocese had asked for someone to help the local Church face up to change, not only in light of Vatican II but as a result of steadily worsening social conditions. Pope Paul, I read, knew my interests, my background, my pastoral zeal, etc. Without the consultation which I had always advocated, this Westminster priest was translated through Portsmouth to the Metropolitan See in the North he did not know, save in most general terms. On Sunday 14 March 1976 I arrived in Liverpool by train to be greeted by an enthusiastic crowd in Lime Street Station. For the time being it was enough that I was '*our* Archbishop'. But more would be needed.

That evening I sat with my Portsmouth chaplain amidst packing cases in Archbishop's House, Liverpool. The front doorbell rang and one of the few faces I knew came round the door. Armed with a bottle of wine, my first visitor, Bishop David Sheppard, had come to say 'Welcome'.

2 CONVERSION TO CHRIST AND TO THE CITY

by David Sheppard

Making a firm start to the Christian journey took for me the form of a classic evangelical conversion. In one sense the turning round was sudden; in another it was the coming together of many loose threads.

When I went to Cambridge University at the age of twenty, I had drunk in much of the tradition of belief and service from my background. My father, who died when I was eight years old, was a solicitor, a founder-member of Toc H (which took its name from Talbot House in Poperinghe, where many soldiers came for fellowship in the 1914–18 war), and started the Chelsea Boys Club. On occasion, I acted as ADC to the Reverend Tubby Clayton, the founder-padre of Toc H, who was my father's first cousin. The ideal of service was strong in public school life and Sherborne, where I went, was no exception. I was confirmed at thirteen years of age. My voice did not break until I was sixteen and I was the leader of the trebles in the choir. The war was in progress: we went to chapel every day and religion was strongly connected with turning over pages in a Book of Remembrance of Old Boys of the school who were killed in the war.

Most important of all, my mother gave me the solid base of a loving home. We discussed all manner of subjects very freely, though boarding school and adolescence meant that I learnt to keep most of my deep feelings to myself. She gave her love wholeheartedly to those she allowed within her closest family circle; outside the circle she had her fair share of prejudices. She was particularly suspicious of socialists and Roman Catholics. As my faith grew, she entered into much of my development with me. She even overcame her initial puzzlement at my very close partnership with the Roman Catholic Archbishop of Liverpool.

These were the loose threads, which added up to a belief in a good and purposeful Creator and an assumption that I wanted to be on his side. Yet the belief was becoming increasingly remote. When the framework of school chapel and an outwardly conforming community was removed, my faith did not seem to be very robust. Two years of Army National Service left me much less sure of where I stood.

At Cambridge a friend, John Collins, invited me to the mission run by the Christian Union. They had invited a blunt and aggressive – and not at all ecumenical – preacher from the United States. Donald Grey Barnhouse aroused strong feelings during the week of his preaching Mission. Neither at that time, nor since then, did I agree with everything he said. But one great truth penetrated my defences and has stayed at the heart of my faith ever since. Again and again Barnhouse returned to his theme that no one can climb up to God by his own efforts to be kind, neighbourly or religious. Only by the totally undeserved love and grace of Jesus Christ can we be accepted by a holy God.

Part of the strength of the Christian Union was the readiness of many of its members to invite friends to their services, and to speak of their own faith. I went back from a Barnhouse sermon to John Collins' room. Here was someone of my own age for whom the loving presence of Christ seemed the greatest reality of his life. Late that night I walked back to my room in Trinity Hall. It felt more important than anything in the world that I should become right with God. I knelt and prayed in my own words, asking Christ to come into my life, to forgive me and to be my saviour and friend. Then I prayed, 'Lord, I don't know where this is going to lead me, but I want to go with you. Please make me willing.'

What were the ingredients of that evangelical conversion? At the heart of it was an overwhelming sense that in the presence of a holy God I was a sinner who came far, far short of his goodness. Yet I could know that I was accepted by that holy God, because of what Jesus Christ had done for me on the cross. Equally important was a whole new awareness of the presence of the living Lord. We learnt to talk about the friendship of Jesus. That led at times to expecting him to reveal some special guidance, when he was intending us to think responsibly for ourselves. I have had to learn that he makes no promises to protect his friends from suffering, failure and uncertainty. But that strong sense of his continuing presence has remained at the centre of all my Christian journey and growth.

I entered into the evangelical emphasis on the Word of God. Every morning there needed to be a Quiet Time of Bible reading and prayer. Recently I came across a notebook from those early months of my Christian journey; I had been reading Romans,

Chapter 8, and had written at the end of some notes I had made, 'Read it again. It's terrific!'

The excitement that there was good *news* was a strong motive in making me want to share it. I had known what it was to experience life without any personal knowledge of God. Now I invited many of my Cambridge friends to Christian Union services and talked with them about how they could enter into this faith. There were times when perhaps I pressed our good news too eagerly on people who were not ready for it. I needed to learn much more about respect – to listen and understand where other people stood and that they had often grown up without the strong moral and religious background I had been given. True evangelism must include that respect, listening and understanding. Yet sharing the good news about Jesus Christ has always remained a powerful motive in me.

An important ingredient which followed very quickly on my conversion was to belong to the worshipping fellowship of Chris tians. In the Christian Union students ran their own Bible studies and prayer meetings; for someone brought up in a rather formal, middle of the road, Anglican tradition everything was new about praying out loud without any written prayers, 'giving your testimony' and singing choruses and hymns, from Moody and Sankey to Billy Graham. I thought to myself, 'I did not know there were people like this.' I did not mean that they were perfect; rather that they took it as perfectly normal to expect the living God to guide and help them. There was warm encouragement and expectation that more new Christians would be added, if we prayed faithfully.

One of the strengths of the Christian Union was that Christians from many different denominations belonged. It planted in me a sense of belonging to one great Church beyond any one denomination. We accepted that these Churches worshipped in different ways. Part of the price of avoiding controversy within Christian Union ranks was that the Eucharist received a comparatively small place in our life. Our language hid from us some of the assumptions we were making; we talked about being 'real Christians'. We would not have expected Roman Catholics to be real Christians or to belong to the Christian Union.

Within a year of my conversion I was travelling to Australia and New Zealand with the England Cricket Team. Another member of the team, John Dewes, and I were known to be evangelical Christians. We were invited to speak at a number of meetings for young people. We were also welcomed into Christian homes of various denominations. That network of prayerful welcome and support strongly coloured my understanding of what the whole Christian Church could be.

I had to work out the daily practice of my faith as a cricketer, believing that God wanted Christians in the world of cricket as much as in any other corner of life. I wrote an 'appreciation of the situation', as I had been taught to do in the Army. This proved to me with ample logic that I should stay in cricket and use the many opportunities which were coming my way to serve God there. I prayed that God would confirm this 'logical' direction to my life, if that were his purpose, or pull me back, if he wanted me to go in another direction. I started to take steps to find a job which would allow me to play cricket regularly. As I pushed on that door and subsequently thought about other possibilities, I came to realise that this was not the way, and that I must think again. Increasingly every task which attracted me involved my being ordained. Slowly I arrived at a deep conviction that I should offer myself for ordination.

I was recommended for training and soon arrived back in Cambridge, this time at Ridley Hall Theological College. I came as a very raw and new Christian, suspicious of influences which would make 'churchy' or threaten the clarity of the gospel I believed. Gradually I learnt to put away some of those suspicions. Theological college helped me to want to belong to a wider, comprehensive Church, while holding firmly to a Christ-centred gospel. Our understanding of a 'wider Church' rarely stretched beyond the Church of England. There was little awareness of belonging to the worldwide Anglican Communion; nor was there any thought of ecumenical partnership, certainly not with Roman Catholics.

My introduction to inner-city church life was as a curate at St Mary's, Islington. Its strength included a strong belief in the power of Christ today, loyalty to the Bible, a warm welcome to those who came to us, a determined insistence on standards of behaviour, courageous personal discipleship, great care with baptisms, weddings and funerals, faithful visiting of homes by staff and some of the congregation, compassion for individuals in need, individual care for black immigrants who were then newly arriving, concern for children and the elderly.

Leadership in the parish was largely either in the hands of the paid staff, or of those who now lived in the suburbs, or who had moved into the district as students or professional people. As young people grew up within the church organisations, the patterns of leadership to which they looked up were those which would have been suitable in a middle-class town parish. The young people who stayed in church life were those who were willing to fit in with such patterns. Typically of many parishes, members of the congregation of St Mary's would largely have found themselves uncomfortable, say, at an Islington wedding party, or at being involved in secular groups that asked questions about the welfare of the neighbourhood concerning housing, or education or play facilities. Certainly some prayed for their neighbours. Some would go visiting. Nowhere did they share a common life with the majority group in the district. The staff had endless slight contacts with neighbours in visiting and through baptisms, weddings and funerals. But we did not know what to do next, unless someone was willing to come straight into the circle of fully committed Christians.

In June 1957 Grace and I were married; that was the beginning of another part of growing of which I shall write more later. I was given the opportunity to go to Canning Town in the East End of London, as warden of the Mayflower Family Centre. This was to be a new project, taking over a longstanding work in old buildings, which the Dockland Settlements were wanting to hand over. One night I drove to Canning Town, and walked the district through the early hours of the morning, to try to think myself clear. There was a somewhat romantic conversation with God, which highlighted how I saw things: 'Lord, we say we believe you are God the Father Almighty, and that we can bring up children to your glory – provided we have a nice garden and trees in our street. But we don't believe that is possible in a district like this.' It seemed to me then, as it does now, that a gospel which had nothing to say to those who lived in inner-city areas – except that they should move away from them – was no gospel.

Being plunged into the inner city, in which we lived and worked for twenty years in East and South East London, brought me into a whole new world. It would not be too much to say that I experienced another conversion – conversion to Christ in the city. The ingredients of this conversion included an insistence that the Church is called to serve the whole community, in particular the poor; secondly, a commitment to the Kingdom of God and his justice in a needy world.

When we went to the Mayflower Family Centre, church life had largely collapsed. There were six regular communicants. Twenty might come to a special service. It was plain that we should give the lion's share of our time to our neighbours, who were right outside the life of the Church, and to the life of the wider community in Canning Town. That meant being ready to listen to what was important to people whose social and economic experience of life was enormously different. I have often wondered whether I would have given that time outside the church community, if there had been a congregation of seventy or eighty members to keep us on a busy pastoral round.

It helped me to make the comparison with a Christian missionary going to other parts of the world. Suppose I had been called to India, I hoped I would not have assumed that I was coming from Europe and a superior culture to an ignorant India. Rather I hoped that I would have known I was coming from one culture to a different culture. The key word would have been respect. Similarly in East London, it was important to renounce old attitudes which had assumed that the educated classes would come from a superior to an inferior culture. Again the key word was respect.

Respect means not just listening to people; it involves entering into the argument. I was much more ready to do that in the second six years in Canning Town than in the first. Accepting a different culture, which had a right to work out its own values, sometimes led to defending Canning Town, right or wrong. I do not believe that is something for which such a newcomer need have been ashamed; it may be necessary to love uncritically before a continuing love produces real discernment.

I recall a midnight conversation in a flat in one of the new high-rise blocks of the 1960s. I had gone to visit a young couple who were staying away from the Mayflower. The man's comparatively new-found faith was more full of imaginative insight than that of many steadier Christians. But he was finding it very hard to accept the corporate decision-making of our Church Council when decisions did not go his way. That night he was in a bitter mood. He went on and on about the disadvantages he and people in Canning Town had experienced, which I did not understand. Eventually I exploded; I said I knew I had been born on the right side of the tracks, and that my place of birth in 1929 decided a great deal about opportunities. I knew I could not enter into all his hurts, but I insisted that Christian love could reach across such barriers.

Canning Town was then a solidly white working-class area: it had no owner-occupied housing. Those who went to grammar school or did well in a youth club or a church were expected to go up in the world and move out to a suburb. The consequence of this pattern of selective mobility was that parents usually had low expectations of what their children could achieve. It was not that they did not care about their children's education, but that they did not know how to support what schools had to offer. Their low expectation spread from parents to teachers, to employers and, most damagingly of all, to young people themselves. I came to feel indignation that so much God-given ability and intelligence was being trampled on and wasted by the circumstances of urban life.

A key figure in the staff team at the Mayflower and in my own development was George Burton, the senior youth leader. We worked together for eight years until his death at the age of fifty-one. On the surface he was a loud-mouthed fat man who insisted that his only task was to tell people about the Lord Jesus Christ. When no rival was in sight, and when he was with the roughest of local young people, there was a patience and sensitivity which led many to trust him deeply.

His personality had been savagely scarred as a boy in Glasgow in the years of the Depression. It remained scarred till his death, though there was a great measure of healing. The love and support of colleagues held him, when he wanted to run away from the Mayflower. He was a disturbing person to work with. He used to say to me, 'I've been fighting you educated people all my life.' He could identify with Canning Town young people because of his own experience. He knew that the ability was there and set himself to encourage local leadership at every level. I have often thought of George in subsequent years, when I have met disturbing community leaders. I have realised that if I am only prepared to do business with calm and steady characters, I will avoid dealing with many of those who can do most to change matters for the good.

Our older teenage youth work was at two levels. First, there was an open youth club, 'A street corner with a roof on.' It had a minimum of rules, but George Burton was able to crack the whip when it was needed. The most demanding job I ever did was following his death. No youth leader was available to take over, so for a year I dropped the rest of my work and ran the youth work. I would never have dared run the club on such a loose rein, if I had not seen George at work. The strain of soaking up the anger of some young people, the disappointment of seeing others get into trouble with the law again after renewed promises and hopes, made me realise both how much youth leaders bear and their own need of understanding support.

Side by side with the open youth club, George Burton started the Sunday Group. As well as belonging to the club, its members met in his flat and had a number of weekends away together. The invitation to join the Sunday Group included an expectation that they would come to church on Sunday evenings and be willing on occasions to enter into discussions about the Christian faith. A number of strong Christian leaders have emerged from that group.

The experience of those twelve years in East London led me to some hard reflection on what the gospel had to say in such a world. Part of my background was to believe from my experience of life that there was a good and purposeful Creator. Soon I realised that I could make no such assumption about the life which many East Londoners experienced. Their experience is of creation spoiled.

At the heart of the teaching of Jesus in the gospels was a whole series of stories and comments on events which began, 'The Kingdom of God is like . . .' Only after that did Jesus go on to say, 'Follow me.' The Kingdom of God was not the same as the Church. The Church was to be the servant of the Kingdom, which was the establishing of the reign of God in the whole world. The idea was not an easy one for western minds: the Kingdom of God was just round the corner, it was at hand, it was coming, it would come in power. It was among them. People were called to enter it. It was to be proclaimed. The roots of the idea were borrowed by Jesus from the Old Testament prophets, who wrote about the coming of a King who would reign in justice. Their emphasis was both on the knowledge of God in the heart and reflecting the character of God in intervening in a spoiled creation on behalf of the poor and oppressed. A good summary of what the Kingdom of God means is 'creation healed'.

The cry for justice from the Old Testament prophets had not been part of the Bible which the Christian Union speakers and books highlighted. They had generally turned to the prophets to point to texts which illuminated the coming of the Saviour. Now in East London the message of the prophets about God's saving justice seemed highly relevant. Our neighbours were only likely to believe our words about following Christ, if they saw that we were working for the healing of creation.

When I was ordained, I believed that the gospel was about changing individuals from inside out. The hope was then that individuals would change other individuals and gradually we would change the world. At no time have I moved away from that belief that Christ changes individuals. But I came to see that Christians must be concerned with something else too: we are called to change the course of events, as far as that lies within our power.

For example, if I wanted to love my neighbour in respect of his or her housing or their child's schooling, individual action had severe limits. My headed notepaper might get them a hearing denied to others in the queue. So if I 'got them a place', it might only be at the expense of someone else. If I was to help bring about changes which would open up opportunities to whole groups at present excluded, I found I had to ask questions or involve myself in political arguments which made me unpopular in the Town Hall.

My earlier involvement as a Test cricketer drew me into public and political debate during these years. The Duke of Norfolk had for several years invited me to captain his team in the opening match of the tour against overseas teams. In 1960 he invited me to captain his team against South Africa. I had done some hard thinking about cricket and South Africa for a while. As a curate, in 1956 I went to a meeting at the House of Lords for people in sport and the arts, which was addressed by Father Trevor Huddleston. He walked along the terrace by the river with me after the meeting, and told me that he thought nothing would more helpfully bring pressure to bear on white South African opinion than if England refused to send a cricket team to South Africa. It was clear to me in 1960 that under those circumstances I should not play. It was a wholly new thought that I should enter into a very public debate by making my refusal known. As I tried to think my position through, I pictured African Christians being taunted all over Africa with the charge that the Christian Church was an institution which supported white dominance. I read passages from the great prophets, like Isaiah 58, 'Cry aloud, spare not, lift up your voice like a trumpet; declare to my people their transgression . . .' (RSV). The chapter goes on about loosing the bonds of wickedness, letting the oppressed go free.

English newspapers' interest in South Africa was at boiling point. At Sharpeville a few weeks earlier sixty-seven Africans had been shot dead by the police after a demonstration. On the eve of the South African cricket team's arrival the media guessed, or got wind of, my position, and came to ask me about it. So my refusal to play and my reasons were headlined over all the newspapers on the day of the team's arrival. For the first time I learnt something of sustaining a controversial position in a very public debate.

In 1968 cricket and South Africa came to the fore again. Basil D'Oliveira, a coloured South African, unable to play first-class cricket in South Africa, had established himself in the England cricket team. After a rather unsuccessful series against Australia he vindicated himself with a fine innings of 150 in the final Test, the day before the MCC team to tour South Africa was to be selected. He was not included in the team and there was an uproar of protest. I became the focal point for opposition within the cricket world. When another member of the team was declared unfit, D'Oliveira was picked instead. The South African Prime Minister, Dr Vorster, said the players had now been picked for political reasons and that the team would be unacceptable.

A group of members of the MCC called for a special meeting to censure the Committee for their handling of the matter. I proposed that motion in the meeting in Church House, Westminster. Mike Brearley seconded it. There was a very bitter atmosphere, as we were criticising our friends and challenging a very basic sportsman's creed, 'No religion, no politics in sport.' One piece of humour lightened the atmosphere. My appointment as Bishop of Woolwich had recently been announced. An elderly member in the course of a lengthy and personal attack on me said, 'I don't know how the Bishop of Woolwich can wear his MCC tie.' A voice from the gallery called out an answer, 'Down the back!'

I was glad that I began to think about race relations, not only in South Africa but also in Britain, while I was living and working in East London. My everyday experience made me realise that too many people, black and white, were being excluded from the good opportunities of our society.

That growing concern about justice was an important part of my growth on the outward journey. Equally important has been continuing growth on the inward journey. Nothing has influenced that inward journey more than my marriage to Grace Isaac and the way we have been working out that relationship for thirty years now. This is not an attempt to hijack this joint book for an agreed statement in favour of married priests! It is, I hope, saying something important for all Christians, married and unmarried.

Wholehearted Christian living can be confused with busy and successful work for the Church. But in the incarnation we see a pattern of living in which obedience to God's truth is worked out in learning to handle close human relationships, male and female. My marriage has been the most significant context in which I have gradually learnt to open myself less fearfully, noticing and expressing deep feelings, and in the mutual sustaining and cherishing with another person.

I was in great danger of becoming a platform Christian when I was first married – being in demand to speak about all manner of subjects, and kept so busy at meetings, that I allowed no time to work out the relationships immediately around me. That tension between public and private has not been comfortably settled yet, but I am convinced that married partnerships cannot thrive without making prime time for each other and not just the fag end of the day or the week.

Grace and I have been aware that the issue of public life versus private life is one of the particular pressures which a clergy marriage faces. We invited Dr Jack Dominian to Liverpool for a series of ecumenical meetings on Christian marriage. One meeting was for those in Christian leadership and ministry with their partners. Someone asked, 'If your calling to Christian ministry and your calling to marriage seem to be in conflict, which should you put first?' Jack Dominian replied, 'You should put your marriage first.' He allowed a long pause before going on to say, 'I know there is such a thing as sacrificial living. But if you are called to that, you should make decisions about your response jointly.' The sense that the calling to serve God in the ordained ministry overrides all other callings can not only lead the husband to squeeze out good time with his partner; it can also lead to self-deception that what he has to do as a priest is so important that he can take his partner and closest friend for granted.

In his lectures and writings Jack Dominian makes a robust defence of the institution of marriage. It provides the firm framework of lifelong commitment, the safe place of trust in which we slowly risk revealing our feelings to our partner and to ourselves. Then it can be the framework for healing, growth and creative partnership.

I came to ordination and to marriage as a public person. I was beginning to learn then, as I still need to do, the distinction between the private person and the feelings inside my skin, and the public role, labelled 'cricketer', 'priest', or 'bishop'. For the family the public label can at times be exciting, taxing and often very confusing. Even returning from our honeymoon we had to kiss one another for the national press. It has been a continuing fight to guard our privacy and to make good time for each other.

Early in our marriage Grace became quite nervously ill. This was an unexpected and painful blow to both of us, and to our high hopes and expectations. Yet it became a major plank on which our closeness was to be built, and for me both as person and clergyman a vital ingredient was introduced. We were faced with the disturbing question, 'What's to be done, when self-confidence slips?' One answer would have been to snap my fingers in Victorian fashion and say, 'Pull yourself together.' Thankfully we were both helped to see that a better way was to accept support and stay with the pain and fears until there was a measure of healing. I now know that snapping my fingers would have produced none of the

31

by-products of that illness that have helped to sustain us and other people since then. It would not have helped either of us to understand suffering and pain. I would have grown harder, brittle and invulnerable, and Grace would have lost any confidence that marriage meant an understanding partnership.

During those rather dark days, I felt I was the stronger member of the partnership. With hindsight I realise that the fight which Grace was putting up called for inner resources of great courage in the face of fear.

Eight years later it was a different story. Grace had a sudden operation for cancer and was in the London Hospital for seven weeks, including four weeks of radiotherapy. Through the skill of the surgeon and his team the threat and uncertainty was replaced by steady recovery and no setbacks; she is bouncing with health twenty-one years later. When I went to visit her every day in hospital, I was the one who felt very weak, not knowing how to offer help except by doggedly being there. Grace was extremely ill, but was able to lift me in moments when I was confused and tired. Privately we wanted to keep the facts quiet, but publicly we needed to offer some explanations to people at the Mayflower. I learnt that there are limits to the amount of explaining that one public person can manage. I became painfully aware that I had limits, and that I was not as strong and rock-like as I thought I was.

The knowledge that each of us needs to receive from the other as well as give to the other has gone on developing. Grace has brought courage, sensitivity, a sense of humour, discretion and cherishing to our partnership. So it has been a safe place where we have learnt to share pressures and delights.

The role of women has undergone a sea change in our generation. Like many other Christian women, she found herself examining the possibilities of pursuing a career or a role in a voluntary movement in her own right. That has changed the character of our partnership, introducing more surprises as two people, growing through different experiences, find fresh ways of communicating with each other. As she has developed her strengths in her own work and interests, she has stood her ground more, rather than retiring into the shadows. That has encouraged me not to censor so many of my feelings. Both of us prefer to know what the other is feeling, even if there is some pain about that.

Grace's skills in music, colour and gardening have played an important part in our learning better how to celebrate. This has helped us both to feel on top of life – mostly! Friends often say with apparent surprise, 'You do look well,' as though someone living in

Liverpool would inevitably be weighed down by the cares of the world. Wherever we have lived, she has managed to combine the elements of the private home and a public place, so that a wide variety of people feel relaxed there. Bishop's Lodge is a large house to manage with a helper coming in only one day a week. I feel that Grace has given me space to take on some real responsibility for shaping and maintaining our home too.

This way of growing has, I believe, made my ministry more sensitive to people's real situations. It is all too easy for clergy to deceive themselves by hearing only the comments they want to hear. Grace has been my most honest critic, just as she has been my most consistent encourager. The daughter and the granddaughter of evangelical Anglican vicarages, she fully understands and lives the faith I was brought into. She has shared deeply with me the experiences which I, together with Derek, try to describe in this book. Sometimes her questioning is more radical than mine.

Acknowledging feelings of fear and weakness, learning our need of support, realising we are vulnerable, not made of cast iron – all these have enabled us to grow as human beings and as Christians. Christian marriages and clergy marriages are not shielded from the stresses which threaten all marriages today. Nothing has seemed more important to me as a bishop than helping to create the kind of atmosphere in which married partners can shout early enough for the help they need for the marriage to have a chance to survive.

In 1968 the Bishop of Southwark, Mervyn Stockwood, asked me to consider becoming suffragan bishop of Woolwich. It was an enormous shock. The Mayflower seemed to offer me the opportunities I wanted most, to be involved with the life of urban working-class people, the group in European history in which the Church had been least able to root itself. I had planned a twelve-month sabbatical in Edinburgh, where I could study and try to write a serious book about urban mission. Reading my notebook of the time in which I had listed a series of factors to consider, I see some of my fears about becoming a bishop: 'My usefulness is that I am close to working-class life. When I go to meetings, I listen with my neighbours' ears. If being a bishop meant being cut off from such, I would lose my usefulness'; 'Others have set out with high hopes of reforming the establishment and have been tamed by it. Why should I suppose I could succeed where they have failed?'; 'If we believe that the visible Church is one of Christ's vehicles, we must want to make it more effective. So some of us must sometimes be prepared to work from within the establishment. Otherwise we must state, "Factor: establishment is hopeless. Deduction: we must all abandon the visible Church!"' Gradually I felt that, if I was called to be a bishop, the sooner I started to learn a whole new set of skills, the better.

I was consecrated Bishop of Woolwich at the age of forty by Archbishop Michael Ramsey in Southwark Cathedral. In the traditional charge to the new bishop was included the question, 'Will you be merciful for Christ's sake to poor and needy people, and to all strangers destitute of help?' In South East London I met on a broader canvas the issues I had faced in East London. Bermondsey and Rotherhithe had similar 'villagey' characteristics to Canning Town. I also met inner-city families who had moved to large outer estates like Downham and St Helier. My area of responsibility took in about 150 parishes, including the suburbs and the much more affluent commuter villages of East Surrey.

We lived in Asylum Road, Peckham. The population in the street comprised perhaps equal numbers of black people and white people. I was very conscious of my need to understand more of the black experience in London. I rang up the Rev. Wilfred Wood, whom I knew through the Martin Luther King Fund and Foundation. I said, 'If I give you a whole day, will you take me and educate me?' He took me to visit black families and to meet leaders in the black community in Shepherd's Bush, West London, where he was working. I faced new and disturbing questions when the community leaders insisted that I listened to them on the subject of the police and the black community for more than an hour, before they would discuss anything else with me.

I had to get used to hearing out angry voices from the black community as much as I had in white East London. When I was driving some black community leaders home after a meeting in Peckham, one, whom I knew quite well, made a caustic remark concerning the Christian philosophy about being black. When the others had got out of the car I asked him what he meant. 'About having a black heart,' he said, 'and Jesus washes you, so you can have a white heart.' I learnt never to dismiss lightly the damaging effect of language like that on black children.

Many schools in South East London had large proportions of black children. I realised again how important expectations were. Visiting an infants' school during a parish visit, I was to speak in that day's assembly. As we went in the head teacher said, 'They won't achieve much of course, but we try to make them happy.' What chance did children have of achieving, when such judgments were made before they were seven years old? False assumptions were also made about parents. A black community worker in Brixton told me of a conversation with a head teacher. They both knew a particular girl and her mother. 'The mother simply doesn't care,' said the head teacher. 'As it happened,' said the community worker, 'the mother had been in my office that morning saying, "I can't cope."'

I must have visited all the grammar schools in South East London with the exception of the Roman Catholic ones. In none of them were there more black faces than could be counted on the fingers of one hand, and they were quite likely to be the children of an ambassador. I wrote to the Runnymede Trust asking if they had considered enquiring into the racial effects of selection at eleven years old. They replied, probably correctly, that they acknowledged what was happening, but thought that it was more likely to be attributable to social class than to race. In some comprehensive schools we were beginning to see black boys and girls among their high fliers on the way to university places.

I came to learn that a strong assertion of black consciousness is not a denial of the possibility of true integration. Community development has to go through a stage where a community which has felt itself powerless develops the strength of its own culture and life. This cannot be in organisations which are indefinitely controlled by white people. Sometimes leaders of such a community will speak aggressively before true dialogue can be achieved on equal terms.

I was chairman of the Martin Luther King Foundation while I was Bishop of Woolwich. We concentrated on training opportunities for employment. These were the years before the Manpower Services Commission offered large funds for youth training and it was a struggle to stay afloat. But with its black leadership the Balham Training Scheme did stay afloat and offered good training for a steady flow of black trainees. I handed over the chair to Wilfred Wood, by now the vicar of St Laurence, Catford. When I instituted him as vicar, the large black congregation showed me how black people are willing to respond when the Church takes them seriously. When Wilfred Wood was consecrated as Bishop of Croydon, he became the first black bishop in the Church of England. Half the great congregation in St Paul's Cathedral that day was black. Much of the drift of black people away to black-led Churches from the mainline Churches, in which so many grew up, was because they did not feel recognised as Christians with God-given talents. Instead they felt they were tolerated only up to certain levels and in certain proportions.

My years in East and South East London increasingly led me to see the importance of ecumenical partnership. That began with recognising the different traditions within the Church of England, which is in a way its own ecumenical movement. When Bishop Wand ordained me deacon in St Paul's Cathedral in 1955, the party traditions among those being ordained were very visible. Half of the men genuflected and crossed themselves at the appropriate moments in the service. Half of us stood motionless at those moments. After the service concluded, we had to go in line to receive the papers of our orders from Bishop Wand. Many in front of me knelt as they received their orders and kissed his ring. I knew that 'we' did not do that, but being anxious to show my respect for the bishop I gave a bow as I took my orders from him. He did not let go. I went cold down my spine, thinking, 'I haven't shown enough respect!' What he knew, that I did not, was that he had agreed for a press agency photographer to take a photograph of this Test cricketer receiving his orders, and he was waiting for the photograph to be taken.

In Cambridge it felt as though each of our theological groups knew precisely where we stood about every issue. We had largely kept company with those we agreed with. In East London the secular winds blew very cold. We could not afford the luxury of working only with those we agreed with about everything. Over many issues it became very clear that Christians of other traditions and denominations were standing up for what seemed most important to me. My closest allies among my neighbours and contemporaries in Canning Town were an Anglican Franciscan, Brother Bernard, a neighbouring Anglican vicar in the Catholic tradition, Robin Bennett, and a more radical-minded Baptist, Colin Marchant. We were still very cautious with our Roman Catholic neighbours. Those were the years in which we learnt that we could now begin to say the Lord's Prayer together.

In one of our talking groups at the Mayflower Family Centre, one of our local lay people put me on the spot: 'You go off and meet these other Christians,' she said. 'Why don't you invite some of them to come as preachers and lead groups here? Don't you think we are strong enough as Christians to hear different ideas?' The evangelicals among whom I began my ministry were inclined to accept invitations elsewhere, but not to invite clergy of other traditions in return. Now the penny dropped, and I saw how paternalist I was being – protecting 'my people' from the possible pain of meeting different ideas.

When I became Bishop of Woolwich, I realised that I must serve all traditions among the 150 or so parishes for which I now had responsibility. I learnt much about being a bishop from my diocesan bishop, Mervyn Stockwood. He did not keep the presence of different Church traditions as an unspoken and unfortunate underground reality. Each was respected for the particular positive contributions which it could bring to the whole. Mervyn Stockwood brought the issue of churchmanship out into the open with a lot of humour and teasing. For instance, every five years he asked rural deans to write some brief comments on each clergyman in the deanery. To bring some light relief to the chore of writing these reports, he asked them to include a note of how the man would currently regard his churchmanship. To assist in this process, the bishop sent the rural deans categories of churchmanship. In one direction the categories became more and more High Church until one description was, 'Thinks the Pope is a lapsed Catholic since Vatican II!' In another direction they became more and more Low Church until a description read, 'So Low Church, he would be in the cellar. Only he wouldn't keep any alcohol in it!' The categories began with: 'Sensible and central, i.e. like the bishop!'

I followed John Robinson as Bishop of Woolwich. It was therefore natural that many clergy and lay people in the diocese were asking radical questions about the Church and society. One of the damaging effects of party controversy in the Church is that the different protagonists avoid at all costs using the language that their opponents employ. So we collide without listening to each other, and bounce further away from brother and sister Christians. It is part of the privilege of being a bishop that many clergy and lay people open their hearts to say in private what they would not utter in public. So radical-minded clergy told me that they could no longer bring themselves to use the traditional language of Catholics and Evangelicals. For them such language was bound up with not really caring for people as people, but only as potential worshippers. Yet in private conversation I was able to ask such 'radicals' whether they felt there was an obligation on them to help those who had grown up altogether outside the Church to understand what it would mean to 'name the name of Christ'. They agreed that they did have such an obligation and were very ready to talk about how the gospel could be presented in terms to which their contemporaries could respond.

At the time when John Robinson wrote *Honest to God*, it seemed as though a 'radical party' might emerge in the Church alongside the more traditional parties. I do not believe that has happened. Rather, many Christians from different traditions have learnt to ask radical questions. For them the Bible and Christian tradition themselves contain very radical questions which tidy systems of belief, practice and conformity have kept submerged.

When I became a bishop I made it a matter of particular prayer that I should be able to worship from the heart when I was leading worship in so many different traditions. I like to believe that prayer has been answered very positively. In the majority of parishes in Southwark Diocese worship is centred very firmly in the Eucharist. I found myself increasingly set free to make that central in my own worship. At Cambridge we had emphasised the importance of the differences in eucharistic worship. I had then felt that emphasis on the real presence in the Eucharist was a denial of belief in the living presence of Christ throughout daily life. I had also then felt that to talk of an Offertory Procession – 'We have this bread to offer, work of human hands . . .' – was a denial of the movement in the Eucharist from God to man. For me nothing can take away from the couplets I learnt in my early years of new-found faith:

> O Saviour I have naught to plead
> In earth beneath or heaven above,
> Save only my exceeding need
> And thy exceeding love.

I came to believe that when God accepts us in Christ he calls us to bring the work of our human hands to offer to him in gratitude. To speak, then, of our entering into the movement of his self-offering is positively a response to that primary movement from God to man. In my own worship and devotion the abiding presence of Christ in every moment of life continues to be at the centre. But increasingly, as a bishop, I have come to understand other traditions and to see that to emphasise the real presence of Christ in the Eucharist need mean no denial of his presence throughout daily life.

I less and less felt the need to be suspicious of the experience of Roman Catholic Christians. In my East London years that change in attitude was inclined to be confirmed through personal meeting with individuals. One such memory was talking the night away with Derek Worlock in his presbytery in Stepney. We found we had much in common in our understanding of the Christian task in the inner city. When Grace and I moved to Peckham, there was an increasing number of opportunities to meet Roman Catholics and see something of their life as brothers and sisters in Christ.

Our closest co-operation was in the new town of Thamesmead. I was chairman of the Thamesmead Christian Community. The Methodist Church, the United Reformed Church and the Anglican Church committed themselves to build joint buildings in Thamesmead and to consult very carefully about our appointments to the joint team ministry. The Roman Catholic parish priest, Frank Sullivan, was thoroughly involved in the life of the team. He would ask me to go and see the Archbishop of Southwark, then Cyril Cowderoy, to try to persuade him that we should share the main place of worship, rather than build separately in the town centre. He thought I had a better chance of persuading Archbishop Cowderoy than he had. I went to make the case to the Archbishop. 'Your predecessor sat in that chair and made that case,' he said.

He spoke of the wish of Roman Catholics to have their own visible aids to worship in their church buildings. However, the door was not closed; we had many discussions with the architect over plans for a moveable or a permanent wall dividing our two centres of worship. After I had moved to Liverpool I came back for the dedication of the church. It has a joint baptistry in the middle. Through glass partitions you look through into the two places of worship.

When my appointment as Bishop of Liverpool was announced, the first telegram of congratulation was from the Archbishop of Liverpool, George Andrew Beck. It was very clear to me that with Liverpool's history our collaboration was going to need a much higher priority than I had yet given to ecumenical partnership. I saw a good deal of Archbishop Beck during my first few months in Liverpool. When illness led to his retirement, Mervyn Stockwood asked me if I would come to dinner with the Apostolic Delegate, Archbishop Bruno Heim. It was carefully planned for us to be left alone together for an hour, in which he asked me to speak about the priorities for the appointment of the new Archbishop of Liverpool.

3   COMING TO LIVERPOOL

'What's it like coming to Liverpool?' It was a question which we were both repeatedly asked. There were supplementary questions, spoken and sometimes unspoken. The spoken variety usually included, 'What do you think of Liverpool?', and before very long, 'Which team do you support?' If you hesitated about the former, your questioner almost invariably supplied the answer which was wanted: 'We're very warm, you know, very warm.' As for the football team of your choice, even though your answer would have no denominational significance, it was best to be evasive if you wished to avoid becoming involved in a spirited argument. The unspoken question was more insidious: 'What's it like coming from the smooth South to the rough North?' In fact both of us had spent long enough in the East End of London to have experienced already similar characteristics and even background. There is more than one South and more than one North.

That we were in a different setting, with another orientation and with some different values, there was no doubt. Many years later we are still struck by the environmental contrasts if, walking in London by St James' Park on the way to Westminster and looking at some of the great stone buildings and fine Georgian houses, we think of some of the rubble and tips remaining not far from our cathedrals. But there is more to it than that: a difference of feeling. It took us both some time before, catching the train at Euston, we could think of ourselves as coming home rather than going away. It is interesting that Londoners, arranging meetings, still seem to feel that it is further and more expensive to travel to Liverpool than to come from Liverpool to the nation's capital. There was another consideration with which to come to terms in this early process of adjustment. The problem of accents was mutual. Wondering whether the school-children were joking when they said 'tha kingdom cum', it was necessary to be sensitive to a smiling parent who said 'Every time you speak, you sound like the Duke of Edinburgh.'

IDENTITY

First impressions of Liverpool include a fierce sense of identity. Of late this has been all too easily equated with militancy, but even when translated to 'solidarity', it is still not as simple as that. It has to do with the most intense loyalties, which are themselves reflected in a strongly expressed possessiveness. Some of these loyalties have been inherited through many generations and are rooted in family ties and in attachment to large family firms, like Tate and Lyle and Crawford's Biscuits, which provided employment for one member of a family after another. The same intense loyalties are to be found with regard to churches, football teams, trade unions, districts, and recently with Merseyside as a whole.

There is a strongly positive side to this sense of identity. Possessiveness is matched by a sense of belonging, responsibility for each other – 'our Mark's ill' – generosity within the local community, and dogged persistence if it comes to a strike for survival. Solidarity may find expression in the quickness, sharpness, wit and anger of a people united in vigorous response to an enemy. In the past that enemy might have been the new migrants on the one hand, or the hostile host community on the other. It might be the 'corpy' (corporation or local authority), the employer, visiting social welfare workers or officials from London. They all fell into the category of 'them'. More recently the common enemy has been the growing bogey of unemployment. Although that may seem more impersonal, its cause is usually identified within that same corporate category of 'them'.

There can be a negative side to this strong sense of identity too. At times it can lead almost to a kind of tribalism which is inward-looking, self-protective and exclusive: an automatic distrust of 'the others'; 'our group', to be defended right or wrong; a retreat into a fortress mentality which is closed to any argument or explanation if it seems to threaten tribal custom. Then the quick wit ceases to be good-humoured and develops an aggressively defensive tone, keeping strangers at arm's length.

As newcomers to Liverpool, we were both struck by the strength of family ties which seemed stronger than those we had known in other cities. Sadly, this did not exclude the element of marital breakdown; but family relationships and concern for other members of the family all fitted into this picture of a tight but not closed community. Couples often shop together. Young fathers take their children out. When they are older, they will go with their sons to football matches or take them fishing. Blood is thicker than water.

In the older inner-city areas married women who have been born and brought up in the district are still known by their maiden names. Some of the spirit of the old terraced streets, where everyone knew and had concern for each other, has survived removal to other parts. If a city church in a depopulated area has a centenary celebration, it is packed out by those who have had to move away. It is evident that even in dispersal they have retained contact with one another and maintained their sense of family responsibility. On the perimeter estates, where there is a high proportion of single-parent families, the relation to mothers and grandmothers continues to be very strong.

Some observers have suggested that ideas of village-style communities, or close parish communities within urban areas, are an anachronism and are merely romantic hangovers from the past. That was not our impression. Their connection with their local history and culture has a clear bearing on many of the values they seek to preserve today. It was in Liverpool that we learnt the definition of culture as 'the way we do things around here'. This is not a wallowing in the past. There is a strong sense of present identity in many districts, especially in the inner city, and it has a great deal to do with how the people of a district wish to stay together as they face today's needs.

By the time of our coming to Liverpool many of the near-ghetto-like segregations within the general community had largely been dispersed. But parish identity was still particularly strong where the roots of the community lay among Irish immigrants of the last century, who had needed a rallying point to survive in hostile surroundings. Roman Catholic families, asked where they came from, still did not offer an address or the name of their district but replied with the name of their parish. Interestingly those who are now in overspill estates outside Liverpool will still give you the name of the parish of their birth and upbringing in the inner city. The names reflect their history and background, even the history before the Great Famine brought so many Irish to these shores. In the Roman Catholic Archdiocese of Liverpool, with 229 parishes, no less than forty-seven are dedicated to Our Lady under one title or another; but Irish traditions are well represented with St Malachy's, St Finbar's and a clutch of St Patrick's. If it was disarming to be told that someone came from 'Blessed Sacrament', the situation was not helped by the Liverpool custom of short forms, pet names and the process of adding a 'y' to the first syllable, now known as 'diddymisation'. To be told that someone was a 'Malachite' did not present an insoluble problem. Even 'Jimmys'

43

could be traced to St James's, Bootle. But you had to be careful of 'Sillies', who turned out to come from St Sylvester's in Vauxhall. This warm-hearted custom is not reserved to Roman Catholics. Anglican parishes have very similar loyalties with St Cyp's, St Ath's, St Phil's and of course the 'Shrewsy' (Shrewsbury House).

By the middle 1970s huge movements of population had already taken place. The population of the northern end of the inner city of Liverpool was in many places no more than one tenth of what it had once been. The famous Jesuit parish of St Francis Xavier, which used to house thirteen thousand Roman Catholics, had through demolition and dispersal fallen to under nine hundred, many of whom were elderly and for much of the year almost housebound. In a church built for a congregation of one thousand, they demanded and expected as many Masses each Sunday as had been required in the numerical heyday. Quite apart from the obvious pastoral problems such a situation presented, there was resentment against the generally accursed 'planners' both among those who had been left behind and those who had been transplanted to the new estates. A generation after the dispersal, the children were still being taught the song:

> Don't want to go to Kirkby,
> Skelmersdale or Speke,
> Don't want to go from all we know
> in Back Buchanan Street.

Loyalties and the strong sense of identity were often very localised. The negative expression of this could be seen from the reluctance of a family to move house from Everton (North End) to Toxteth (South End), a distance of no more than two miles. The teenage children expressed great fear at the reception they expected. Where feelings are so intense, change, even of surroundings, does not come easily.

DEREK WORLOCK: Within months of my arrival I was required to produce a pastoral plan, and in it may be found an early reflection on this problem:

> *Of great consequence are the steps we must take to deepen the faith of our people. This archdiocese is rightly renowed for its loyalty: a loyalty to a way of life as well as to people and even buildings. But if this has usually been unquestioning – a holy allegiance which is a combination of religious devotion and at times near-militant*

adherence to traditions and customs – it has also to a great extent been doctrinally uninvolving and uncommitting: more the 'faith of our fathers' always to be preserved, rather than the fulfilment today of cherished responsibilities handed down to us from the past and flowing from our baptism and confirmation and membership of the Church.

I am hesitant to appear in any way critical of this, because so much of it is part of our history and the inherited beauty of our past. But we must recognise that such an approach is under pressure and threat today from secular values and considerations. Without involvement there is no sense of responsibility: without responsibility there is no active sharing in the life and mission of the Church. Often there is alienation. Move the loyal adherent from his customary surroundings or demolish those surroundings, and he can be confused, if not actually lost. For he can no longer recognise the externals of what has commanded his loyalty. There must be commitment of mind and heart to survive such changes: and there have been many such changes.

('Pastoral Plan for the Archdiocese of Liverpool', September, 1976)

When we came to Liverpool in 1975/6, the dream of great new housing projects already lay in ruins. On the wall of a large block of flats on Everton Brow, now demolished, was a commemorative plaque which read, 'The Braddocks: opened by the Rt. Hon. Hugh Gaitskell, 1957.' The hope, which so many shared, was that such high-rise blocks would get rid of the long waiting lists for housing and of the mean, grey, terraced streets. With this went the belief that it would relieve the gross overcrowding of the past and that families would be given a flying start, if they could move from the over-populated inner city into spacious estates on green field sites. So rigorously was this policy pursued that a quarter of the whole population of Merseyside lives on those great estates around the perimeter of the city.

DAVID SHEPPARD: Our first year in Liverpool saw the production in the Everyman Theatre of the play Love and Kisses from Kirkby. *It was keen observation, often bitter, sometimes sensitive. There was Bessie Braddock, five feet square, dressed in red from head to toe, explaining the pressure of ten thousand on the housing list. There was the family buying new furniture and making everyone take off their shoes to enter the house. There was the councillor taking the blame when reality fell short of a dream. And then came the smashing of the dream – the broken glass, the endless delays for repairs, costly travel to see grandparents left behind, poor shopping facilities, the collapse of employment . . . Within fifteen years of being built, the great blocks of Netherley were deserted, then demolished.*

Undoubtedly some of the sense of community moved with the people and is recognisable in the outer estates. People in one block of flats in Speke told us that, because through unemployment one family had moved out, all the other families in the block felt, as it were, bereaved and were contemplating trying to move away themselves. There have been a number of local community and estate festivals, such as 'Speke Together', which seem almost to try to emulate the street-parties of the past. Living and working in this sometimes dispiriting context, one vicar said, 'I would hope more than anything that people's confidence in themselves and in God might grow against all the odds. The odds include lack of confidence, anger, the risk of mental breakdown and the shortage of money.'

Those long odds were part of the reality which met us when we both came north to Liverpool. Beside them must be set the sense of identity and the resilience of the people, their uncrushability which prevents the recognition of defeat foretold by others. Not easy to explain, it is for many people part of a deep sense of belonging to Liverpool and to Merseyside. There was to be an astonishing expression of this at the Milk Cup Final between Everton and Liverpool at Wembley in 1984. The cars and coaches travelling south had blue scarves and red scarves flying from the same windows. Once arrived, the two bands of supporters could not be separated into different parts of the ground: they came from the same family, the same street. At the end of a hard-fought good-tempered drawn match the two teams made the lap of honour around the stadium together, while the whole crowd took up the chant, 'Mer-sey-side, Mer-sey-side'.

MANY LIVERPOOLS

Archbishop's House and Bishop's Lodge are within one mile of each other in Mossley Hill and Woolton. These are prosperous suburbs of Liverpool. Many professional people, moving to Liverpool, have been warned that life here would be a grim experience. They have found, as we have, a city which captures the heart. It provides varied opportunities. In addition to the attraction of its two famous football teams, there is easy access by car to well-known golf courses, cricket and rugby. North Wales and the Lake

District are no real distance away, and in Liverpool itself there are good walks by the River Mersey and in long-established parks. Sefton Park and Croxteth Park bring the whole of Liverpool together. It was in the latter that two small boys were heard talking in the thickest of Scouse accents and with sheer delight of the field they were passing: 'It's the one where the robins were.' Ainsdale Beach also, with its miles of sand, is a place where people from all over Merseyside go for relaxation with their families.

The arts in Liverpool also present lively opportunities. We found three hundred children from Liverpool schools coming together every Saturday morning in orchestras and bands. The Philharmonic Hall is a focus for the world of music in which both cathedrals play an important part. Theatres and clubs have helped develop much local talent. The city is rightly famous for its Liverpool-born comedians, but it has also bred its actors and actresses, artists, poets and musicians The scope of its culture is wide. When the Royal Ballet visits the city for a week each year, the largest theatre is packed out night after night. All this is a very different picture from that presented by the all too frequent, if sadly accurate, reports of Liverpool's bad housing, vandalism and unemployment.

Among our suburban neighbours we found sharply different attitudes to many features of Liverpool life. We soon discovered, for example, that the Beatles were hated as well as loved in Liverpool. Their songs were still sung. Some of their contemporaries admired their success and the fact that they had 'got on'. But as many were critical of their lifestyle and of the way they appeared to have abandoned the city which had given them a start. Similar polarised reactions were aroused by such topics of conversation as Liverpool dockers, poverty, investment in Merseyside, and racial discrimination. Some with whom we would try to discuss these matters were judgmental, arguing that those who were disadvantaged had brought their troubles on their own heads through laziness, incompetent management or strike-happy militancy. Others of our neighbours reacted very differently. They saw Liverpool as their city and, feeling keenly the human hurts of a declining economy, were determined to stay and fight.

Quite quickly we came to see that there were two Liverpools. Then, as we became conscious of these very different attitudes, some of which were related to social class and others to difference of experience, we began to realise that in fact there are many Liverpools.

Part of the knowledge which we brought with us about the North-West concerned the painter L. S. Lowry. He rejoiced to call himself 'a Manchester man'. That was part of a pointed comparison from the nineteenth century: 'A Salford lad, a Manchester man and a Liverpool gentleman.' The edge of the comparison was against Liverpool, which at that time had more millionaires than any other British provincial city. In a manufacturing city like Manchester it was easier for the workers to improve their situation. A fair proportion would find their way on to the staff or into management. Liverpool never had a large sector of manufacturing industry, except for the 1950s and 1960s, when attempts were made to attract car firms and other large industrial concerns by means of regional policy grants. The pattern of life in 'busy, noisy, money-getting Liverpool', as it was described at the time, was established by its merchants in the nineteenth century. The city was largely a commercial and distributive centre. Its industrial sector chiefly wanted low-paid unskilled workers. The docks encouraged casual labour. Relatively few Liverpudlians found stable employment.

Part of our introduction to Liverpool consisted in listening to those in the trade union movement. We were told of the lasting influence of the dominant culture of the Dock Road. For generations dockers had had to stand 'on the stones', trying to make themselves visible to the foreman in the hope that he would choose them for the job in hand. That culture of the Dock Road, which introduced competitiveness into solidarity, bred among the dockers themselves a deep suspicion of all who held formal institutional positions of responsibility. A mate who became a trade union official was suspected of having sold out to the big institution; you stopped drinking with him. When young trade union hopefuls were sent off to university, they were often thought to have lost contact with those they were meant to represent. They joined the ranks of those who lost credibility with the community from which they had been drawn and to which they could seldom return. There is a long background in Liverpool's history to the mistrust which the local shop stewards' committee has on many occasions shown towards national officers of their own union.

In every large city in Britain there has been a certain segregation by social class. From the very beginning Liverpool was more divided than most. Haphazard housing development took place in response to the erratic need for labour in the commercial sea-port, and to the arrival of impoverished migrants from the countryside in Ireland, England, Wales and Scotland. The dominant philosophy of self-improvement meant that the quest for education and success in finding a steady job led out of areas like Scotland Road into private housing. This segregation within sectors of the city's community was compounded when vast one-class corporation estates were built. The clergy in such areas learnt from hard experience that those young people, whose leadership for Church and community they tried to develop, almost invariably sought advancement and employment opportunities outside the area in which they had been reared.

It was the hope of those who took pride in their city that the many Liverpools, with their variety of identities, could make for rich potential. They believed that the city possessed a tolerant, cosmopolitan character, which encouraged its many migrant groups – Irish, Welsh, Scottish, Jewish, Asian, Chinese and black – to keep their distinct characteristics as a contribution to the life of the whole community. Jewish, Chinese and Asian migrants were best placed as they included a high proportion of business people. The efforts of each group to emphasise its distinct character has often been fortified by religion. But sadly some of the groups have found that a disproportionate number of their members have become entrapped in a vicious circle of the poorest opportunities in jobs, housing, health, schools and other services.

One distinct Liverpool group has been excluded from the life of the city to a markedly greater degree than any other. We refer to the black community. When we first arrived in Liverpool we were repeatedly told by white people that Liverpool had no race relations problem. This proved to be merely their perception: they rarely saw any black people and there was very little trouble to disturb them. As we started to meet Liverpool-born black people and listened to those who were close to them, a very different picture began to emerge. In an early discussion we heard: 'Don't call us an ethnic minority. We are disadvantaged Liverpool blacks.' Wally Brown, a black community leader in Liverpool at that time, has written: 'In Liverpool we are dealing with generations of under-achievement; those of school age see around them parents and grandparents who have not achieved, and thus feel that there is no point in trying.' Earlier a working party, as far back as in 1939, had interviewed two hundred and six black heads of household. Seventy-four per cent were unemployed. At that stage white people spoke of there being 'no seamen's jobs' available.

The leader of the Methodist youth club in Princes Road spoke to us of the difficulty he had when trying to encourage black young people to go after good jobs. Their reply was fair enough: 'You are not just wanting us to be twice as good at the job as white people. You are expecting us to be pioneers, going after jobs where no black people have gone before.' There was also the account of the black girl in the fifth form at Paddington comprehensive school, near the top of Edge Hill, which runs down into the city centre. 'Why don't black people get jobs in Liverpool in the big stores or on buses and trains?' she asked. 'They do in London. I know because I've lived there.'

By comparison with South London we saw only small numbers of black people in churches, and of these only a small proportion had been born in Liverpool. We met little or none of the vigour of the black-led churches, so strong in more recently settled black communities in Birmingham and in South and West London. Liverpool has had a substantial black community for at least one hundred years: some say two hundred years. Yet we found that there were no black MPs or city councillors, and hardly any Liverpool-born black lawyers, doctors, teachers, managers or, for that matter, clergy. 'Frankly,' we were told, 'they are not the sort of families to produce that kind of person.' Although the word 'alienation', owing its origin to Marx, was not at the time in popular use, we met a whole community which felt itself excluded from the normal workings and opportunities of the city which was their home.

ECONOMIC DECLINE

On our coming to Liverpool we were quickly made aware of the problems arising from the change in the city's fortunes. The Roman Catholic clergy, on being consulted by those concerned with the appointment of a new archbishop, had indicated the grave social questions which would have to be faced as a result of the movement of people and the economic decline. The recently constructed Metropolitan Cathedral, which was called 'Paddy's Wigwam' by all except the Catholics, who spoke of the 'Mersey Funnel', had been built of new materials by new methods in record time; but the roof leaked, the debt remained, and much of the area had been depopulated by university development. For the Anglicans the change in Liverpool's fortunes was even more significant. The massive Anglican Cathedral was still in the process of building. It was to be completed in 1978 after seventy-four years' continuous work. In 1904 a powerful Laymen's Building Committee had reflected the confidence of Liverpool's giants in setting out to build the largest Anglican church in the world. As it neared completion, it served the poorest city in England.

As newly-arrived bishops we soon found ourselves listening to the very different reasons to which divided Liverpool attributed its economic decline, which dated from much earlier than many of its critics supposed. None could deny that the economic base was weak. It was also clear that many of the decisions affecting the local economy and the employment situation were being made elsewhere: often in London, but in the case of multi-nationals much further afield. All manner of diagnoses were offered. One set of perceptions accused 'bloody-minded dockers' of making the port unworkable. On factory closures they pointed the finger at 'wreckers' who, abusing worker solidarity, were allowed to lead the work-force by the nose into pricing themselves out of the market. Those who viewed the problems in this way were opposed to further government intervention through regional policies. On the other hand there were those who stressed the bitter history of the docks industry and who warned of the poor consultation in commerce and industry. They pointed to remote boards of directors with no stake in Merseyside, to inadequate management often brought in from outside and unfamiliar with the character of Merseysiders.

Liverpool now found itself in the wrong place, on the wrong side of the country. The market of the European Economic Community had replaced that of the Empire. Air travel had taken over from passenger lines. This was an accepted fact, but the extent of the reversal was not always appreciated. The port had always dominated Liverpool's economy. In 1800 three quarters of British slaving ships had sailed from Liverpool, in peak years carrying fifty thousand slaves. There were vast imports of raw materials and a major export trade for the north of England and the Midlands. Between 1830 and 1860 trade trebled. It trebled again between 1860 and the outbreak of the First World War in 1914. By that time one third of all British exports and one quarter of all imports passed through Liverpool.

Liverpool's decline dates back to the Depression which followed that First World War. At the same time as Britain's overall commerce slumped between 1919 and 1939, Liverpool lost an annual average of one per cent of its trade to other British ports. By the early 1930s unemployment in Liverpool had reached twenty-eight per cent. Throughout the 1930s it was one and a half times the national average. In the late 1940s, immediately following the Second World War, it was two and a half times the national average. Then, in the 1950s and 1960s, government policies brought new jobs to Merseyside, including twenty-five thousand in the car industry. That growth was soon reversed, and in the ten years before our arrival, between 1966 and 1976, employment in Merseyside fell by fourteen per cent.

At this time hopes for growth in employment were shifting towards the service sector, which had always been stronger than the manufacturing sector in Liverpool. Most service jobs were in the 'blue-collar' sector, in nationalised industries, transport, retailing and distribution. Significantly, high-status jobs in insurance, banking, finance, business, professional and scientific services, actually declined in Liverpool in the 1970s, while nationally they grew. Meantime the pattern of ownership was critical to the weakness of Merseyside's economic base. While some effort was being made to promote local small businesses, they never existed in Liverpool on a scale comparable with, say, Birmingham.

The trend of moving the head offices of traditional Liverpool companies to London or Southampton was long established. We were told that the city's commercial decline had commenced when Cunard moved its head office to London early in the century. The real vulnerability lay with the large firms, many of which were controlled from outside the region. Between 1965 and 1975 the proportion of Liverpool's manufacturing firms which were under control from elsewhere rose from fifty-one per cent to seventy per cent. Decisions about investment or disinvestment were made by directors with no particular interest in Liverpool or commitment to its people. When this is linked with the problem of Liverpool's so-called 'image', which is widely believed in business communities, the inevitable follows. When major companies and multinationals consider the rationalisation of their operation in times of recession, the first cut-back invariably falls in Merseyside. Conversely, when we successfully persuaded the managing director of a large company to consider opening a new branch in Merseyside, he informed us subsequently that his bright young men had advised him and his colleagues that it should only be attempted if his company were in a philanthropic mood about throwing away good money.

BITTER FEUDING

In the summer of 1975 Archbishop Donald Coggan of Canterbury issued a Call to the Nation. It sparked off a whole number of ecumenical meetings at which members of different Churches sought ways together of bringing Christian principles to bear on English public life and morals.

DAVID SHEPPARD: Soon after I arrived in the city I received an invitation from Owen Doyle, the Roman Catholic Lord Mayor of Liverpool, to call on him and discuss what sort of response could be made to the Call to the Nation. I gladly accepted the invitation on the understanding that Archbishop George Andrew Beck would also be asked. As a result of this discussion, the Lord Mayor invited a wide-ranging group of people in public life in Merseyside to meet the leaders of the Churches. Subsequently there was a private meeting between the Church leaders and the leaders of the three political parties in Liverpool. I suggested to the next Lord Mayor that he should call a similar meeting with the leaders of the parties, and that we should discuss the subject 'Continuity in Government'. Somehow that further meeting was never called. Political bitterness developed over generations dies hard.

The week before I came to Liverpool, I sat by the bedside of Bill Hamling, MP for Woolwich West. It was only a few days before his death in Westminster Hospital. Bill had been born and brought up in Liverpool and he talked to me of his memories of those early years. 'I suppose I ran away', he said, 'because the politics were so bitter.'

Behind the bitterness Bill Hamling had known in the 1930s were years of animosity in which sectarian feelings produced the deepest divisions of all, divisions in which party politics and religious sectarianism had become intertwined. Orange Lodges had first been formed in England in Manchester in 1798, then in Liverpool in 1807. As the Famine years brought more and more Irish immigrants into the dock area of Scotland Road, so the native-born section of the community looked down in fear and threat from Everton Brow on what they saw as an 'alien green flood', sweeping in to take whatever employment existed. Militant Protestantism took an even more aggressive turn with the coming of George Wise to Liverpool in 1888. He would burlesque Roman Catholic rites in the streets and John Kensit vied with him in making still more extreme attacks. Bishop Chavasse said, 'I am often ashamed of the unwise and unchristian conduct of some who call themselves Protestant.'

A Protestant Party was formed in 1903 and had an uneasy understanding with the Conservatives until 1972, when the latter determined to put up their own candidates in every ward. Whereas Home Rule had been the issue which most inflamed passions at the turn of the century, ritualism in the Church of England was another target raised as an enemy by George Wise and later, at the time of the 1928 Alternative Prayer Book, by his successor, the Reverend H. D. Longbottom, leader of the Protestant Party. The following year there was a storm when the Roman Catholics wished to buy the nine-acre site of the Brownlow Hill Workhouse in order to fulfil Archbishop Downey's dream of building 'a cathedral in our time'. But amidst cries of 'Rome on the rates', the abiding bone of contention was the issue of denominational schools. The case for Roman Catholic schools had been fought almost since Catholic Emancipation but it remained a matter of bitter contention in Liverpool. When the city council refused to implement the 1936 Education Act, which empowered it to give grants for the building of denominational schools, a special Liverpool Act had to be passed in 1939 to secure the position of the Roman Catholic schools: an anomaly which vanished with the Butler Education Act at the end of the war.

There were of course Roman Catholics who were ready enough to respond in kind. A 'Sunday Music in the Parks League' came into conflict with sabbatarian restrictions: in the ensuing riot several Protestant homes in Toxteth were wrecked. During the September of 1904 the police reported that almost nightly disturbances occurred without special occasion or warning. It is no exaggeration to say that in 1909 the city was torn by sectarian civil war. 157 Catholic families (833 persons) fled from their homes in Netherfield Road in the heart of the Orange Lodge territory. Forty Protestant families left their homes in Scotland Road and Vauxhall. Gangs consolidated uniformity street by street, workplace by workplace. There was a Protestant Defence Committee and the Roman Catholic Bishop Whiteside sanctioned a Catholic Emergency Association. To make matters worse, this sectarianism was being practised against a background of industrial disputes and violence.

Anarcho-Syndicalism, with international links with Spain and the United States, was strong in Liverpool. It stressed direct action to bring about change rather than recourse to parliamentary legislation. Syndicalists argued that when working-class representatives were returned to Westminster, they were seduced by the 'club' atmosphere of Parliament and failed to stand up for their constituents. There was no shortage of social problems to provide industrial action, and in 1911 seamen, dockers, railwaymen and other transport workers came together in a prolonged strike. A demonstration on St George's Plateau attracted ninety thousand people and ended as 'Bloody Sunday' with two hundred people injured. No less than 2,300 soldiers were introduced to patrol the streets of Liverpool and the Anglican Bishop Chavasse gave judgment, declaring that many urban dwellers had resisted 'alike the laws of God and man', being ever ready to 'riot, plunder, maim and destroy'. But he claimed that the well-to-do were also transgressors: 'their selfish, unsympathetic attitude, absorption in getting money or in seeking pleasure, are some of the chief causes of the present labour troubles'.

Reaction was inevitable. The Labour Party, which had increased its poll in the municipal elections, now lost every election in 1912 and 1913. While the Conservatives were firmly organised under the leadership of Archibald Salvidge and Sir Thomas White, the Labour supporters were riven with feuds. It was said that they hated each other more than they hated the Tories. The allegation that some were over-committed to Irish nationalism was countered by charges that the others were the proponents of atheism. In the 1920s Archbishop Keating agreed to the formation of the Catholic Representative Association (the 'Catholic Party'). It proclaimed itself against 'divorce, interference in Catholic schools and the Revolution'. But it was short-lived. When Richard Downey became Archbishop in 1928, he immediately forbade the use of the title 'Catholic' to any political party and banned electoral activity by priests. This did not in fact bring sectarian violence to an end. The continuing question of aid to Catholic schools led to recurrent feuds with extreme Protestants under Councillor Longbottom. The annual outings and marches of the Orange Lodge could be as explosive occasions as were the processions in the Roman Catholic areas of the city.

Indeed violent clashes continued until much more recent times. Some of the episodes have passed into religious folklore and are related to this day, though frequently with a smile. Two incidents are often recalled. In 1932 when Canon Dawber, parish priest of St Malachy's, was celebrating his jubilee, he was pushed through the streets in a carriage bedecked with flags and ribbons. This proved too much for the Protestants in the South Docks area, who attacked the parishioners, drove them into the church and besieged them there for three days. The local police would not intervene and a force had to be brought up from Birmingham to effect relief. The second incident was the notorious stoning of Archbishop Heenan in March 1958. Be it said at once that the Archbishop at the time and those with memories today insisted that the episode was exaggerated by the press. When visiting St Anthony's parish in Scotland Road, the Archbishop had chosen to visit a sick woman on the edge of the parish bordering the Orange Lodge quarter. On foot and clad in cassock and cloak, the Archbishop was soon joined by cheering schoolchildren, much to the alarm of the Protestants who, fearing an attack, put out their Orange flags and bricks began to fly. No great damage was done and the Archbishop, perhaps with undue optimism, told the press: 'I imagine that they were enjoying themselves. I am sure that when they come to know me in those streets, where I shall continue to visit the sick, we shall become friends.'

John Braddock became the leader of the Labour Party in 1945 but was not able to embark on many new initiatives. Now there was a strong Roman Catholic presence in the party and Braddock himself, though not a religious man, devoted himself to the old Roman Catholic districts in central Liverpool from which so many were now being removed through new housing developments. Between 1955 and 1961, Labour controlled Liverpool City Council for the first time. Bill Sefton became leader of the council from 1963–67 and introduced a number of plans for modernisation, education, housing and transport. But the massive urban renewal and slum-clearance programme proved unpopular. Dislike of large-scale housing and anger at poor repairs turned many working-class tenants against Labour and prepared the way for the revival of the Liberal Party in Liverpool, with its emphasis on community politics. The population of many of the old Labour wards had dropped, the councillors had grown old and the 1974 Housing Act stressed the rehabilitation rather than the demolition of housing. In 1975 wholesale local government reorganisation changed boundaries, names and responsibilities of local authorities. The new councils were often to be run by inexperienced councillors with newly promoted officers. That year the Liberals took over the new Metropolitan District of Liverpool. It had new neighbours, faced different tasks and there was a new and powerful Metropolitan County Council. To this situation the Liberals brought a tight control over rates and, as we shall see in chapter nine, a change in direction in housing policy.

RELIGIOUS AWARENESS

We were quickly told that in Liverpool, 'Two things count. One is football and the other religion.' Certainly it seemed, and seems, a much more religious city than London. That is not merely to make an observation about church attendance. Simply to describe a group of people as 'secularised' is a very different matter from acknowledging that they are 'un-churched'. Again, believing and belonging are two different religious responses which do not always go together. Even to claim that people have faith is to invite the questions: 'What sort of faith? What kind of God do they have faith in?' Some years ago a famous answer was given to an enquiry into religious attitudes. In response to the question, 'Do you believe in a God who can change the course of events on earth?' the reply was given: 'No. Just the ordinary one.'

This brief sketch of the history of divided Liverpool will have shown that there was a great deal of belonging which did not necessarily imply believing. On the other hand the movement of people to new estates frequently left them with little or no sense of belonging, and belief was put to the test. The very hostility between the Orange and the Green had proved a rallying point and a strength against the threat which each felt the other to be. Now with the movement of people there were new challenges to be reckoned with. Augustine Harris, who was an auxiliary bishop in Liverpool when we both arrived, made this comment to us about Roman Catholic church life in Liverpool: 'The Church really depends for its practice on a strong community. There may be several reasons for such a sense of community: there may be other people's hostility; or there may be external pressures such as hard times, or internal pressures such as strong faith and fellowship. As the external pressures ease off, because Catholics feel themselves fully accepted into the wider community, the religious practice drops off.' In the old-established inner-city parishes, where the belonging of the men was matched by the believing of the women, the religious processions on the great festivals brought large numbers on to the streets; but on arrival at the church the women went in for devotions, the men mostly remained outside, officially on guard. The situation with the Orange processions, which still march today, was not so very different.

DEREK WORLOCK: One of the strongest impressions I received on coming to Liverpool from the South was that the intense loyalty of northern Catholics was directed primarily to externals, such as 'our' parish, 'our' priest, 'our' archbishop and even 'our' social club. This was not always a blind thing, but it did not imply much understanding of underlying belief. Resistance to change was probably tougher about the threatened closure of a presbytery in a depopulated area than it would be about some new insights into the nature of the Church's mission. It also meant that if the externals were changed, as when people were uprooted to new estates where church, priest and fellow parishioners were different, believing could cease when there was no longer a sense of belonging. On reflection it struck me that in the South there was less

*concern with externals, which could the more easily be changed or
re-ordered without realising the extent to which they might be propping
up belief.*

Social mobility has meant that in the post-war years strong
Roman Catholic parishes have developed in professional and
middle-class areas of Liverpool. Here, as might be expected, a
higher proportion of parishioners are regular Mass-attenders.
Educational opportunities have also been an important factor in
this, resulting in a single family experiencing in a few years
changes which were previously accomplished over several
generations.

Anglican patterns of church-going had long been very different.
Twopence to Cross the Mersey is Helen Forrester's own story of a
well-to-do family coming to Liverpool after bankruptcy in the
1930s, and becoming steadily more destitute. As a teenager Helen
was asked what Church her family belonged to. 'We are Church of
England. That is . . .', I hesitated, 'that is, when we are clean and
rich we are Church of England. I suppose that at present we are
nothing.' In 1974 Jim Hart made a study of the Protestant churches
of Toxteth. He looked at ten evangelical churches, of which three
were Anglican. Of the worshippers 331 lived in the area, and 1099
came from outside. Two of the Baptist churches had very substantial commuting congregations. The three Anglican churches had
sixty per cent of their congregations coming from within the area.
But the majority of lay people holding office in the churches came
from outside.

The sense of still belonging to a church, even if not a regular
attender, was certainly true of many Anglican parishes. When the
population had declined enormously and a scheme was published
to make a church redundant, the opposition was likely to be fierce.
It was often fiercest among those who were not church attenders
but who still spoke of 'our' church, with its association for them
with baptisms, weddings and funerals. Anglican church-going
proved to be much stronger in the suburbs. Close relationships
between the denominations had sometimes developed there; but
the pattern was patchy. Old sectarian 'gut feelings' were not
always set aside with the achievement of affluence or higher
education. In the 1950s Bishop Clifford Martin moved to Woolton,
where Archbishop Downey lived. They started to walk their dogs
together. Suburban Woolton was scandalised.

On our appointment to Liverpool, it seemed to both of us that,
given Liverpool's sectarian history, it must be right for us to give

higher priority than ever before to ecumenical relations and the work of reconciliation which must be involved. We both sought advice. Both of us received firm warnings that we should be very cautious, lest by trying to push forward too quickly the promotion of Christian unity, we might upset the precarious balance that had been achieved. Over and over again we were advised to leave well alone because it was impossible to tell how close to the surface there still lay the sectarian violence and hatreds of the past. We both weighed the advice as seriously as was merited and decided that we must press ahead.

LIVERPOOL: CITY AND DIOCESE

We have used the term 'Merseyside'. That word was not invented for the short life of the Merseyside County Council, whose abolition we greatly lamented. The term has long had a reality. The great estates of Knowsley all have their roots in Liverpool. In the borough of Sefton, districts like Formby, Ainsdale, Birkdale and Southport have a high proportion of Liverpool commuters. Economically they are part of Merseyside. At any dinner of professional people in Liverpool it is likely that up to a half of those present will have come through the tunnels from the Wirral. Whether they like it or not, economically they too are part of Merseyside.

The Roman Catholic archdiocese and the Anglican diocese both have the Mersey as their southern-most boundary and so do not include the Wirral. Both include the Lancashire towns of Ormskirk, Skelmersdale, Wigan and St Helens, and the (now) Cheshire towns of Warrington and Widnes. The archdiocese also extends to Leigh to the east and to Chorley and the outer reaches of Preston to the north. Lancashire town and country parishes, both Anglican and Roman Catholic, have strong family networks. Hard times have been faced with resilience which draws much of its toughness from staunch family life. The decline of a specialised industry, on which a town has depended, hits a whole community very hard. The smaller communities are often less prepared for change than the urban dwellers. Wigan and St Helens feel strongly that they, as well as Liverpool, have priority needs.

Community strength, built up over generations, is also reflected in active church membership. Anglican church attendance in Wigan is stronger than in any other part of the diocese. Once it had thirty-two coal mines. They have all been closed for some years: yet thirty Anglican parish churches, each with its church school, continue to keep the identity of those communities strongly alive. 'Catholic' Lancashire, in the archdiocese of Liverpool as well as in its neighbouring dioceses of Lancaster and Salford, is proud of places retaining their faith without break from pre-Reformation days. Today, with probably a smaller proportion of professional people in its membership than other Roman Catholic dioceses, the archdiocese of Liverpool remains numerically the largest diocese in Britain. In 1975 the numbers from the archdiocese were 550,000 (now, through emigration, 515,000), of whom about thirty-six per cent are at Mass on any one Sunday. In practice that means as much as sixty per cent in some rural and small town parishes, and maybe only twelve to fifteen per cent in the more deprived inner-city parishes with a high proportion of old people. Anglican attendance figures are on a different basis. The average Sunday attendance of those over sixteen years old in 1986 was thirty-one thousand. That of course does not take into account occasional church attendance.

With much the same territory, therefore, we quickly came to realise the temptation of the more remote parts such as Southport, Warrington and Chorley to want to distance themselves from Liverpool. In effect they were saying: 'We don't want to belong to them.' We were even advised to use our surnames rather than the title of the diocese when dealing with certain areas. It is now a commonplace to say that Britain has become polarised. But such feelings were not general. In most parishes in our dioceses we found people whose roots were in Liverpool. Sometimes they had turned their backs on those who had remained behind or failed to push themselves up into a new society. Often there was sympathetic understanding of the effects of unemployment and poverty, and a strong sense of being 'members one of another' in the Christian body.

4 MEETING-POINT

We had not been together in Liverpool for many weeks before we became convinced that the living Lord was calling us to face the challenge of trying to present a common witness to his teaching. It would be wrong to pretend that we had any real vision of the size of the task or the many aspects of the mission apparently opening up before us. Nor did we see ourselves as called to break through any ecumenical barrier. It just became increasingly clear that in attempting to shed the light of Christ's gospel on the problems facing Merseyside, we should try wherever possible to speak with one voice.

It was in fact a central day in the Church's life of worship which brought us more closely to what we now recognise as a meeting-point. Over thirty years earlier, at the height of the war, William Temple, Archbishop of Canterbury, had one Good Friday taken up his pen to write to Cardinal Arthur Hinsley, Archbishop of Westminster. Both were near the end of their lives. William Temple's greeting was simple: 'We meet at the foot of the cross.' On Good Friday 1976 the telephone provided for us the chance of just such an exchange. From that first real meeting-point a new sense of sharing arose.

DEREK WORLOCK: I had been in Liverpool just three weeks and was finding it increasingly difficult to disguise my sense of bereavement from the diocese of Portsmouth where I had left so many friends. Liverpool relationships had not yet grown and, in spite of all the tentative brotherhood offered to me by the priests the previous day, I had that Maundy Thursday known something of the loneliness and desolation of Gethsemane. On Good Friday evening David Sheppard rang. It was soon evident that there was no official business on hand. The call sprang from a wish to reflect together on the very centre of our faith. We talked unhurriedly about the Lord's death on the cross for us. When I put down the phone half an hour later, I realised the significance of our 'meeting at the foot of the cross'.

Every subsequent Good Friday we have made a point of meeting and of helping each other to meditate on the cross. Eight years after that first telephone conversation, we went together on the evening of one Good Friday to the first shared Anglican/Roman Catholic church built by our two dioceses. As a sign of our commitment to the project we had presented a large crucifix, specially carved and tinted, to hang on the wall behind the sanctuary. Standing together before it, we experienced again that essential unity of faith in the crucified Redeemer of mankind. Later we moved slowly around the new Stations of the Cross, sharing the thoughts provoked by each of these scenes of the Passion. They had been given particular poignancy by the wood-carver, David John, who had introduced certain well-known contemporary figures into the groups about Christ. The suffering, death and rising again of Jesus are for all time, even now. Of that we must both be a sign.

WORD AND EXAMPLE

Our acknowledgment of that common purpose and our recognition of one another as brother Christians, worshipping together at the foot of the cross, has been neither original nor unique. It has been rooted in our common faith in our Redeemer and in the central truths of the gospel. It has echoed the profound theological statements of recent times, though some people have found it difficult to recognise the link between our relationship and the inevitably heavily-worded theological reports of, for example, the Anglican/Roman Catholic International Commission (nowadays known as 'ARCIC'). This international group of theologians was set up by our two Churches in the aftermath of the Second Vatican Council to examine the differences between us and to evaluate the degree of agreement which already exists. Against that background, we have tried to give a practical example of partnership in action. Just as our partnership also involves other Churches, attempts at organised dialogue are not restricted to the Anglicans and Roman Catholics. There are, for example, bilateral talks in progress between the Methodists and Roman Catholics, and between the Anglicans and the Reformed Churches.

One of the most important tasks the ARCIC theologians have faced has been to try to find a common expression for their faith. Some of the differences of the past have been found to be at least related to language, and significant progress has been made in mutual understanding and the agreed expression of shared belief.

The task of this Commission is not concluded. ARCIC I completed its agenda and has been succeeded by ARCIC II. Our task has to a great extent been to live, reflect and sometimes to try to build on the agreement which the theologians have reached. If the language of the theologians in their Statements is inevitably 'churchy' and rightly precise, it is not easily understood by ordinary folk. To many people nowadays example strikes home before the word. Yet clearly we believe that our partnership is theologically based. Our Good Friday meeting-point and the partnership which has followed from it must somehow be seen to be related to, for instance, ARCIC's Windsor Statement on the Eucharist:

> God has given the Eucharist to the Church as a means through which the atoning work of Christ on the cross is proclaimed and made effective in the life of the Church . . . In the eucharistic prayer the Church continues to make a perpetual memorial of Christ's death; and his members, united with God and with one another, give thanks for all his mercies, entreat the benefits of his Passion on behalf of the whole Church, participate in these benefits and enter into the movement of his self-offering.
>
> (*Windsor Statement*, n. 5)

If it took the theologians of ARCIC I years of agonising to reach what they called 'substantial agreement' about terminology of this kind, it is not surprising that some people have failed to recognise in our concern for social justice 'the atoning work of Christ . . . made effective in the life of the Church'. But it is our belief that often it has been the common concern of the Churches for the real problems of how people in Merseyside live, which has led to a lessening of the old sectarian hatreds and to the beginning of a desire for Christian unity.

'Ecumenism', or the promotion of unity among Christians, is not a word which comes easily to English tongues. The extent of the unity of all believers in Christ, which is the aim of the Ecumenical Movement, may be seen from the Greek word *oikoumene*, meaning 'the whole inhabited world'. In practice there are many divisions even among those professing the same Christ. True ecumenism takes place between Churches and not simply between individuals. The point is made by the Second Vatican Council's Decree on Ecumenism: 'Those who take part in the ecumenical movement invoke the triune God and confess Jesus Christ as Lord and Saviour. This they do not merely as individuals but as corporate bodies, everyone regarding the body in which he heard the gospel as his Church and as God's Church.'

The need to reconcile separated Churches has existed ever since differences appeared among the early Christians. This is evident in the Acts of the Apostles and in the letters of St Paul. After the great division between the Eastern and Western Churches nearly a thousand years ago, various attempts at reunion were made without success. In the centuries following the Reformation, further sporadic efforts were made, often discoloured by nationalist considerations, but the real impetus of the Ecumenical Movement was not generally experienced until more recent times. The sheer wastefulness, rivalry and duplication of effort in much of the missionary work of the Churches, notably in India and Africa, were contributory causes for the Edinburgh Conference of 1910 which began a new search for unity. (The earlier sorry state of affairs is reflected in a recent survey of Toxteth, with its population of perhaps forty-five thousand inhabitants. The enquiry revealed no less than fifty-nine different Christian congregations.) Even then many of the early initiatives appear to have been of a pragmatic character rather than the expression of a clearly worked out theological position.

It was some time before biblical theology, deeply affecting Protestant and Roman Catholic thought, led to a new emphasis on the organic and unified nature of the Christian community, as described by St Paul and St John. We began to hear a great deal about the one 'people of God'. One-ness in Christ was recognised as the foundation on which all rests. The World Council of Churches had been inaugurated in 1948. Increased contacts, often in matters of social rather than doctrinal concern, led to increased knowledge. Various reunion schemes were proposed in which Anglican and Protestant Churches attempted to find a way forward. By the time Pope John XXIII summoned an Ecumenical Council in 1959, there was already evidence of new enthusiasms for the growing relationships between Christians of different traditions.

RECONCILING DIVISION

In Merseyside, as elsewhere throughout the country and indeed the Western world, such enthusiasms were patchy. Some questioned the very desirability of what Roman Catholics called 'the fullness of Christian unity'. Others questioned the need for it, being quite content merely to coexist in a state of non-belligerence. Realistically, Vatican II had spoken of 'one visible Church of God' as something for which 'almost all long, though in different ways'. Ecumenism is all about this longing, 'though in different ways'.

The Church is to be a sign of the unity of those who believe in Christ. It cannot be a faithful sign if it is itself divided and torn apart. This is where the content of unity, the agenda of ecumenism, is so important. The task of reconciliation in the world calls for what some describe as 'the wider ecumenism'. It is not just bringing divided Churches together by ecclesiastical 'joinery'. It is about the depths of unity grounded in the life of the Blessed Trinity, expressed in the human community of all the baptised. Our efforts to break down human barriers, such as those established through race, class and sex, may lack credibility unless we also face up to the divisions between the Churches. But the reverse is also true. Ecumenism is in danger of becoming an academic nicety unless it also takes account of the human divisions in society today.

Many people rightly attach great importance to the account, given by St John, of Christ's prayer to his Father the night before he died, that his followers might be one 'so that the world may believe it was you who sent me' (John 17:21 NJB). It was not to be just a notional relationship. So close was this bond of unity among his followers to be, that it must reflect the relationship between his Father and himself. The only thing that could stand in the way of the task he was entrusting to his disciples was sin. So Christ prayed that they and the believers who would follow them would be holy and be united in belief and in witness. Filled with the joy and the hope that came from his resurrection, they should be able to experience the strength of the bond of unity between them and draw mutual support from one another.

Scriptural teaching on this matter is clear. What in reality has happened? The rivalries and differences between groups of Christians have been so sharp and widespread as to have earned the description of being a 'scandal', a stumbling-block. Not only have they diminished all reasonable thought of mutual support and collaboration, but they have affected the credibility of the gospel entrusted to us. It makes matters worse that most of the differences have been held conscientiously and have become deeply rooted in religious loyalties. At various times and in different parts of the world, what started as doctrinal differences led to active persecution, leaving behind a trail of hatred, mistrust and fear. As we have seen in the previous chapter, for one hundred and fifty years

Liverpool experienced the consequences of differences just such as these. At times the bitterness which was aroused obscured almost all trace of a common belief in Christ. Collaboration on religious grounds became under the circumstances unthinkable.

A fresh impetus to progress in relationships came as a result of the Second Vatican Council. But the study, development and growth of understanding have been present in almost all Christian Churches. Where the differences have been most acute, there has been obvious urgency about the need for reconciliation. It was Pope John XXIII who said that 'the road to unity is the path of love'. But he was doing no more than reaffirming what John Wesley had written in the eighteenth century in his *Letter to a Roman Catholic*: 'If we cannot as yet think alike, we can at least love alike.' To describe ecumenism as love is not mere sermonising. Love alone is capable of healing the wounds of disunity and of casting out the fears that come from lack of trust in one another's motives. It helps to banish the prejudices which have often hung on from insufficient knowledge of each other's beliefs and inadequate loyalties. It enables people to rid their hearts of the bitterness left behind by recollections of less happy days. Yet this love cannot be mere emotionalism. It is prompted by the Spirit which enables Christians to overcome natural weaknesses and antagonism, to develop the respect which is a prerequisite for the bond of Christian unity, and to have the courage which is needed to tread new paths – or paths untrodden for centuries.

THE BOND OF BAPTISM

Looking back at the development in the work of reconciliation during the last twenty-five years, we believe that the breakthrough has at least been linked with a new approach to the understanding of baptism. For to recognise the bond of baptism is to acknowledge a common faith in Christ and makes it possible for the baptised to know each other as fellow Christians. St Paul, writing to the Christians in Rome, provides an insight into what baptism stood for from the very beginning, probably quoting words used in an early rite: '. . . if you declare with your mouth that Jesus is Lord, and if you believe with your heart that God raised him from the dead, then you will be saved' (Rom. 10:9 NJB). In many parts of the early Church it was usual for new Christians to be baptised on Easter morning. Christianity was cradled in warm Middle Eastern countries, so that baptisms normally took place out of doors, in a river or a lake. While the new Christians stood in the water, the Easter story would be told, that Christ was risen from the dead. When forgiveness and new life in the risen Christ were offered, the new Christians made their response in words of repentance and faith. Then they were baptised by immersion, right down into the water – not just a gentle trickle of water from a silver shell, as so often today. 'You cannot have forgotten', St Paul reminds his readers in that same letter to the Romans, 'that all of us, when we were baptised into Christ Jesus, were baptised into his death. So by our baptism into his death we were buried with him, so that as Christ was raised from the dead by the Father's glorious power, we too should begin living a new life' (Rom 6:3, 4 NJB). But St Paul is stressing the effects of baptism as well as the cleansing from sin. 'If we have been joined to him by dying a death like his, so we shall be by a resurrection like his' (Rom. 6:5 NJB).

In emphasising baptism as the root of the relationship between us, we are acknowledging a bond which is forged, not in mere terms of human friendship, but in Christ's life, death and resurrection. Recognising each other as brothers in Christ is not simply the result of sentimental warmth. It is not even a pragmatic arrangement, based on the fact that we work well together and enjoy doing so. It matters deeply to us that our relationship and partnership are derived from the Christian doctrine we hold and teach. Now that much of the old language of controversy has been cast to one side, we recognise that we hold Christian truths in common. We believe that by our baptism we are drawn into the death and resurrection of Christ, sharing in the divine life by the gift of the Holy Spirit, and becoming members of the Christian community which we call the Church. The links between those who have been baptised are summed up by St Paul in the words 'one in Christ Jesus' (Gal. 3:28 NJB). There can be no more profound a bond and relationship than that.

For the early Christian, baptism was a decisive and glorious event, marking the beginning of a new life in Christ. Recent insights into the nature of baptism have tended to stress the importance of the response required of the person baptised – or in the case of a child, the response of the parent, acting in the context of the believing community – as a balance to the emphasis formerly laid on the effect of the act of baptism upon the recipient. A relationship comes alive when it is acknowledged and given effect. There is indeed a need to hold the balance between the marvel of God's gift and the nature of our response. If we are asked which is the more important aspect, we would both reply that it is God's gift and that there is a certain objectivity in the visible sign of God's love for each person who is baptised. But by God's grace we are also given the power to respond. In that response, which is the beginning of a lifelong process, we are able to express our relationship not only with Christ but also with those others who are our brothers and sisters in the body of Christ.

Much of this is reflected in the document *Baptism, Eucharist and Ministry*, which was prepared in 1982 by yet another Commission of theologians drawn from all the main Christian Churches, including our own. They had been brought together by the World Council of Churches at Lima in Peru and the document they agreed on is known nowadays as the Lima Statement. In it we read: 'Baptism is both God's gift and our response to that gift . . . The necessity of faith for the reception of the salvation embodied and set forth in baptism is acknowledged by all the Churches. Personal commitment is necessary for responsible membership in the body of Christ' (*Lima Statement*, n. 8).

This emphasis on response as an outward sign of personal commitment and as a strict requirement for the acceptance of baptism has inevitably led to variations of pastoral practice, especially where infant baptism has been concerned. In the last two or three decades, the pendulum has swung back and forth in the light of both teaching and experience. Some priests have with a fair amount of reason been concerned lest baptism be seen almost as magic by parents demanding that their children be 'done' as soon as possible after birth, regardless of their own religious practice or lack of it. Clergy in both our Churches have often insisted on at least delaying the baptism of the infant while the parents are carefully instructed in their responsibilities to ensure the Christian upbringing of the child. This created an obvious problem in those parishes where baptisms had customarily been held each Sunday afternoon in church and any baby presented for baptism was duly baptised. Now baptisms were arranged 'by appointment' to enable the minimum requirement to be explained to the parents over a course of weeks, if the need for adequate response and personal commitment was to be met. The letters of protest from irate parents and still more irate Liverpool 'nans' (grandmothers) showed that no amount of patient explanation could translate what they saw as a 'refusal of baptism' into the delay for instruction which was intended.

As the years have passed, preparatory talks and even parish-based sacramental programmes have become more acceptable. Undoubtedly some progress has been made in this regard, though not without the occasional ecumenical hiccup when an affronted but lapsed Roman Catholic mother has stormed out of the presbytery and gone in search of the nearest 'vicar', who more often than not sent her back. Perhaps also in the light of experience, greater understanding has been shown. A recent check on baptisms revealed that seventeen per cent of the children baptised in the Roman Catholic churches of the archdiocese of Liverpool were either 'one parent' or born out of wedlock – at least as recognised by that Church. Even then, that figure can disguise the fact that, with a much lower percentage in this category in some of the Lancashire parishes, the corresponding numbers in certain deprived areas of inner-city Liverpool were often around forty per cent. Clearly pastoral practice has eased or at least better contact has been maintained. That is the reality of the situation which theologians discuss. It is against this background that enthusiastic ecumenists must learn to evaluate their commitment to the bond of baptism.

As members of Christ's body we must recognise its wounds. Fellow Christians must in all humility acknowledge their failings and weaknesses. Even shared baptism and membership of the mystical body of Christ have not prevented the separation and sometimes bitter divisions among his followers. We commend those attempts by our clergy to share the preparation of parents of both our Churches for the baptism of their children. The work of ecumenism calls for repentance and humility. But our failings and even our sinfulness do not remove the unique and indelible act of our baptism. They do not destroy the bond of baptism. Martin Luther, going through a dark night of the soul, would remind himself: 'I was baptised.' He knew his own response and failure well enough. In dark moments he needed most of all to know that God had truly put his hand upon him. Christ, becoming truly human, shared every aspect of our lives. In our union with him through baptism we should not be surprised if sometimes we are drawn into that sense of desolation which he knew as his agony approached.

A TASK FOR ALL CHRISTIANS

'The restoration of unity amongst Christians', said Pope John Paul II when preaching in Liverpool during his visit to this country in May 1982, 'is one of the main aims of the Church in the last part of the twentieth century, and this task is for all. No one can claim exemption from this responsibility.' In spite of the enthusiasm and joy which bound most of our fellow citizens together on that astonishing Whitsunday evening, we would have to admit that by no means every Christian feels the closeness of the bond of baptism which we cherish. The sharply marked-out boundaries of the one, true Church of Christ, and the conviction of being absolutely right to the exclusion of all other Churches as being absolutely wrong do not disappear overnight.

DAVID SHEPPARD: Evangelical and Protestant Christians had marked out the boundaries of the one, true Church quite as sharply as had their Roman Catholic counterparts. Some years ago now a parish in Toxteth invited me to discuss ecumenical matters with their members. After a while a man took me up: 'Bishop, you have repeatedly referred to Roman Catholics as "our brothers and sisters in Christ". That is the point. We do not believe that they are our brothers and sisters in Christ.' For evangelical Christians like him the boundaries of being a 'real Christian' must be a conscious response to Christ in the heart of each believer. They have not felt that the Roman Catholic Church has taught this. Sometimes evangelicals have assessed the validity of the response by whether the inward experience was expressed in particular words.

In Liverpool many Christians have stayed in the trenches, fearful of betraying truths for which their forefathers fought and sometimes died. It is altogether understandable if, in defence of what they have perceived as their history, they have kept folklore rather than tradition strong, reminding themselves of old aggressive statements and attitudes which they can at least allege that the other Church produced one hundred years ago – or was it four hundred years ago? Some have perhaps relished the exhilaration of seasonal hostilities. Some have been content to pray for rain on the day of the Orange Order's outings to Southport or the Corpus Christi processions for the Roman Catholics. A not inconsiderable number have kept their heads down, afraid that if they climb out of the trenches and start to talk and work together with 'the others', the clear faith and witness of their parents may become blurred and confused.

DEREK WORLOCK: For Roman Catholics also the process has not been easy or swift – though too swift for some who have denounced ecumenism as disloyalty to the heritage of their Lancashire martyrs for the ancient faith. Before taking a step forward it has been necessary to clarify one's present stance, otherwise it could be one step forward and at least two back. The Roman Catholic bishops, in their 1986 statement to the Inter-Church Process Not Strangers but Pilgrims, *make clear our belief 'that the Church of Christ is historically embodied in all its essential elements in the Roman Catholic Church, without substantial corruption or defect, however imperfectly. We readily accept also that the Church of Christ is not co-extensive with the Roman Catholic Church. We recognise sanctification and truth existing in other Christian communities which are rightly called Churches.'*

If that statement seems guarded, it is also clear, providing the basis of a true relationship between the Churches. In some ways, of still greater importance are the words in the Statement which follow: 'We come to the work of ecumenism, not with the intention of trying to achieve an amalgam of Churches but of working with others to build up into its proper fullness the one Church of Christ. We accept that within the Church of Christ there will be limited diversity, and different expressions of the same faith.'

We would want to pay due tribute to the work of theologians, notably but not exclusively in ARCIC, who have made outstanding efforts to clarify points still at issue between the Churches. It is of the greatest importance that this academic task be carried forward and the points listed in the Joint Statement at Canterbury by the Archbishop and the Pope be carefully studied 'with a view to their eventual resolution'. But the work of growing together while those official discussions continue, remains the responsibility of the individual members of the Churches concerned. Both levels of endeavour – official, doctrinal commissions and individual grass-roots Christians – need one another. Understanding between individuals builds planks into the bridge which draws Christian communities together. But no matter how close their association, individual Christians cannot resolve the problems of disunity on their own. Groups from different Churches who decide to go it alone in trying to achieve their own working arrangement over some doctrinal problem or discipline, are in danger of doing no more than creating yet one more fragmented Church. On the other hand, without the efforts and experience of those in the field, the effective work of the theologians is seriously restricted.

SHARING IN THE MISSION OF CHRIST

Many Christians undoubtedly feel that there is nothing which they personally can do about ecumenism, or even about acting together with the other Churches, until the fullness of unity has been achieved. They are perfectly willing to coexist so long as, like parallel lines, they never actually meet. To us that seems a failure to recognise the immediate consequence of our common baptism. We have been baptised into the mission of Christ. It is both natural and right that we should recognise each other as partners in the mission field in which we have been placed. This is not make-believe. Nor do we try to disguise that there are some matters of belief and religious practice about which we are not in full agreement. But such differences as there are must be seen within the comprehensive commitment to Christ which we share. Ours is not a reluctant partnership made expedient by opposition. It is a joint obedience to God's call.

There is a close connection between the belief that God sent Jesus and our efforts to ensure that Christians are united. We have already noted that unless it can be seen clearly that we are working hard and conscientiously on the divisions between the Churches, our efforts to break down the barriers in today's society lack credibility. But there must always be regard for conscience and absolute concern for integrity. A highly successful, if somewhat anxious businessman, said to us: 'I give you fellows five years to get it together or else it's the bomb.' He was not reassured when receiving the reply that we shared his desire that we should get it together, but concern for truth and regard for conscience would have to outweigh the threat of the bomb. Disunity has had a number of knock-on effects within society, much more widespread than the academic disputations between theologians. Divisions can mean barriers, and barriers limit vision and areas of concern. For example, many Anglicans have grown up without noticing that there are Roman Catholics living in the same street, and *vice versa*. Failing to recognise one group of neighbours leads to a habit of not noticing other groups whose pattern of life does not coincide with your own – religiously, or socially, or racially.

DAVID SHEPPARD: Once, while visiting an inner-city parish, church members and representatives of the local community came to meet me. One senior church member said: 'This district is like a transit camp nowadays: people are always moving.' Another told me that she had lived in that parish all her life and then added: 'There are no children in the parish any more.' The head teacher of a local nursery school was present and told us all that she had eighty-nine children on her school roll. Perhaps the former lady saw the life of the parish entirely through her church experience. Once upon a time many local children had come to Sunday school. Now few did. The children living in the parish were now of a different social grouping from those she had known before. Many were black. She failed to notice their existence.

This failure to notice one another can undoubtedly happen between different church memberships, though the occasional unity service in the area has increased people's consciousness of others, sometimes with a shock. But such limited vision and self-concern have an effect on the belief of others. The world will not believe in the values which Christians teach if we spend all our time on ecclesiastical business, working at the niceties of ecumenism while ignoring the needs of society, local or Third World for that matter. The love for one another, which Jesus said was to be the mark of his true followers, was not to be restricted to neighbours or fellow parishioners. 'Every one of you that has been baptised has been clothed in Christ. There can be neither Jew nor Greek, there can be neither slave nor freeman, there can be neither male nor female – for you are all one in Christ Jesus' (Gal. 3:27, 28 NJB). Now we see the significance of *oikoumene* meaning 'the whole inhabited world'. The Ecumenical Movement is concerned not merely with church congregations but with one world. That means helping to break down the barriers which divide our world today: between men and women, black and white people, management and labour, Europe and the developing world.

Our commitment to ecumenism is challenged by the reality of the situation all around us. It has things to say about the real problems of people's lives. We share Christ's concern for such matters. Some time after we had written an article in *The Times* about the Militant leadership in Liverpool City Council, the author Peter Hebblethwaite wrote to us, linking the article with the partnership between the Churches in Merseyside and their intent on tackling real live issues together. He quoted the Jesuit, Jon Sobrino, who had told him that the Church in El Salvador was transformed once it had a 'project'. Hebblethwaite added:

People change not because of exhortation to change but because they are engaged in a project which cannot be carried through without change. In the same way, ecumenical dialogues stagnate so long as we are just gazing into each other's eyes, and warily wondering what to think about each other. They take wing, or at least begin to get off the ground, if there is some common task. That seems to me to be the significance of what is happening in Merseyside. People will *learn* to work together.

With varying degrees of likelihood, a number of people of different background, office and political persuasion, have claimed – for better or for worse – to have had some part in our near-simultaneous appointment to Liverpool. Pope Paul VI made it plain that the Church must concern itself with the social and economic problems of the people. Pope John Paul II, on his visit to Liverpool in 1982, said:

> Our times present us with many challenges and difficulties. The problem of unemployment is a tragedy which affects every aspect of life, from the material and physical to the mental and spiritual. It therefore very much affects the Church, which makes her own the hardships and sufferings, as well as the joys and hopes, of the men and women of our time. It is a matter of vital importance and it deserves the attention and prayers of all people of good will.

There is nothing directly denominational about such social problems. The challenge is to all people of good will. For Christians the response is more effective when it is undertaken ecumenically. The need is immediate.

IN THE SERVICE OF THE COMMUNITY

Ecumenism is not only about belief but about the Christian response to the problems of human life. For both of us, involving ourselves in human needs in Merseyside has meant facing complex situations and conflict issues, which neither seminary nor theological college ever trained us to handle. Our experience has been that we have frequently been taken out of our depth. That has forced us back time and again to our spiritual resources. Far from the secular squeezing out the spiritual, it has positively driven us to our knees in prayer, to seek the guidance of the Spirit, to find wisdom from each other and to receive much in terms of advice and understanding from a wide variety of people. Father Austin Smith, a Passionist priest who has lived for many years in the heart of a deeply hurt but vibrant community in Liverpool 8, often reminds us that while the Christian emphasis on giving is obviously right, we all need to learn also about receiving both from other Christians and from people right outside the Church. His favourite puzzled phrase is: 'There is a creation thing going on out there.' So we need to listen, to enter into the argument and to be open to receive from what the Creator has given to our neighbours.

In all this our experience is not of course unique. Edward Patey, formerly Dean of Liverpool, liked to say that he spent more time on his knees in preparation for a meeting of the Merseyside Community Relations Council, which he chaired for its first ten years, than he did for meetings of the Cathedral Chapter. This was because he was conscious that he needed God's resources all the more. In another part of Liverpool's inner city, the local Roman Catholic leader of a team ministry holds a weekly staff meeting of the priests and religious men and women working under his leadership. All attend the business part of the meeting. When it comes to the time of reflection and discussion, half of them leave. The division does not seem to be between older and younger. It has more to do with theological stance. For some there is a faith 'once and for all delivered to the saints'. It belongs to the Church and the Church must tell the world. For the other clergy and religious, there is also a living Lord present in all the human situations where they serve. That Lord is calling them to take the risk of facing up to new experiences and setting those experiences in the light of the gospel and of the faith handed down. It is a demanding process which some at least need to undertake together.

We both believe that the Church in Merseyside is called, in the words of our Methodist colleague Norwyn Denny, to stand alongside the poor. For many clergy and for many suburban laity that means new experiences. It is nothing new to say that God speaks to us all today in the voice of our neighbours if only we have ears to hear. In today's setting this includes listening with real attention to those whose voice, humanly speaking, counts for little and is often bitter and disquieting. It means having a proper respect for the God-given knowledge and intelligence of many people who have been excluded from the normal life of the city and its institutions. It can mean at times trying to make those unheeded voices and attitudes more coherent and more widely noticed; or intervening as partners to try to help provide resources which will enable people to help themselves.

When we have acted in such ways, we try to reflect on the lesson for ourselves. We invariably discover that we ourselves now see matters from a new angle, perhaps because people have come to trust us and share their insights with us. If we are to discover God's word for today, we need to commit ourselves to reflection as well as action. It is an ongoing process because one must lead to the other. Having reviewed the situation in the light of the gospel, we must seek how best the next action is to be carried through in the setting of God's revelation in Christ. But each new experience calls for an act of faith in the power of the risen Lord.

THE SHARING OF GIFTS

To affirm that we have one Lord should make us appreciate the gifts which he wills that his whole Church should possess. In addition to the gifts given to the individuals for their personal holiness, there are the gifts or charisms which are freely and lovingly given by the Holy Spirit, not so much for the sake of the individual recipient but for the benefit of others. St Paul wrote to the Christians at Ephesus:

> To some, his 'gift' was that they should be apostles; to some, prophets; to some, evangelists; to some, pastors and teachers; to knit God's holy people together for the work of service to build up the Body of Christ, until we all reach unity in faith and knowledge of the Son of God and form the perfect Man, fully mature with the fullness of Christ himself.
>
> (Eph. 4: 11–13 NJB)

St Paul develops the same idea in writing to the Corinthians, when he emphasises that 'The particular manifestation of the Spirit granted to each one is to be used for the general good' (1 Cor. 12:7 NJB).

Once the sharing of our common baptism is accepted as uniting us in the Church of Christ, we may recognise how the gift with which our particular congregations and traditions have been endowed may be for the enrichment of the whole Christian body. Through different communities, with our different histories and traditions, the Holy Spirit can enrich the whole Church of Christ. To say this is not indifferentism but a recognition of what may truly be shared in faith. This is not to try to tamper with truth: the ecumenical aspect of our possession of the gifts of the Spirit gives us new insights into the truth. As separate Churches we have through historical differences tended almost to divide up our heritage. The renewal of liturgical worship in both our Churches highlights this point. It is sometimes said that as a result of the Protestant Reformation, the Reformers lost sight of the significance of the Eucharist, while the Catholics lost sight of the importance of the liturgy of God's Word. That charge can be hard for both of us to bear, but it is worth dwelling on for a moment.

DEREK WORLOCK: *After being brought up to defend the Mass against the extreme Protestant charge of being a 'blasphemous act', our people still express surprise when they are told that the first task of a bishop and a priest is to proclaim God's Word. So central to our lives has been the Mass that the celebration of the Eucharist customarily tops the list of priestly tasks. Yet the Second Vatican Council's Decree on the Ministry and Life of Priests says plainly:*

> *The People of God finds its unity first of all through the Word of the living God, which is quite properly sought from the lips of priests. Since no one can be saved who has not first believed, priests, as co-workers with their bishops, have as their primary duty the proclamation of the gospel to all.*

> *The ministry of the Word is carried out in many ways. In the celebration of the Mass, 'the proclamation of the death and resurrection of the Lord is inseparably joined to the very offering whereby Christ ratified the New Testament in His blood'* (Presbyterorum Ordinis, n. 4).

The renewal of the liturgy, with due prominence given to the Word (now customarily read in the vernacular) and in preparation for the Eucharist, has been a revelation to many Catholics. While the former rite, celebrated in Latin, still holds attractions for a minority, for many – especially those who were without missals as well as without Latin – the whole process of renewal has been a most exciting experience. The old sacristan at St John's Cathedral, in Portsmouth, served Mass most days of his life. Now he added to his privileges the task of reading the Lesson at Mass each weekday. I shall never forget the reverence with which he read God's Word to those present. Especially with readings from the Old Testament, there was wonder in his voice because, as he once told me gratefully, he was discovering the marvel of the Scriptures for the first time.

DAVID SHEPPARD: *In just the same way, many members of the Church of England reacted against what they saw as Romish tendencies by under-playing the Eucharist. The parish in which I first experienced regular church life had a shortened form of Holy Communion following Morning Prayer. If you wished to receive Holy Communion, you stayed behind among a small minority after the majority had left. That, or 8 a.m. Holy Communion, was the usual pattern for very many parishes. All this has now changed on a very wide scale. The Series 2 and Series 3 Services and the Alternative Service Book have drawn together different traditions within Anglicanism to make the Parish Eucharist and the Family Communion the central act of worship for most parishes today. This development has restored something which Bible-loving Christians should never have abandoned. The scriptures show that the first Christians seem plainly to have broken bread together on the first day of the week as the central part of their worship.*

On one of our many journeys together Derek once said to me, 'I feel totally disorientated any day until I have had the opportunity to celebrate Mass.' I replied that I often felt just the same until I had had the opportunity to study and meditate on a passage from the Bible. This difference in church tradition calls for great sensitivity and mutual concern. It exemplifies well the enrichment of the sharing of gifts which our coming together has brought us.

The sharing of gifts is not restricted to the pair of us. But whoever is involved there must be mutual trust. The Merseyside Church Leaders Group brings together those responsible for the leadership of the Methodist, United Reformed and Baptist Churches and the Salvation Army, as also our own suffragan and auxiliary bishops and ourselves. In addition to our regular business meetings, we also meet twice each year for a long evening, which includes an hour's discussion of a chosen subject about which we expect not to be in agreement. This discussion is followed by a time for devotion and prayer, and finally we all sit down to a meal together. Whatever our differences, there is always sensitivity but frankness. The guiding principle of this group and of our partnership is never to allow ourselves to get into a 'no go' situation about any issue. We claim that for ourselves in private there must always be an 'open' agenda, though as far as possible we try to keep away from public expressions of difference. This means also avoidance of pushing one another into defensive positions in public. Private dialogue, which respects each other's tradition, leads to mutual confidence and to trusting each other enough to raise what may be more controversial issues. The sharing of gifts leads to increased understanding, not to the blurring of conscientiously held differences.

CONSULTATION AND SUPPORT

Between the two of us the basic principle is habitual consultation. We soon learnt that it is not a truly ecumenical partnership when one Church plans an event and then invites the other to be present and to take part. We agreed that we must go back to the base-line and decide on each new issue if we wished to make plans together. Link that with the Lund principle of acting 'together in all matters except those in which deep differences of conscience compel you to act separately', and the number of decisions about collaboration is very considerable.

Because it is known now that we come to many meetings and services together – and more recently in the company of the Free Church Moderator – there is a steadily growing number of joint invitations and joint consultations. If official duties have taken one or other of us away from Liverpool for a week, it is normal for us to need – often on a Sunday night – a full hour on the telephone to check the 'shared' correspondence and agree how to respond to the various approaches. This can often mean delaying a responsible decision until we know each other's mind. That does not mean giving each other a 'veto' so much as automatically checking out what the other feels, and being sensitive to his views.

That degree of consultation is extremely costly in demands on heavily committed diaries. But as a result we have discovered whole new resources. Mutually agreed decisions are that much stronger. Over the years we have come to know each other's minds to the extent that in an urgent situation where direct contact is impossible, the one can with reasonable assurance speak for both. As the demand for appearing, acting and speaking together grows, we have always to ask ourselves whether such joint action is really necessary or whether it is mere duplication. When pressed for the basis on which we make such a decision, we admit that the principle for acceptance must be 'when one plus one adds up to more than two'.

In public ministry we have found that such consultation and partnership have made us a little braver as well as, we hope, a little wiser. There are occasions when the heat in the kitchen of public life becomes intense. One is able to give a very special kind of support when the other is under pressure of attack or misrepresentation. This does not always call for a public statement of support, though on occasions this may be helpful. Often a bishop has to remain silent even in face of misrepresentation because the mere divulgence of the true story in his self-defence can mean the destruction of someone else. At such a time the support of another who knows the true situation and the values involved is an enormous help.

DAVID SHEPPARD: Two or three years after we came to Liverpool, a journalist I had never met wrote an article about me in a local newspaper. In a real hatchet job a vicar in a more well-heeled part of the diocese was reported as saying: 'If you're not poor, black or unemployed, he does not want to know you.' That part of the attack was good enough for dining out on. However, much of the article seemed seriously to misrepresent my way of working. I was away the day the article appeared, but Derek Worlock immediately rang my wife Grace to talk the whole thing through with her. He was sensitive to the fact that a partner sometimes feels more of the hurt than does the public figure himself. When next we were together, Derek said to me: 'I know that you can be quite a tough soldier but that kind of attack leaves wounds.' For the same reason, some years later, when Derek's position regarding the black community was totally misrepresented in a Panorama *programme on Toxteth, I made sure that I was the first person on the phone to him as soon as the programme was over. That was even more important than writing to the producer to demand the apology which was eventually given.*

It is not only the need to respond to Merseyside's more complex problems which drives us to our knees in prayer. We both value worship as the first priority of the day. But there are many times when we find strength in prayer together before taking on a difficult interview with a government minister, or going to plead with an industrial mogul for a threatened factory, or facing a challenging television appearance. A regular occasion is when one of us has a quiet day in the chapel and for a time both come together for prayer. In our early years in Liverpool people thought it necessary to introduce us to one another at receptions, as if we had never met before. It was at that time we were asked to do a joint interview on Radio Merseyside. We agreed that we would finish the interview with a prayer. We realised how suspicious people still were after the long years of religious strife, and how they would suspect that two separate recordings had been spliced together. So we agreed that one would begin an extempore prayer and the other would interrupt and continue it. Then we said the Lord's Prayer together.

To those who say that the steam has gone out of ecumenism we have to reply, 'not when it speaks about problems and differences which are real to people'. There are also those who speak of intercommunion as if with its arrival the Kingdom of God will have come, but that until then there are nothing but stopping-posts on the path of ecumenical progress. To them we reply that intercommunion may be a sign of unity achieved, but it is not the only way in which we can profess our faith in the Lord who has called us. There are those who say that there is nothing our divided Churches can usefully do together until the fullness of Christian unity is achieved. We have to ask whether the responsibilities flowing from our common baptism are to be regarded as post-dated.

Christ calls us to be partners in mission. That is authority enough for our collaboration. Joining hands in tackling some of the deep human needs which face us in Merseyside to some extent outflanks but does not ignore the attempts at theological agreement which inevitably take so long. The two approaches to Christian unity are complementary. Serving people in the world together in God's name, and sometimes going through fire in the process, breeds a trusting relationship which is of great importance in facing the tough theological questions. We have long climbed out of the trenches of static theological confrontations. We can dare in the atmosphere of trust to express our deepest feelings, questions and fears. The point is made in the last paragraph of ARCIC's *Final Report* of 1982:

Contemporary discussions of conciliarity and primacy in both communions indicate that we are not dealing with positions destined to remain static. We suggest that some difficulties will not be wholly resolved until a practical initiative has been taken, and our two Churches have lived together more visibly in the one *koinonia*.

Early in this chapter we referred to the difficult word *oikoumene*, meaning 'the whole inhabited world'. We conclude with the even more difficult Greek word *koinonia*, used in the New Testament to denote communion, sharing, fellowship, and here seeming to imply 'the common life', 'the living bond of fellowship of Christ'. The precise meaning of difficult words is understood more easily when it can be related to the real problems of people's lives. There is the story of the journalist who asked the Liverpool docker the meaning of 'ecumenism'. The scouser thought for a bit and then said: 'I suppose that it's those two bishops standing up for our jobs.' As a description for ecumenism in practice, perhaps we should settle for that.

5 CALL TO PARTNERSHIP

Whatever progress has been made in ecumenical relations in Merseyside in recent years is often attributed by others to the fact that 'of course the pair of them are good friends'. Personal friendship is not to be discounted, but it cannot be adequate if one is thinking of a relationship between Churches. The personal element is important, but some structure must be devised and recognised if more than a good understanding between individuals is to be achieved.

On our arrival in Liverpool we reminded ourselves that, with the limited opportunities for close contact which existed in the past, our predecessors, Stuart Blanch and George Andrew Beck, had enjoyed good friendship. We hoped that it would be the same for us. We agreed that we should try to build upon that good base and should look for some imaginative events which might push ecumenical partnership forward.

Opportunities have not been lacking. If at the beginning we had to seek out occasions when it might prove possible for us to act together, nowadays our collaboration is taken for granted in so many matters that sometimes care has to be taken to avoid duplication. At times it has proved possible for us to promote shared events. On other occasions it has been a matter of giving a fair wind to the invitations of joint groups or institutions anxious to work together.

Quite frequently it has been a case of reacting together to situations not of our making and out of our control. But to respond quickly and thoughtfully to events which just happen, there have to be certain enabling factors. There must be a willingness, if necessary, to give the new situation priority, even to the extent of dropping existing engagements. There must be habitual mutual contact and consultation, leading to open communication between each other. And of course there needs to be sufficient organisation to make it possible for Churches to consult and actually plan together. We soon learnt that true ecumenical partnership is not fostered by one Church making its plans and then inviting others to join in. Customarily it means starting together from the same base-line and planning jointly.

Over the years in many parts of the country a certain pattern had emerged. The occasional meeting, addressed by an Anglican, a Roman Catholic and a Free Church representative, had been an important first step in the 'getting to know you' process. In certain areas it had given way to an occasional ecumenical service, the joint nature of which referred more to the congregation than to the form of worship. But collaborative action was evident more in social matters, for the most part of a fairly 'churchy' nature: for example, attending each other's Christmas parties for old people, church bazaars and fund-raising events. All this represented a step forward from the sectarianism of the past. But if truth be told, for the majority of church people the alleged new enthusiasm for ecumenism represented little more than a degree of mutual politeness. Seldom was more involved than support for an annual joint service during the Week of Prayer for Christian Unity, held each January.

But things were stirring. The 'Call to the North', made by Donald Coggan shortly before he left the archbishopric of York for Canterbury, had already produced certain results at church leader level. In Merseyside a Churches' Ecumenical Council had also been formed, largely through the initiative of Edward Patey, the then Dean of Liverpool's Anglican Cathedral. A Baptist minister, David Savage, had been appointed full-time Ecumenical Officer. In July 1976 a Church Leaders Group was formally established. This was serviced by the Ecumenical Officer, who was responsible for ensuring the implementation of any decisions which were reached.

From the beginning there was determination that this group should be more than a talking-shop. Items included in its agenda in the first few years reflect this and give some of the flavour of our discussions: planning a two-day conference on ministry; arranging an annual Shrove Tuesday party for mayors, civic officials and their partners; responding to the Government's inner area study; making the Liverpool Industrial Mission an ecumenical enterprise; planning the Queen's visit to the Church in Liverpool; leading a youth pilgrimage to Taizé; establishing a World Development Centre; supporting a new pastoral counselling project called COMPASS; launching a joint clergy orientation course; involvement with the Roman Catholic National Pastoral Congress in Liverpool; a score of other items listed in the agenda and including police liaison, episcopacy, marriage and family life, and a joint pastoral letter to all the Churches at Pentecost. To be the Ecumenical Officer in Merseyside was no sinecure. With closer collaboration over the years, the work has developed. David Savage was succeeded, after completing his fixed term of office, by a Roman Catholic priest, David Williamson, who in due time was succeeded by an Anglican, Canon Michael Wolfe.

Over the eleven years of its existence the Church Leaders Group has had remarkable stability of membership. Trevor Hubbard, the North-West Superintendent of the Baptist Union, and John Williamson, the Moderator of the United Reformed Church Mersey Province, were here before us and throughout this period. Norwyn Denny, the Methodist Chairman, came within the same year as we and continued until 1986, when he was succeeded by John Newton. Colonel Lily Farar, followed by Major Douglas Rayner, was the senior Salvation Army officer and played an active part in the group and its activities. In addition we have had the collaboration of Michael Henshall, the Anglican suffragan bishop of Warrington; Bill Flagg, an assistant bishop in the diocese of Liverpool; and Kevin O'Connor, Anthony Hitchen and John Rawsthorne, the three Roman Catholic auxiliary bishops in the archdiocese.

To have been together over so long a period has been a privilege and an enormous benefit. Knowledge of one another developed into real personal friendship. Such friendship leads to trust and mutual confidence. Although the pair of us, initially at least, were accorded most of the publicity, the Free Church leaders were from the beginning thoroughly supportive of us. They recognised the difficulty of a group of half a dozen attempting to draft a text together or speaking to the media. Wherever possible, drafts would be exchanged and consultation achieved. But such a process is not always possible. An opportunity can be lost or silence misrepresented in a matter of moments in an age when 'instant wisdom' is often required. To overcome this difficulty there has to be a general agreement and a knowledge of each other's minds and areas of sensitivity. For the same group to have been together over so long a period proved an immense advantage.

We crossed an important bridge when in 1977 each denomination received from the Department of Environment a copy of the substantial Inner Areas Study report on Liverpool 7 and 8, with a request for comment. After calling together a group of clergy and lay people serving in the inner city, the members of the Church Leaders Group met to discuss what our individual responses should be.

DEREK WORLOCK: Suddenly it struck me how ludicrous it was that we should be contemplating individual replies on a denominational basis. I remember thumping the table and saying, 'If we cannot produce one joint response on a subject like this, what is the point of all our ecumenical activity? What right have we to stress the importance of our unity?' After some extended discussion of what we wanted to say, the other church leaders said that they would be happy if David and I would agree a text and send it to the Secretary of State in the name of all of us. That was really the beginning, but it also meant burning the midnight oil later that week at the Northern Church Leaders Consultation at Scargill House in Yorkshire.

WITH THE FREE CHURCHES

When it became more generally expected that in certain matters the pair of us would speak or write together publicly, there were occasions when almost inevitably critics would ask where the Free Church leaders were. One such critic wrote to *The Guardian* when we had both been interviewed together on television, following the occasion when in March 1982 the Archbishop of Canterbury had been shouted down by a group of extreme Protestants during a service in Liverpool Parish Church. The Merseyside Free Church leaders wrote in reply:

> Most of us were in Yorkshire at the annual consultation of Church Leaders of the North of England, where we were expressing Merseyside's concerns and seeking to act on behalf of our Anglican and Roman Catholic colleagues, while they, with our full approval, were in Liverpool, facing up to the media. We meet with the Bishop and the Archbishop regularly throughout the year, and by now have learned to trust each other, whilst appreciating the different convictions and points of view which still divide us. We have found that on such occasions they are both sensitive to our positions, and try to represent all the Churches and not just their own.

None the less it indicated a gap in the expression of the Christian voice in Merseyside which needed attention. At about that time a working party was set up by the Merseyside Churches Ecumenical Council to make recommendations for joint decision-making. In its report *Call to Partnership* (with which we will deal more fully later), the members of the working party proposed a new initiative by which a Free Church Moderator for Merseyside would be appointed by the Free Churches to be 'a recognised spokesman to stand with Bishop and Archbishop in the corporate witness of the Churches'. They urged that the Free Churches should find effective ways of offering support to their Moderator. They would have to undergird him financially and would also need to find ways of freeing him so that he might share in responding jointly to unforeseen and immediate demands.

In 1985 the Free Churches were ready to make such an appointment and our colleague John Williamson, the United Reformed Church Moderator, was chosen for this post. Within a few months the three of us were trying to pick our way through the minefield of the Liverpool City Council rates crisis. This involved private meetings in London with successive Secretaries of State for the Environment (first Patrick Jenkin and then Kenneth Baker) and with leaders of the other political parties. In the crisis of the previous year the two of us had acted together and it was an added strength in that we now comprised direct representation of all the mainline Churches. Before we could embark on such discussions, we spent many hours together, talking matters through and listening to a series of advisers inside and outside our Churches.

This triple partnership provides an additional dimension and gradually we have worked out how practically to consult and share in producing the common witness. Sometimes it can be easier spoken than written, though the reverse can also be true. Going to see a government minister together is often a problem for several diaries, which is why the Moderator needs someone to cover prior engagements for him, just as we would use one of our assistant bishops. The agenda must also be prepared together, and agreement reached in advance as to which point is to be raised by whom. In the same way we have learnt how to consult before the first draft of a statement is prepared by one of the three – and usually re-written or amended by the others subsequently. There is little practical difficulty about the acceptance by the media of a joint statement, or even of a letter to the editor signed by the three of us. But as yet newspapers have been unwilling to accept that an article can have three joint authors.

For example, in July 1985, at the height of the rates crisis, the three of us produced a joint statement in which we made clear our belief that the reduced Rate Support Grant left Liverpool with grossly inadequate money, but we sharply criticised the policy of confrontation being pursued by the Militant Tendency leadership. When just over two months later we had to develop this theme, we approached *The Times* about their publication of an article. It was made clear to us that a 'two bishops' authorship would be very welcome since our partnership was sufficiently well known. Triple authorship must take the form of a letter to the editor: and the publication would be subject to a different set of rules. When the article appeared, Tony Byrne, the chairman of the city's Finance and General Purposes Committee, challenged us to appear before the committee next day. To this we agreed and the three of us went and supported our criticisms in a session lasting over an hour. As the crisis mounted in succeeding weeks, again the three of us circulated a paper with suggestions for emergency action which would be required if the city went bankrupt and its services collapsed. Together also we issued a call to prayer for the city at this time of grave anxiety and tension.

As far as possible we have tried to ensure that the triple leadership is evident also in radio and television coverage. But as yet few interviewers have found their way past their producers or editors, whose primary concern is often to reduce yards of tape or film to a twenty-second clip. In such conditions it can be a case of 'too many cooks' rather than 'the more the merrier'. The result often calls for patience and understanding, and indicates the need for each individual to avoid personal points if in the end only one voice is to be heard for all the Churches. The 'triple technique' develops with practice.

Inevitably some approaches continue to be made to the two of us. We have worked so closely together for our eleven years that it is natural to go on consulting and following through some of the engagements to which we are invited as a twosome. In June 1987 John Williamson's time as URC Moderator came to an end and he left the area. He had been a trusted friend throughout our Liverpool years and brought careful preparation and insight to the partnership. It is in the nature of public life that the media tend to pick out names they have come to know best. The three of us felt ourselves called to work at the practice as well as the notion of our partnership, perhaps preparing the way for our successors to take it on in a new style. John Williamson was succeeded as Free Church Moderator by the Methodist Chairman, Dr John Newton, who brought great experience and fresh gifts to the role.

NATIONAL AND INTERNATIONAL STEPS TO UNITY

What has been happening in Merseyside has occurred against a background of a series of Christian unity initiatives taking place on the national and the international scene. In 1976 the 'Ten Propositions' appeared. Following the failure of the General Synod of the Church of England to give a seventy-five per cent vote for the Anglican/Methodist scheme, there were talks about talks among all the mainstream Churches in England. Each was asked to respond to the Ten Propositions which were prepared by the Churches' Unity Commission. The Roman Catholic Church in England felt unable, 'especially on its own', to accept those propositions dealing with Holy Communion and the recognition of ministries. The Baptist Union also gave a 'qualified No', claiming that the propositions gave inadequate attention to the concept of unity in mission and presented difficulties regarding episcopacy.

DAVID SHEPPARD: I sat next to Derek Worlock at a discussion in Liverpool about the Ten Propositions. We had just heard a speech in which 'No salvation outside the Church' was unreservedly restated. Others seemed to be making very heavy weather of the details of the Services of Mutual Recognition. I recall that Derek pointed me to the section of his paper which dealt with the characteristics of the nature and life of the Church. 'That is the essential part,' he said.

At national level, the Methodist, United Reformed and Anglican Churches pressed ahead with proposals to find a way forward through the mutual recognition of ministries. They established a Churches' Council for Covenanting which duly prepared a report with a final chapter on joint decision-making. Thus it was that in Merseyside the leaders of the Churches involved in the proposals for covenanting met to take a careful look at how joint decision-making might be approached without constructing a great juggernaut of additional committees. Trevor Hubbard, the Baptist Superintendent, asked if he could join them. There are vivid memories of a gathering of these Churches' leaders, each kneeling on the floor drawing decision-making charts of districts, circuits, synods, etc.

DEREK WORLOCK: I also have a vivid memory of being with the other Church leaders soon afterwards and of realising that they had been discussing a further gathering of which I was not due to be part. I felt left out in a way I had not experienced since I had come to Liverpool. I also realised that this development might well prove to be the parting of the ways. So I told David my feelings and my fears. He approached the others, who immediately said that if Roman Catholics felt able to be part of this attempt to achieve a process of joint decision-making, they would be happy that I should join them.

89

Although at national level the Covenant proposals failed, just as the Anglican–Methodist scheme had failed, to obtain the special majority in the House of Clergy of the Church of England General Synod, the Merseyside conversations about joint decision-making continued. It was this initiative which ultimately led to the Covenant between the Church leaders at Pentecost in 1985, but in the meantime there were a number of national developments and detailed preliminaries to be effected locally.

DAVID SHEPPARD: In supporting the Covenant proposals I argued that Anglicans needed to go forward both with the Free Churches and with the Roman Catholic Church. A closer understanding with Rome must not be at the expense of our relationship with the Free Churches. Addressing the Liverpool Diocesan Synod in 1980 about the national Covenanting proposals, I said:

> *So I come back to those who fear that by entering into the Covenant, we will make further steps forward with Rome more difficult. My Liverpool years have made me believe that we could and should go forward with the Roman Catholics. What would that involve for the next step? Perhaps that we recognise the Pope in some way such as the ARCIC Statement on Authority suggested, and that Rome recognise Anglican Orders. Let us suppose for a moment that we were now considering such a step forward; let us also suppose that, in order to take that step, we must abandon inter-communion with the Free Churches. If such a 'package' were brought forward, you would certainly find me digging in my heels against it – and together with me, I am confident, would be the great majority of Anglicans. We are not going to wave good-bye to our Free Church brothers and sisters. And in any case what makes us think that Rome is only interested in union with the Anglicans, and not with the Free Churches too? Just because I want to go forward with Rome, I believe that it is crucial that we commit ourselves to the Covenant with the Free Churches. How can we expect to heal the rift with Rome if we are not willing to heal the rifts which are within our power to heal now?*

In one sense it was ironical that 1982 marked not only the failure nationally of the Covenant proposals but also the visit of Pope John Paul II to Canterbury, where he met British Church leaders and expressed the hope that 'our meeting this morning will not be the end of this fruitful exchange, but rather a beginning'. In fact the Churches moved into what was called the 'post' age: post-Papal visit and the encouragement given for closer collaboration; post-ARCIC I, whose *Final Report* had been published the previous

March; and post-breakdown of the Covenant proposals. For some it was clearly a question of finding new heart as well as a new way forward. Clearly there was need for a new initiative, but only after frank, if private, consultation.

DEREK WORLOCK: The Roman Catholic bishops resolved to throw the focus on what became known as the 'ecclesiological question', dealing with the very nature of the Church. They decided to devote their annual In-Service Conference to this matter and invited leaders of other Christian Churches in England and Wales to join them at New Hall near Chelmsford in January 1984 to share ideas on the subject. Speaking for our bishops I told our guests:

> *We are well aware that much dialogue and effective pastoral action, some of it by covenant, already takes place at local level and occasionally on a regional basis. But there would seem to be a danger that ecumenical dialogue in matters of faith is left to the theologians, and not always reflected in the preaching and teaching of the leaders of Churches and Christian communities. For different Church bodies there are different concepts of leadership. But we would suggest that wherever leadership exists in the Church at a national level, there the regular opportunity for dialogue must be given and with it the opportunity for consultations on matters of concern for the Church and nation.*

This consultation was followed in the spring of that year by a long weekend of recollection and prayer together at Canterbury. After this, perhaps because of it, a series of initiatives followed. The Spring Assembly of the British Council of Churches resolved 'to consult the member Churches and other Christian bodies on their readiness to share in a process of prayer, reflection and debate together, centred on the nature and purpose of the Church in the light of its calling and for the world'. The Roman Catholic Bishops' Conference, not itself a member of the BCC, came up with a very similar suggestion and, as a result of several meetings and long negotiations, an Inter-Church Process was launched in 1985 which became known as 'Not Strangers but Pilgrims'.

This was a three-phased programme, spread over two years and having regard for developments at local, national and international level. It was accepted by all the mainstream Christian Churches and, for the first time, by a number of black-led Churches in Britain. Of great significance was the widespread interest expressed in this whole Inter-Church Process, and revealed by the very large number of groups throughout the country which took part in the discussion of the topics raised through local radio in Lent 1986 on the general theme, 'What on earth is the Church for?' Often quite fundamental questions must be asked when the way ahead for ecumenical pilgrims appears to be marked 'No Entry'.

In the spring of 1987, national conferences, drawing together representatives of all the participating Churches, were held at Nottingham, Bangor and St Andrews. These showed that ecumenical relations were at different stages in the three countries concerned. There were varied priorities but it was plain that if there was to be development in ecumenical partnership, how Churches saw themselves was related to the way authority was exercised and the manner in which each Church operated. It also affected how they viewed other Churches and what kind of ecumenical organisation or instrument might be needed to service the Churches in their future partnership. In September of that year representatives of Churches from the three countries, this time including their accepted leadership, met at Swanwick for five days to assess where the process had brought them and to try to determine the way forward.

In the following September over three hundred representatives of no less than thirty-three Churches, including for the first time several of the black-led Churches, met at Swanwick, in Derbyshire, for a five-day conference. The presence of observers from Ireland meant that all four nations were represented, this time with the accepted leadership of the Churches concerned. We were both amongst the delegates whose purpose was to assess progress in the inter-Church process, to try to determine the point reached in the common pilgrimage and to decide whether there was adequate basis of shared faith to continue the journey together. If so, what 'instrument' would be required for the future to service the fellow-pilgrims, or participant Churches, in their onward journey to Christian unity?

After much frank discussion of underlying theological differences and at the same time the common bond of faith and mission, the delegates turned to the difficult matter of future co-operation. There was no desire to establish yet more ecumenical structure demanding additional meetings. There was already a network of groups and councils operating at local and regional levels. The lacing of these together and the development of committed or covenanted relationships could be achieved quite simply by a 'slimmed down' version of the BCC. But this future 'instrument' must not be a super-Church, representing member Churches and telling them what to do. Its authority must lie in each member-

Church with its own decision-making machinery. Thus it would service its members, help to co-ordinate the efforts of individual Churches and regional groupings, and hopefully would have the effect of drawing the Churches together as they came to work and pray together. The direction of this as yet deliberately nameless instrument would be in the hands of the leaders of the member Churches who could choose to act through a management committee and small secretariat. Most important, there could be a large assembly, meeting perhaps annually, to stimulate and monitor progress.

Although this re-structuring was important, of far greater significance was the re-vitalised spirit which emerged from Swanwick. No one who was there is likely to forget the intense joy and feeling of confidence and trust in the presence of the Holy Spirit amongst us. This was most evident in the eucharistic celebrations at which we all assisted during the week, acknowledging the pain of separation but recognising the real but imperfect union already amongst the Churches. All this was summed up in the intervention made by Cardinal Hume towards the end of the conference and in the immediate and positive response from Archbishop Runcie.

The Cardinal spoke of his hope that, in answer 'to a gospel imperative' and as official policy, we could move from the situation of co-operation already existing 'to one of commitment to each other'. We should commit ourselves to praying and working together for Church unity, and to acting together, both nationally and locally, for evangelisation and mission. 'We should have in view', he said 'a moving, in God's time, to full communion that is both visible and organic.' But he went on to point out 'that there will not be uniformity but legitimate diversity'. We should be seeking that fellowship already outlined in the Acts of the Apostles, remaining 'faithful to the teaching of the apostles, to the brotherhood, to the breaking of bread and to the prayers' (Acts 2:42 NJB).

The atmosphere at that moment was variously described: 'momentous', 'historic', 'electric' and 'as though everyone present had won the pools'! The Kingdom of God had not come then and there, but a consensus was that this was the breakthrough for which the Churches had been waiting.

MERSEYSIDE ECUMENICAL ASSEMBLY

Amidst the set-backs and progress at national level, the Merseyside Church leaders reaffirmed their commitment to try to find a way forward in shared decision-making, while remaining absolutely loyal to their own Churches and traditions. A working party was set up under the chairmanship of Bishop Michael Henshall to see what practical recommendations could be made and on how extensive a basis. The working party invited each of the Churches to respond to four questions:

1. What activities could we possibly do together effectively which are at present done separately?
2. What specifically would your Church wish to continue to do separately?
3. What can the Churches do together, which should be done and is not at present being done?
4. Are there areas of work which your Church might be able to carry out on behalf of the other Churches?

The working party's report contained a clear recommendation for the establishment of a Merseyside and Region Churches' Ecumenical Assembly, inevitably to be called MARCEA. Its object would be to draw the denominations concerned into a fuller understanding of the gospel; to promote the visible unity and mission of the Church at every level of church life; to encourage the Churches to make decisions together where possible, and to give effect to the Lund principle of doing together everything except that which in conscience must be done separately.

To achieve this there would be an Ecumenical Assembly of about two hundred persons drawn from all the Churches, with a Standing Committee, a Church Leaders Group and with departments with interdenominational membership for Ecumenical Affairs, Social Responsibility, Ministry, Education and International Affairs. Although that might look like the administrative juggernaut we had sought to avoid, it proved to be a practical means of working together without undue overlapping. Indeed twenty-two of the proposed committees to be incorporated into the various departments already existed; so it would ensure a better co-ordinated effort. Each Church was asked to consider the whole package of proposals carefully, to see whether denominational committees might in some cases cease to exist and be replaced by ecumenical committees to which each Church would elect representatives.

The report *Call to Partnership* spoke of the concept of a continuum. This envisaged an overall strategy for advance along a line from competition to communion. 'Co-existence, co-operation and commitment are significant points along the continuum,' we were reminded by the authors of the report, writing with a fine sense of alliteration. A clear distinction was made between the process of decision-making (in which all were consulted and collaborated) and decision-taking involving commitment in certain specific matters, such as the deployment of ministry and the provision of finance. It would be understood that certain major decisions of the Ecumenical Assembly, which would meet in plenary session twice a year, would require ratification by the appropriate synod or council of the member Churches.

In the spring of 1985 the proposals of the full report were laid before the representative bodies of the various Churches and received overwhelming votes of support and commitment. Thereupon the Church leaders agreed themselves to enter into a covenant, pledging their commitment to God and to one another in the pilgrimage and search for the visible unity of Christ's Church. The only qualification came from Major Douglas Rayner, who was restrained from formally signing the Covenant by a national decision of the Salvation Army, but who none the less joined us in the prayer asking God to 'bind us together now as partners with you and with one another in the task entrusted to us, that obedient to your command we may proclaim the Good News and make disciples of all nations'. Most suitably the Covenant was signed at a great service held on Whitsunday 1985. The celebration began in the Roman Catholic Cathedral and concluded in the Anglican Cathedral after a joyful procession along the connecting road, called Hope Street.

People have often commented upon the coincidence that this road between the two cathedrals and just half a mile long should be called Hope Street. When the Roman Catholic Cathedral was opened in 1967, the then Anglican Dean, Edward Patey, who did so much to develop ecumenical relations in Liverpool, made great play of 'the Street called Hope'. In recent years the Churches have tried to give practical expression to the desire that the coincidence should become a meaningful symbol. With no desire to imitate sectarian marches of old, but remembering the Whit walks in so many parts of Lancashire, we have on a number of occasions invited Christians to walk with us along Hope Street.

The first occasion was in the Queen's Jubilee Year of 1977. In a joint pastoral letter the Church leaders called on Church members to celebrate the Jubilee in their own local churches on the Sunday morning, and then to join us in the afternoon in a service of thanksgiving and dedication. This began in the Anglican Cathedral and finished in the Roman Catholic or Metropolitan Cathedral, as it is often called by way of distinction: the dedication of both cathedrals is to Christ. Between the two points of the service the great congregation walked together along Hope Street. There were a few rumbles from Liverpool's sectarian past when some tried to make capital out of the direction the procession took, ending up in the Roman Catholic Cathedral. But balance was restored when a few days later the Queen made the journey in the reverse direction, while the primary school-children of Liverpool took part in a pageant between the cathedrals and along Hope Street. Needless to say, a fine ecumenical balance has been preserved in the many processions which since then have taken place in each direction along this route.

Hope Street was crowded to its roof-tops at Pentecost in 1982 when Pope John Paul II visited first the Anglican Cathedral to greet and pray with the 'other Churches', before travelling along this route in his 'Pope-mobile' to celebrate Mass in the Metropolitan Cathedral. For the following two years at Pentecost we repeated a joint service between the two cathedrals, and it was at Pentecost 1985 that the great Covenanting Service took place. So the route had been well prepared. The occasion was wonderfully well supported. There was a huge congregation for the opening of the service in the Metropolitan Cathedral where Dean Patey, who had returned to Liverpool from retirement for this fulfilment of his dream, preached of the sign which this historic step might be to the rest of the nation. Then we moved in procession to the Anglican Cathedral, gathering still greater numbers on the way. When we reached the end of Hope Street we looked back to see the whole route filled with a joyful surge of people, from all parts of Merseyside and of all ages. Afterwards we were told, 'If at that moment the Church leaders had wanted to turn back, they couldn't have. The crowd would have carried them forward.' In the Anglican Cathedral we solemnly signed the Covenant. Towards the end of the service, we all sang 'Bind us together, Lord' and the Church leaders spontaneously joined hands. Immediately an old lady reached out and moved across the nave aisle – a distance of some twenty feet – towards the person on the other side. Within half a minute the whole aisle down the length of the cathedral had disappeared as the entire congregation joined hands and the great divide closed.

The whole area of feelings – feelings after God, feelings for one another, 'gut' feelings of mistrust – is so important that we devote a whole chapter to the subject later in this book. But the point is made over and over again throughout this record of our years together in Liverpool. Shared events alter the way the participants see one another. One of the earliest shared ventures which we promoted was the Merseyside Youth Pilgrimage to Taizé. In this we shared the leadership with Norwyn Denny. It was the first of several such pilgrimages which we have led and we spent days on end living and sharing with young people, often facing for the first time the challenge of religious differences. The eight days' pilgrimage to Taizé was the longest as well as the first and it marked a major step forward for the three of us. On our return we published a rather grand-sounding Taizé Declaration. In the course of it we said:

> We are conscious that the relationship of Christian friendship and common purpose, which already existed between us, has been deepened by our time together . . . The regularity of our worship together has served to strengthen the sense of community amongst us. We desire to share this with others, and we hope that our experience may serve to encourage those who for long have shared these ideals.

LOCAL PARTNERSHIP AND JOINT INITIATIVES

Against this record of apparent success and enthusiastic support, it must be said that in both our dioceses the pattern of ecumenical partnership at local level remains patchy. There is a small, if growing, number of local ecumenical projects in which both our Churches share. The number in which the Anglicans and Free Churches are involved is greater. We have tried to experiment in projects where a church is not only shared but jointly owned, and also in those where – sometimes to defeat the legal demands of ecclesiastical officialdom – there is shared use of buildings owned by one or other denomination.

When in 1982 a shared church was proposed for a large estate at Hough Green near Widnes, the Anglican Planning Adviser visited the parish to consult local people. He wished to make sure that the proposal was not being foisted on the people by over-enthusiastic clergy. He found that they fully supported the plan. Some told him that they had grown up amidst division in Liverpool: they wanted something different for their children. In the event a fine new shared church was built by the Catholic archdiocese between presbytery and vicarage. All facilities and usage are shared. In the sanctuary, to one side, is the baptismal font which was specially constructed using parts of the fonts used previously in the separate chapels. We presided together at the opening celebration and jointly presented the church with a large hand-carved wooden crucifix for the sanctuary wall. The obvious friendship between the members of the two congregations represented several years of preparatory work by the clergy involved. There is already evidence that this relationship and arrangement have survived change of the leading individuals concerned. The Anglican vicar has moved to another assignment and the Catholic priest, a much loved Irishman, died suddenly while visiting the home of an Anglican family. The vast numbers present at his funeral were testimony, if such was needed, to the deep commitment of both sets of parishioners to this pioneer example of local ecumenism, which continues to thrive under different leadership.

In another parish in Warrington New Town, lay people pressed that the two Churches should be equal partners in ownership of the proposed new church building. They felt that shared usage alone was inadequate evidence of their commitment to such an important ecumenical venture. As important as anything in the working of a formal local ecumenical project is careful consultation before appointments are made by either Church. Commitment to the ideals such a project represents is an obvious prerequisite. But there must also be sensitivity in bringing forward particular names.

In one large Anglican team ministry there are three churches; one is shared with the Roman Catholics, and the other two with the Methodists. An Anglican priest, who happened to be divorced and remarried, seemed in himself a suitable choice as team vicar for one of the churches shared with the Methodists. The idea was dropped in order not to make matters difficult in the partnership with the Roman Catholics at the other end of the area. On the other hand, the Roman Catholic authorities, unaware of this issue, subsequently ran into trouble with the Methodists for consulting only with the Church of England on the appointment of a priest to the church shared with the local Anglicans. New relationships, even at one stage removed, can have growing pains. Even where informal relationships have developed, consultations about the appointment of clergy have great importance. Years of trust can be destroyed by appointing someone out of sympathy with carefully established relationships.

DAVID SHEPPARD: On one occasion Derek told me of the death of a young priest, of whom he had a very high opinion, and who had served in an inner-city parish. Some days later I saw our Anglican vicar in that parish. I said that I had learnt of that young parish priest's death. The vicar, a man in the evangelical tradition, said to me: 'That priest was my brother.' He went on to tell me of how they had begun to co-operate in an area where in the past sectarian divisions had been very bitter. I described this conversation to Derek, who at the funeral sought out the vicar to console him and who promised me that he would make sure that the new appointment was of someone who would be in sympathy with ecumenical partnership.

DEREK WORLOCK: More recently another priest died suddenly in a Wigan parish. At the funeral I was handed a letter from the Anglican vicar telling me how keenly he felt the loss. He wrote: 'This was a very lovely person. We prayed together. We planned our Good Friday processions together. I shall miss him acutely.' As a result of receiving that letter I asked my auxiliary bishop who carries through the appointments of our clergy to discuss the vacancy with me again. In the light of the information I had received, we agreed to change the nomination we had been considering.

There have been many other examples where clergy fraternals have provided the contact which has led to real brotherhood and partnership. Often such personal friendship leads to a Christian partnership in which two parishes come in time and in some measure to share. There are signs that such development can lead groups of local churches to enter into local covenants of a kind similar to that made by the Merseyside Church leaders. Of late there has been a considerable number of these local covenants. One example is that between the Anglican Liverpool Parish Church and the Roman Catholic St Mary's, Highfield Street, together with the Methodist Central Hall. For several years the clergy had worked closely together in the City Centre Ecumenical Team Ministry, which operates in a part of the city which is busy with people working in shops and offices by day but from which increasingly local residents have been moved. Both parishes have their regular supporters, many of whom are weekday rather than Sunday parishioners. A series of study days and growing activity between the two congregations led them to the point where clergy and lay representatives of the parishes signed a local covenant. To give this practical effect four active committees were established to deal with worship, witness, study and social matters.

The way in which this partnership developed over the years, despite changes among the clergy who had originally led the way, was impressive evidence that such Christian collaboration need not be the prerogative of the priests. Undoubtedly in this case the lay parishioners drew great strength from shared prayer and occasional joint services in each other's churches. Their witness was often given in their professional or commercial life, where mutual support was of great consequence. We cannot think of church life merely as activities associated with church buildings. The networks of urban life by which Christians meet one another are not necessarily associated with any one parish. They may lie in employment, education or leisure activities. These sectors are often places where creative sides of life are to be found and where burdens are to be borne as much as in the home neighbourhood. Lay people are the proper leaders of the people of God in these sectors which prove natural places for ecumenical co-operation.

The Liverpool City Centre Ecumenical Team includes Anglican, Roman Catholic and Free Church clergy. Their ministry is directed towards people in the world of work. They visit stores, offices, hospitals, the press and local government, if possible in twos but in any case never merely in the name of their own particular Church. To go visiting with two clergy from different denominations is to realise the kind of authority which can exist when people cannot dismiss such a visit as representing only one of many Churches. On one of her visits to Liverpool the Queen kindly allowed us to introduce members of this city-centre team to her. They explained their work and she asked one young Anglican priest if he really thought that those he approached in a large shopping store did not mind if he were an Anglican or a Roman Catholic. 'No, ma'am,' was the reply. 'So far as most of them are concerned, I am just "religion".'

The Liverpool Industrial Mission has been in existence for over forty years. For a long time its life focused on six Anglican industrial chaplains who visited factories regularly and helped networks of Christians from different Churches to think out the nature of their calling at work. In 1978 we felt that the time had come to develop this group of chaplains on an ecumenical basis and we therefore established the Liverpool Industrial Mission Ecumenical Council (LIMEC).

It is evident that the Churches have different styles of presence in commerce and industry. While the Church of England has concentrated largely upon industrial chaplains, Roman Catholics have attached great importance to the movement founded by Josef Cardijn and known in this country as the Young Christian Workers. Founded here just fifty years ago, the movement has always been strong in the North-West and has produced leaders who have gone on into local government and the trade unions.

When we first arrived in Liverpool, the Lord Mayor of the city was a former YCW, as were the mayors of St Helens and Wigan. The movement concentrates on the personal formation of the young workers, and its meetings, following the See, Judge and Act method, comprise a gospel enquiry, a review of life, and a consideration of responsibilities in facing the problems and opportunities of working life.

In 1978 some of their more experienced members were drawn into LIMEC. In the same way the Free Churches brought in groups of lay people who drew strength from one another and from their study of the questions raised in the world of work. But their contribution was not entirely from their lay members. The United Reformed Church supplied one full-time and one part-time industrial chaplain to join the Anglican clergy in their team. These different styles of presence reflected the Merseyside community at work. In the 'winter of discontent' 1978–79, if we brought together a group of Christians from the factory floor, the great majority was likely to be Roman Catholic. When some years later we invited senior businessmen to form the Michaelmas Group, concerned with the regeneration of Merseyside, the majority of practising Christians among them were Anglicans or Free Churchmen.

There are of course in Merseyside other sectors where Christians of different Churches are brought into partnership, sometimes explicitly noticed and encouraged, sometimes hidden. Informal partnership frequently comes about in response to human needs. For many years now, Christians have come together for the relief of hunger and for world development. There is good collaboration between Christian Aid, the Catholic Fund for Overseas Development (CAFOD) and The Evangelical Alliance Relief Fund (TEAR Fund). A World Development Study and Resource Centre was established by the Churches in the Liverpool Institute of Higher Education, where it serves the community at large.

In hospitals, social work, the voluntary movement, youth and community work and in local government, human issues arise which do not call for denominational viewpoints, but for Christian insight and support. If we ask why the Christian voice is so often silent, one of the first answers is that Christians who are present often feel terribly isolated. Sadly it is also suggested their Church has not always kept their work issues on its agenda. We betray lay people in some very demanding and exposed positions if we do not offer them the opportunity to think through their problems and responsibilities with other Christians.

Education is the sector which historically caused many of the most bitter divisions in Liverpool. We recognise the importance of children receiving a good grounding in the knowledge of their faith; but we have seen no contradiction in encouraging closer co-operation, wherever possible, between denominational schools. The falling rolls of recent years have not provided an easy context for collaboration. Parents and teachers have inevitably struggled vigorously to preserve 'our school'. It is the old story that rationalisation is reasonable so long as it applies only to the others. It has been a particularly difficult situation for the Roman Catholic archdiocese. When John Carmel Heenan was Archbishop of Liverpool from 1957 to 1963, he maintained strongly that 'you can never build too large for Catholics'. He led a vigorous campaign for school-building as well as church-building, convinced that the number of children would never fall. The policy was for total provision at both primary and secondary level. Almost every parish had its own infant and junior school and a share in the local secondary school. On the other hand the Liverpool diocese had 140 Anglican primary schools but only four secondary schools. The movement for 'responsible parenthood' and even more the movement of population, in particular from the inner city, has meant a dramatic fall in the number of children and a large number of redundant school buildings. In the ten years prior to our coming to Liverpool, the number of baptisms in the archdiocese fell by just on fifty per cent. For parishes which made great financial sacrifices to build new schools it has been a heart-break to see their costly achievement declared redundant due to falling rolls, the development of large inter-parochial comprehensive schools and the justifiable demand for economy by the local authority.

Although there are a number of cases where Anglican parents choose to send their children to a Roman Catholic all-abilities high school in preference to the local county school, we have as yet had no success in establishing a joint or so-called 'Christian' school at secondary level. We have made it plain that in principle we are not opposed to such a scheme but, where possible, parental wishes must be observed and experience suggests that such a venture would be easier and more successful in an area where altogether new secondary provision is required. The difficulties of such a project, if it is to be formed from existing schools of unequal numbers and of different traditions, appear almost overwhelming.

When, due to falling rolls, we were asked to consider the establishment of a joint 'Christian' school in an area served by a Roman Catholic secondary high school and one county comprehensive school, we found it difficult to explain to governors, staff and parents that what was being proposed meant a new venture and was not just a matter of admitting Anglican pupils to the existing Roman Catholic school. It then became clear that if one form of entry from the Anglican primary school were diverted each year to the joint school, the county comprehensive might well become inviable because of reduced numbers. In such circumstances, the suggested joint venture was a non-starter. With our advisers we then proposed, with the encouragement of the LEA, that special provision be made in the county school for the religious education of all the children, including the Roman Catholics. In the event, most of the parents elected to 'bus' their children across the district border to the neighbouring authority where there were places in Roman Catholic high schools. Quite simply, we remain enthusiastic about the possibility of establishing in suitable circumstances joint Christian schools or joint sixth-form colleges. But to have a chance of success, it must be in conditions where such a school can flourish rather than as a measure forced on reluctant parents in order to stave off the closure of a school due to falling rolls, and sometimes at the expense of another school.

In the realm of higher education there is good co-operation between our chaplaincies in Liverpool University and the Polytechnic. The resources of the chaplaincies and of some departments and staff have been shared on various occasions, notably in 1981 for a four-day conference on Faith, Hope and Technology.

The contraction of numbers caused by reduced public expenditure has provided a difficult climate for one of the most important ecumenical initiatives of recent years. When we arrived in Liverpool we were vigorously lobbied by staff and governors of our three colleges of higher education, two Roman Catholic and one Anglican. They were most anxious to work steadily closer together in some loose-knit federation. One day it was learnt that cuts by the Department of Education and Science would endanger one if not two of the three colleges. We met immediately with the principals and agreed that no college would seek to secure places if it were at the expense of another. Eventually to help achieve the demanded economy, the two Catholic colleges (Notre Dame and Christ's College) agreed to move to a single site adjoining the Anglican College (St Katharine's). The two Catholic colleges then amalgamated and after many negotiations, the Liverpool Institute of Higher Education was established with two constituent colleges, St Katharine's and Christ's and Notre Dame College. The Institute, under a Rector, was to become a unified academic body, but with each college preserving its distinctive character.

The ease with which the single Institute was accepted by the students was remarkable. The repeated threat of redundancies proved damaging to the confidence of some of the staff in the Institute. We have been chairman and vice-chairman of the Institute's governing council for periods of two years in turn. All of us involved in the development of the Institute have needed to persevere in realising the dream of a Christian Institute, in which Roman Catholic and Anglican characteristics can continue to flourish. It has been a sign of hope, a declaration of intent for the future, and a challenge to be faced at a time of repeated economic cuts and educational changes. But Christian teachers have been trained together, with knowledge of each other and of denominational differences, amidst friendship and collaboration. In the long run this may prove even more important and valuable, so far as educational method and content are concerned, than the spasmodic establishment of joint Christian schools.

ECUMENISM, LOYALTIES AND DIFFERENCES

It has been important while there have been so many developments in the promotion of Christian unity at both national and international levels, to ensure that what has been taking place should find its way into the hearts and minds of more Christians than those enthusiasts regarded by others as 'ecumaniacs'. At two-year intervals the Church leaders of Merseyside have invited some four hundred clergy, ministers, deaconesses and religious sisters to two-day study consultations on doctrinal matters. These have included the various ARCIC reports and the Lima Report on Baptism, Eucharist and Ministry. We have allocated the places at these conferences on a basis of 150 each for the Anglicans and the Roman Catholics and 100 for the Free Churches, reflecting roughly the numbers serving in Merseyside and region. We decided not just to announce each conference on a first come, first served basis. Each of us invited people personally, making sure that not merely was there a good coverage geographically and by age range but also there should be included a fair proportion of names of those unlikely to have taken part before in an ecumenical consultation.

Although in the Roman Catholic archdiocese the priests are mostly drawn from the area and at ordination are committed to it for life, with the Anglican and Free Churches there is a greater degree of movement. To help the recently ordained and new arrivals to understand the relationship between the Churches in Merseyside and the responsibilities and challenges shared, an eight-week Clergy Orientation Course is arranged each year. Another valuable annual course, now of several years' standing, is a joint Course in Pastoral Ministry. This requires attendance for one day each week over a three-term year. At least one participant in this course has said it saved his ministry. He had come into the course in those dangerous middle years of ministry when the whole horizon can seem to offer only more of the same routine. Ministry to ministers can imply mutual support across denominational frontiers.

Such doctrinal study is not for the clergy alone. Just as multi-disciplinary study can carry its own advantages, so a variety of ministries, ordained and lay, can often bring an enrichment of insight and experience. The same is true when a problem is tackled together with Christians from other Churches. For example, at the time when the *Final Report* from ARCIC was receiving a crude and destructive treatment in the press, it was good to meet some quite unsophisticated grass-roots Christians in one area just north of Liverpool whose members had studied the document for themselves. Far from complaining that it was made up of all the big and difficult words of theologians, they claimed to understand it and its significance well. The clue was that over the years, as each report from the Commission was published, two neighbouring parishes, Anglican and Roman Catholic, had met in groups to study it. When one group could not understand why a particular point was being made, the others were likely to explain what importance the matter had for them. The will to understand and to keep pace with new insights cannot be confined to academics. It will not be, if the challenge of ecumenism can be seen in the context of mission.

Especially in our first years here, we found that the very loyalties which had survived the displacement of extreme sectarianism led to great emphasis on '*our* Church' – rather as we had known in the East End of London the importance attached to 'looking after our own'. On both sides there remained deep suspicion of anything other than absolute and unequivocal statements about belief, morals and church life. Quite evidently it was not always easy for Christians, whose strong sense of loyalty was identified with safeguarding 'our Church', to accept some of our early initiatives in collaboration or indeed to understand that it was not disloyal to enter into ecumenical partnership. Development, change, the revision of words and ways in worship, even though fully authorised by our Churches, were often seen as in some way critical of the past and its heroes. To encourage honest debate about complex issues was not far removed from an unwelcome invitation to sup with the devil.

At the end of our first year together in Liverpool, the *Liverpool Daily Post* published an extended interview with the pair of us, which the newspaper described as 'an historic meeting'. In the interview we were led to discuss those occasions when we were pressed to make absolute or definitive statements. We were reported as saying:

DAVID SHEPPARD: I want to take up the point you made about people wanting to be given a definite answer. I think that this puts clergy in a particular difficulty. The cry is, 'In a world where everything is changing, let there be one unchanging thing.' Many say to us, 'Give us a lead.' I regard it as wrong to give a snappy catch answer to a request like that, because the issues are deeper. There is a natural longing to be assured of a cast-iron sort of Saviour, who protects you from all sorts of pain, all hurt, all doubt. I believe him to be a Saviour at a deeper level because he enters into those pains and doubts too.

DEREK WORLOCK: In the past the Church has seemed at times to be autocratic in its methods and its teaching. But there is no instant push-button answer to the new problems, whether moral or social. There is no use our pretending that there is, as it were, a book to which one can always turn to find the page with the right answers. There lies the danger: believing that Jesus at some time on earth gave an explicit answer to every question that has come up for later generations; or believing that in his human nature he knew how to speak French or Latin and that he talked to his apostles about, for example, the morality of spare-part surgery. We must try to be clear about what we say. But I hope that we shall not go back to being knowledgeable know-alls providing instant wisdom through a press-button service for every new question which arises.

Then some words of caution and perhaps even of prophecy are inserted:

DAVID SHEPPARD: Both of us are very aware of the current pressures on Merseyside, the loss of jobs and of opportunities in the inner city.

DEREK WORLOCK: And we also have to face the fact that, when Bishop David and I talk about some of these things, people tell us to mind our own business and stick to church affairs.

When bishops raise awkward questions and even when they try to speak of the awkward questions put to them, they are quickly labelled 'way-out radicals'. We believe that as church members have seen us regularly leading worship and preaching in our parishes, they have realised that for both of us our firm desire is to be wholeheartedly loyal to God's holy word in the Scriptures and to the Church. In making our way around the rather more than two hundred parishes which each of our dioceses comprises, we found that, as we also visited hospitals, factories, coal-mines, schools and football grounds, and were increasingly seen together, people stopped questioning our association and even assumed our joint interest and presence, especially in times of crisis. People still distinguished themselves as belonging to 'Bishop David's flock' or 'Archbishop Derek's flock', though no longer by way of aggression or apology. There was a warm response from a wide range of people, inside and outside the Church, to our interest in issues like housing and unemployment. But it took time. Such acceptance was often at least as difficult for our clergy as for lay people.

DAVID SHEPPARD: For one of our ecumenical study conferences for the clergy, we had agreed that we would attend each other's Eucharist. One evangelical vicar wrote to me before the conference, saying that he had a commitment to speak in his church school at the time we would be expected to attend the Roman Catholic Mass. What should he do? I wrote back suggesting that he could transfer the day when he went into the church school, and hoping that he might feel able to set himself free to attend the Mass. It became clear that there was deep within him a hostility, even a revulsion and fear, at the idea of being present at a Mass. On the day in question, as we came out of the Mass, this vicar approached me and, almost in tears, said, 'I never realised that it was like that.' He had found the service profoundly Christ-centred and was thankful that he had come.

DEREK WORLOCK: Forced ecumenism can be as undesirable and unproductive as forced conversion. For many the problem was: how to start? It was my custom for many years to try to ensure that in areas where there seemed to be no movement or where antagonisms were evident, the local Council of Churches would invite me to preach in a non-Catholic church during the January Octave for Christian unity.

This often led reluctant but loyal Catholics to be present in my support, if not in my protection. But once contacts had been established, good relationships were made and usually preserved. As in so many matters, it was the initial breakthrough and personal contact which overcame the reluctance and prejudice built on misconceptions and ignorance.

In the close partnership in which we have been engaged, it has been important that others should be able to place their trust in us, just as we have known absolute trust in one another. We have always worked on the understanding that there is no matter which we are not prepared to discuss either personally or as part of the agenda for a meeting of Church leaders. With habitual consultation and constant exchange of news and views, there grows an increasing degree of sensitivity, without any pretence or attempt to hide differences of approach and of belief. While we have avoided any unnecessary expression of disagreement in public, there has been no lack of attempts in the media or in political circles to cast us into opposition. There have to be both honesty and balance in such a situation. There have been times when we have been confronted in public on issues about which we not only hold different views but must be expected to hold different views. Some differences inevitably indicate obstacles on the road to unity but not the end of reconciliation. A cover-up would be false ecumenism.

DEREK WORLOCK: One Sunday morning some years ago we took part together in a phone-in on BBC Radio Two. Most of the questions were straightforward enough but one questioner from London pressed me hard as to whether I accepted the validity of Bishop David's orders. I replied that this was really part of a wider question which concerned our two Churches. I did not know the particular circumstances of Bishop David's ordination but I did regard the historical basis of Pope Leo XIII's famous 'absolutely null and void' judgment as being no longer relevant. There were many issues now involved and our Churches were discussing them. In the meantime I was glad to accept Bishop David's ministry as a Bishop of the Church of England and to work with him in our Christian service of the people. Afterwards the producer said that I had ducked the question. Since then the Holy See has made it plain that the issue of orders cannot be seen or judged apart from other matters of belief and practice, especially with regard to the whole sacramental system.

In personal conversation and in clergy seminars we have tried to see the way forward to the mutual recognition of orders and the sharing of eucharistic hospitality – so often called intercommunion – which could follow. Whatever our personal yearning and the hurt which arises from the present separation in the Eucharist, we have always maintained that there is no true way forward in breaking the disciplines of our respective Churches. In its statement on *Ministry and Ordination*, the Anglican and Roman Catholic International Commission made considerable progress in showing the similarity of traditions in our two Churches in the three orders of bishops, priests and deacons, with ordinations performed in the apostolic succession through the bishops. There remains important work to be done on how the distinction should be expressed between the priesthood of the ordained ministry and the priesthood of all the faithful people of God. This is true also of the distinction between the words 'ministry' and 'priesthood'.

ARCIC's 'Elucidation' of this particular statement calls for the reappraisal of the verdict on Anglican Orders by Pope Leo XIII in *Apostolicae Curae* (1896) and adds:

> Mutual recognition presupposes acceptance of the apostolicity of each other's ministry. The Commission believes that its agreements have demonstrated a consensus in faith on Eucharist and ministry which has brought closer the possibility of such acceptance. It hopes that its own conviction will be shared by members of both our communions; but mutual recognition can only be achieved by the decision of our authorities.
>
> (*Final Report*, p. 45)

On this we are in agreement; and it is important to recognise that the question of – as Roman Catholics see it – the validity of Anglican orders in general is distinct from the issue about the ordination of women to the priesthood, which has in recent years caused such a furore and about which we ourselves are divided. The extent of that division was reflected in the much publicised exchange of letters between the Archbishop of Canterbury, Pope John Paul and Cardinal Willebrands of the Vatican Secretariat for Christian Unity. This was published by mutual agreement just prior to the meeting of the General Synod of the Church of England at York in July 1986. In a letter at the end of 1984, the Pope had written that 'the increase in the number of Anglican Churches which admit, or are preparing to admit, women to priestly ordination constitutes in the eyes of the Catholic Church an increasingly serious obstacle to that progress [between our two Communions].' Archbishop Runcie, having consulted the Primates of the autonomous provinces of the Anglican Communion throughout the world, replied that 'although Anglican opinion is itself divided, those Churches which have admitted women to priestly ministry have done so for serious doctrinal reasons'. Some of these he set out in a letter to Cardinal Willebrands, to whom he added, 'Those provinces which have taken this step have indicated to me that their experience has been generally beneficial.'

DEREK WORLOCK: In that exchange of letters, which reflected a welcome development in frank dialogue between our Churches, both the Pope and Cardinal Willebrands reaffirmed the Roman Catholic view that 'the ordination only of men to the presbyterate and episcopate is the unbroken tradition of the Catholic and Orthodox Churches. Neither Church understands itself to be competent to alter this tradition.' Archbishop Runcie claimed that those provinces which had gone ahead with the ordination of women believed that tradition is open to this development 'because the exclusion of women from priestly ministry cannot be proved to be of divine law'. Nevertheless the Archbishop recognised that for 'so significant a theological development it is not enough to assert that there are no reasons against such a proposed action. It is also necessary to demonstrate compelling doctrinal reasons for such a development.' I cannot feel that such a compelling argument for this development has been made.

DAVID SHEPPARD: True ecumenism is not helped forward by holding back from actions we deeply believe to be right. There is an entirely proper fear of hurting or dividing the Church further. Yet we have no simple choices to make about that. I know that Derek has stated publicly that while the ordination of women is from his viewpoint an obstacle to unity, yet if we truly believe it to be right, he can understand why we must see it as the way forward. There are in fact some very hurtful divisions around this subject already. I am keenly aware as an Anglican bishop of that hurt at every ordination service. I am not then able to consider ordaining women to the priesthood, even though they are trained side by side with men and are made deacons with them. Like other bishops, I am told by these women how deeply hurt they feel.

It will not do to say that women bring wholly distinct gifts and therefore should be given entirely different roles from men. Modern understandings of personality make us realise that each of us has some characteristics which we have been inclined to call female and some male. It is a revealing exercise to make a list of characteristics which you believe belong to your own personality and to write down each under the heading of female or male. I believe that there is no hard and fast line between male and female personality which makes them inadequate for sharing in decision-making in society. Yet, so long as women cannot be ordained, they can only be in a minority at best in many places where Church decisions are made.

DEREK WORLOCK: I have always believed and worked to ensure that women should have their full and rightful place in the decision-making structures and processes of the Church. Of course, for me this has to be seen in the context of the fact that, by the very nature of the Church, the responsibility for the taking of some decisions is vested in certain offices in the Church, which is not a democracy ruled by majority vote. But the question of the ordination of women to the priesthood is a theological issue and not to be resolved on sociological or cultural grounds. The role of women in the Church and in society today is of major importance but there are quite different grounds for considering women in the priesthood.

When we speak of tradition, we are not speaking of inherited cultural practices which may become outmoded, but of the constant teaching of the Catholic and Orthodox Churches based on the practice of Christ and the apostles. Cardinal Willebrands expressed this to the Archbishop of Canterbury in these words: 'The practice of the Church to ordain only men embodies her fidelity under the guidance of the Holy Spirit to what was given by Christ.' The Church considers herself bound by Christ's own manner of acting. There is real continuity between the redemptive work of Christ and the sacramental office of the ministerial priesthood. The Vatican's declaration on this subject Inter Insigniores (1976) quotes Saint Thomas as saying: 'Sacramental signs represent what they signify by natural resemblance'; and then it adds:

> The same natural resemblance is required for persons as for things: when Christ's role in the Eucharist is to be expressed sacramentally, there would not be this natural resemblance which must exist between Christ and his minister, if the role of Christ were not taken by a man: in such a case it would be difficult to see in the minister the image of Christ. For Christ was and remains a man.

This is a question of fact but does not imply superiority of man over woman. After all the Son of God became man, taking human flesh from his mother Mary.

DAVID SHEPPARD: I base my belief that women should be ordained to the priesthood and the episcopate on serious theological grounds. I understand the fears of our critics that we are simply following current cultural trends. At the same time I resist any suggestion that matters to do with church life and order are proper subjects for theology, while great *matters of human relationships which affect all people are somehow to be filed away under 'sociology' or 'psychology'. If we believe that God is continuing to be the Creator and Redeemer of the whole world, we cannot wholly separate what we believe to be his purpose for women in secular life from what his purpose is for them in church life.*

Coming back to the biblical evidence, it is true that Jesus chose all males to be his apostles. I make the point that he also chose all Jews and all free men. The great promise in St Paul is that in Christ 'there are no more distinctions between Jew and Greek, slave and free, male and female, but all of you are one in Christ Jesus' (Gal. 3:28 JB). It took the Church eighteen centuries to break down the barrier between slaves and free men, as St Paul's words challenged us. It is perhaps not surprising that we should have taken even longer to break down the barrier between male and female.

As for the sacramental sign, our worship is to be in some sense a reflection of the worship of heaven. When I imagine the worship of heaven, I think of Mary the mother of Jesus with an intimate place of honour in the worshipping circle: and Christ at the centre. One of our clergy, who had always believed that the priest at the Eucharist was an icon of Christ and must therefore be male, told me not long ago why he had changed his position and now believed that women should be ordained. The priest, he said, should indeed be an icon of Christ, but of the risen and glorified Christ, who has taken up all humanity, male and female, into heaven.

DEREK WORLOCK: Our teaching that the priest stands at the altar to make present the once-and-for-all sacrifice of Christ implies that he represents Christ in his saving relationship with his body, the Church. Although in one sense the priest is acting and praying in the name of the whole Church, before all else he is acting in the person of Christ, so intimate is the union between the Eucharist he celebrates and Christ's sacrifice on the cross. This is at the heart of our understanding of the symbolic and iconic role of the priest who represents Christ in the Eucharist. But we must not lose sight of the fact that the ordained priesthood is not the only ministry to be exercised in the life and mission of the Church.

We have set out this difference of belief between us at some length at the conclusion of this chapter on partnership between Churches for several reasons. It would be dishonest to pretend that because there are so many matters on which we collaborate, there can be no division between us. Personally distressing though differences on matters precious to us can be, the very sincerity of the exchange can enrich rather than endanger the relationship between us. We have highlighted this particular issue because our Churches are involved and it is not just a difference of personal opinion. Nor is the issue likely to go quickly away. In their joint declaration at Canterbury on the occasion of the papal visit in 1982, Pope John Paul and Archbishop Robert Runcie charged the new ARCIC to examine

> the outstanding differences which still separate us, with a view towards their eventual resolution; to study all that hinders the mutual recognition of the ministries of our Communions; and to recommend what practical steps will be necessary when, on the basis of our unity in faith, we are able to proceed to the restoration of full communion.

We shall have to live with this and other differences which will not be resolved overnight. Meantime we must not be discouraged. We recall the words of Pope Paul VI: 'Obstacles do not destroy mutual commitment to a search for reconciliation.'

6 THE SERVANT CHURCH IN A HURT CITY

In a country like Britain the Church has far more influence than is often supposed. For that influence to be positive and effective it is necessary for the various denominations to 'get their act together'. This means not only that some form of ecumenical partnership is highly desirable but also that we have a clear idea of what the nature and role of the whole Church is. The theological importance of this has been shown through the responses to the Inter-Church Process, *Not Strangers but Pilgrims*. But there is also the whole sphere of relationships, attitudes, lifestyle, objects of concern and priorities. For these are a reflection of how the Church views itself and the fulfilment of its role.

THE SERVANT CHURCH

Time was when the Church had considerable temporal power. From the age of the Emperor Constantine its leaders frequently approved wars or forbade them. Its institutions questioned and often barred honest research, as with Galileo. Its bishops and religious orders dispensed charity, and pioneered hospitals, schools and universities. While some of its theologians maintained the divine right of kings, behind the scenes its top men often whispered in the ear of the ruler. True enough, this Church of power left behind it much that was good and of benefit to at least part of the community. Yet the possession of power often led it away from the example bequeathed by Jesus in the foot-washing of his disciples, and far from the way in which he dealt with people in their needs.

In their efforts to understand what kind of Saviour God had sent into the world, the writers of the New Testament turned often to the Servant Songs of Isaiah. They found that the book of the prophet contained passages like these about the Servant of the Lord:

He does not cry out or raise his voice,
his voice is not heard in the street;
he does not break the crushed reed
or snuff the faltering wick.
Faithfully he presents fair judgement;
he will not grow faint, he will not be crushed
until he has established fair judgement on earth . . .
(Isa. 42:2–4 NJB)

Lord Yahweh has given me a disciple's tongue,
for me to know how to give a word of comfort to the weary.
Morning by morning he makes my ear alert
to listen like a disciple.
Lord Yahweh has opened my ear
and I have not resisted,
I have not turned away.
I have offered my back to those who struck me,
my cheeks to those who plucked my beard;
I have not turned my face away
from insult and spitting.

(Isa. 50:4–6 NJB)

Like a sapling he grew up before him,
like a root in arid ground.
He had no form or charm to attract us,
no beauty to win our hearts;
he was despised, the lowest of men,
a man of sorrows, familiar with suffering . . .
(Isa. 53:2,3 NJB)

History shows us how the Church, in its structures and in its learning, is often influenced by what is happening in contemporary society and culture. In the present age of a society which knows both affluence and extreme poverty, technological achievement and the wastage of unemployment, superpowers and Third World dependence and powerlessness, the Church has had to make its choices. For human and sometimes cultural reasons, the option has not always and everywhere been the same. But generally it has been a true instinct which in recent years has picked up the theme of the prophet and placed its focus upon the Servant Church.

The call for renewal in many of the Churches has occurred simultaneously with a growing realisation of the inequalities in contemporary society and among the nations of the world. Even before the emergence of liberation theology, with its inevitable political overtones, increasing emphasis had been placed upon human rights and development rather than on charitable relief. Vatican II gave expression to this in its *Pastoral Constitution on the Church in the Modern World*, stressing the new relationship which must exist between the Church and the world of today. Certainly the Church must respect the accomplishments of the world and learn from them, if the gospel is to be proclaimed effectively. But lest it seem that the Church is being encouraged to clamber on to the back of power, we are reminded that just as Christ came into the world not to be served but to serve, so the Church, carrying on the mission of Christ, must seek to serve the world by fostering the brotherhood of all mankind (cf. *Gaudium et Spes*, nn. 3 and 92).

The term 'servant' implies work that is humble, perhaps demeaning. It certainly denotes an attitude which does not claim to have all the answers, rather like the popular song from the musical *Annie, Get Your Gun*: 'Anything you can do, we can do better.' The status of a servant also implies work directed to the good of others rather than for self-benefit. There is a certain limitation in the use of the term if it is implied that the work of the servant is done under orders and not freely. Yet down the centuries Christians have proved the paradox that the service of God is perfect freedom. The mission of the servant is clear. It was spelt out in words which Jesus himself was to quote:

> The spirit of Lord Yahweh is on me
> for Yahweh has anointed me.
> He has sent me to bring the news to the afflicted,
> to sooth the broken-hearted,
> to proclaim liberty to captives,
> release to those in prison . . .
>
> (Isa. 61:1, 2 NJB)

The modern world needs something which the Servant Church, by the very manner of its service and by its motivation, alone can give: faith in Christ, hope in the ultimate coming of God's Kingdom, and commitment to the values of justice and peace. By itself the secular world is more conscious of its need to give and receive service than it is of its search for faith and hope. That is why it can become lost in its quest for power and success. In some measure the Church too has sometimes succumbed to this. When that has happened, the role of the servant has been lost in a take-over which can deny responsibility to others, setting itself up as a rival power to the secular world. The Anglican bishop John Robinson once wrote: 'The house of God is not the Church but the world. The Church is the servant, and the first characteristic of a servant is that he lives in someone else's house, not his own' (*The New Reformation?* p. 92).

In the Servant Songs of Isaiah the astonishing claim is made that God regarded the Persian king Cyrus as his 'anointed one', even though he did not know God. Cyrus was to be regarded by the people of God as a wise and good ruler through whose hand the Lord Yahweh would restore Israel (cf. Isa. 45). This bears a lesson for Christians today. We should be glad when, for example, the state takes on the care of the sick in the National Health Service. God's work is not done only when it can be marked by a flag declaring 'Church-run project here'. Experience suggests that sometimes the Church must endeavour to provide for those who slip through the human network of the institution. But often the calling to Christian people is to serve in as hidden and quiet a way as the servant of the Lord, who did not cry or 'shout aloud in the street'.

The Church's mission has been described as shedding the light of the gospel on the world. Christians have distinctive and special news to proclaim by life and by lip. The service and example demanded of the Lord's followers in no way denies this duty of proclamation to the world. The servant is first and foremost the servant of the Lord. Each morning he is to listen like a disciple, anxious to learn his Master's will. The whole of his life is to be threaded through with prayer. Worship is like a generator which renews hope and energy to serve people in face of the many disappointments experienced in a hurt city. In worship we are to fill our hearts and minds with the triumphs of Christ. But we have also to try to understand what kind of triumphs were his and the methods by which he won them. In learning to measure true progress and success, we are to be upheld by the knowledge that it can be no less Christlike to seem in the eyes of others to fail.

So the Servant Church must put aside all appearance of triumphalism. That means recognising that the calling of many Christians lies primarily in the secular sphere of life. It includes welcoming good-willed persons of other faiths or none: joining hands with others not of our faith in order to serve the whole community. Crucially it insists on our willingness to renounce our desire to control whatever we have a share in. To cede control so that another may grow in responsibility is a sign of the true servant of the Lord. Other signs will include humility without obsequiousness, a readiness to express gratitude and personal concern for the efforts of another, and a willingness to apologise and admit faults even where responsibility is at most indirect. This is true of the Servant Church as a whole as well as of the individual Christian.

DEREK WORLOCK: The earlier mention of Galileo reminds me of an incident which occurred in Rome towards the end of the Second Vatican Council, when the finishing touches were being put to the document on The Church in the Modern World. *At the time there was much beating of breasts for past errors and many gestures of friendship for the future. An historic liturgy of the Word was held in the basilica of St Paul's outside the Walls, in which Pope Paul VI took part with the representatives of the Protestant and Orthodox traditions. A few days later there was a joint declaration by the Pope and the Orthodox Patriarch of Constantinople, Athenagoras I, in which both Churches consigned to oblivion the mutual excommunications of the eleventh century. There was widespread enthusiasm for the mood of reconciliation and forgiveness. It rose to a crescendo when certain of the French bishops pressed for a formal apology by the Church to the memory of Galileo. However, a West African bishop scuppered this by asking: 'What am I expected to do? Must I first go home and instruct my people about who this man Galileo was? Am I then to tell them what happened and demand that they now apologise for their part in it?' Not surprisingly, that particular conciliar business was left unfinished.*

THE PEOPLE OF GOD

This splendid title reminds us of the Lord's covenant, as set out in the words of the prophet Jeremiah: 'Then I shall be their God and they will be my people' (Jer. 31:33 NJB). St Peter saw this fulfilled in the Church which he described as 'a holy nation, God's own people' (1 Pet. 2:9 RSV). Ironically the Greek word for 'people' is *laos*, from which our word 'laity' is derived. Yet for centuries this has borne the negative sense of being 'not of the clergy'. Nowadays it is often said that it is easier to describe what the laity do than define who they are. Centuries of clericalism have cast them in a second-class role.

To be of the laity is to share in the task entrusted by God to all his people. The task is a consequence of that covenanted relationship foretold by the prophet. For our purposes here it means serving God in a hurt world and it is the responsibility of the whole people of God, not just of the 'professionals', the clergy. In just the same way, clericalism has for too long reserved the term 'ministry' for those in holy orders. Only relatively recently have we begun to speak of the diversity of ministries, to realise that they are distinct and that, whoever performs them, they bear true dignity and importance in the life and mission of the Church.

All true ministry, ordained or lay, must bear the distinctive mark of the servant. Christ the Lord instituted in his Church a variety of ministries, which work for the good of the whole. Those ministers to whom has been given particular power and responsibility are themselves the servants of their brethren. For all the people of God enjoy a true Christian dignity. In a Church which proclaims a ministry of service to others, there is to be service between ministries – ministry to ministers.

The avoidance of excessive clericalism among the people of God means taking the laity seriously and trying to ensure that they have the opportunity to express their proper responsibility in the life of the Church. The way in which this is to be achieved is inevitably related both to the nature of the Church and to its source of authority. Our two Churches have been trying to work this out in different ways and at different speeds. Perhaps the basic difference lies in the fact that in the hierarchical system of the Roman Catholic Church, all consultative structures – from the synod of bishops through to parish committees – are strictly consultative, save in purely administrative matters; whereas with the Church of England with synodical government there are major executive powers to be exercised by elected representatives. In practice the difference in outcome may be small. But it is a significant distinction not unrelated to how the source of authority is seen.

In the Church of England the House of Laity of the General Synod celebrated in 1986 one hundred years of the involvement of lay people in the government of the Church. The Church Assembly was succeeded in 1968 by the General Synod, with equal elected representation of laity and clergy meeting together with the House of Bishops, which has particular rights in matters of doctrine. This pattern is reflected in diocesan and deanery synods. At a more local level lay people have for long served as church wardens and as elected representatives on the Parochial Church Council. On occasion these councils are open to the criticism that they are only concerned with buildings and finance. But in fact many attend to the whole task of Christian mission, perhaps appointing sub-committees concerned with mission and unity, social responsibility, liturgy and finance, which report on these matters to the Parochial Church Council at regular intervals.

In the Roman Catholic Church some of the consultative bodies have in certain places existed for many years. But the general mood of dialogue and consultation really began to emerge after the Second Vatican Council had insisted that all the members of the Church had a role to play in its life and mission. The Holy See itself established a Laity Council as part of the Roman Curia, with all save its permanent officials drawn from the various continents, with most of its members lay, and a handful of bishops and clergy as consultors. Later the Canon Law of the Church was revised to provide for the establishment in each diocese of a pastoral council 'to study and weigh those matters which concern the pastoral works in the diocese and to propose practical conclusions'. Such a council 'is composed of members of Christ's faithful: clerics, members of institutes of consecrated life, and especially lay people'. At the end of the legislation are found the words: 'The pastoral council has only a consultative vote.'

Again this can sound very negative, but it reflects the effort to achieve a means of sharing responsibility in an ordered structure: one mission, a variety of ministries, proper responsibilities and authority, one people of God.

Few would deny that in their present state of development the church structures in which the laity play their part are still far from perfect. In fact 'structure' has become for many people almost a dirty word. It is probably true that some structures in both our Churches tend to absorb committed lay people in 'churchy' procedures rather than in working out their ministries in the secular world. Yet there are other considerations. The way in which the local church decides its own priorities – and this is equally true at national and international level – does affect the witness it bears in the world. Our agendas must look outwards as well as inwards. But to be a Servant Church means having specific objects of service. The Lord chose to wash the feet of his disciples rather than to speak in general terms of the humility of that kind of service towards people in need.

A further and important consideration is that, while those exercising a particular ministry may with advantage meet together to exchange experience and counsel, no one vocation or ministry is the whole Church or the whole people of God. Experience of these last years suggests that the danger of over-concern with 'churchy' things is best countered by structures or groupings in which representatives of different ministries have their proper role. A good example of this was the Roman Catholic National Pastoral Congress, in which we both took part with bishops, clergy and laity from all over the country. This was held in Liverpool in May 1980.

This insight into the variety of callings within the people of God makes clear that this development is not a matter of one group taking over from another. Nor is the calling of the laity due to a current shortage of clergy, though this may have been a God-given factor in our increased understanding of the ministry of the laity in both the Church and the world. It is still a question of *one* people of God. Those massive church documents of the 1960s and the teachings they contained were all about relationships, especially among God's people. Today they must be seen in the context of the many ministries in a Servant Church.

SACRED AND SECULAR

In the last few years much has been written about the Church and politics. It is a regular item in the list of questions advanced by any audience if we have been speaking publicly together. Our concern with some of the issues in society today led one national daily newspaper to refer to us as 'interventionist bishops'. The intervention of the Church in secular issues is often resented, though the charge is laid against the bishops and clergy rather than against lay members of the Church. Our critics mutter: 'They should stick to their lasts,' or we are reminded that it is not 'the business of the Church to concern itself with secular matters'. While we question the extent to which the sacred and the secular can or should be kept separate, the real objection of the critics is to the issues of hurt cities becoming part of the regular agenda of the Church. Experience suggests that as long as Church leaders content themselves with generalisations on these issues, they are accused of nothing worse than moralising. When they deal with specific issues which are of current interest and concern, their words come under attack as political intervention.

There is a proper Christian insistence upon the importance of the secular. This is the concern of the whole Church, even though its laity have a particular responsibility and competence in this sphere. The special role of the laity in secular matters, to the exclusion of the clergy, is not claimed any more than that the laity should be excluded from the Church's worship. The laity are not to be excluded from singing in the choir and from reading God's word in the Church's worship. Is the local priest to close his eyes to the cause as well as the consequence of the factory closure which has thrown many of his parishioners out of work? Bishops and clergy must respect the experience and competence of lay people in their own fields. Yet we cannot connive at the total separation of sacred and secular. The Church is in, not of, but *for* the world.

The bearing of Christian witness in the secular world can be for the laity the fulfilment of their prophetic task which is part of their sharing in the common priesthood of all the faithful. Today the presence of someone, lay or clerical, who is known to have connections with Christ and his Kingdom, is a reminder of values all too easily forgotten and yet desperately needed for social justice and community harmony. Sadly the prophetic witness of the laity is not always recognised for what it is, because of the false separation in people's minds between what they regard as religion and real life.

Businessmen sometimes say to us, 'You won't agree with this, Bishop . . .' and go on to describe their regular practice as if it were a mystery to us. Their assumption is all too often that the sacred is idealistic, impractical and other-worldly, with no bearing upon their problems. An honest attempt to hold sacred and secular side by side can often throw a surprising degree of light on a perplexing social or industrial issue. 'Throwing the light of the gospel on the secular world' is indeed an apt description of the task of the Christian laity. The prophetic task of Christ may be brought to fulfilment through the official utterances of bishops and clergy, teaching in his name and with his authority; but it is also fulfilled through the laity.

For the individual as well as for the Church as a whole this separation of sacred from secular can often be quite unrealistic. Even the contemplative holds a place in his or her concern and prayer life for all that is happening outside the enclosure. In truth, Christian theology is built on earlier, Jewish foundations of the God who is Creator and Sustainer of the universe. He asks us to share in his continuing creation. The Old Testament speaks of the God of history. History includes what is happening now. That is not to claim that all so-called progress is good. The mystery of evil present in our world continues. But the God of history has not abandoned the secular world. He cares about reliable structures, just institutions, the quality of life for everyone, good opportunities which match the free will he has given to all his people. If evidence is sought for this, it is to be found in the Old Testament books like Exodus, Deuteronomy, Proverbs, Amos, Isaiah, Micah,

Jeremiah and Ezekiel. It is not the invention of those dismissed today as being socially 'trendy' and politically 'wet'.

Christian belief in the incarnation asserts that God entered freely into the human condition and whole human experience. The great mystery that Christ was the Son of God made man involved his working from within the limitations of human nature. That included earning a living, sharing indignation at the abuse or waste of the abundance with which the Creator had surrounded mankind, reaching out in compassion to those who were most hurt or rendered most abject, experiencing what it was to be powerless in face of human greed, envy and ambition. In a certain sense, the incarnation was not an emergency Plan B because through sin Plan A had failed. The incarnation, decreed from all eternity, was the expression of God's love, to the point of death, for all humankind to whom he had and has given freedom to respond to his love in their daily life on earth.

Christ's taking our human nature means that there is no part of our lives from which we can exclude him. We cannot separate our lives into compartments of varying degrees of concern or unconcern to our Creator – office, industry, scientific discovery, sport, politics, family life and spirituality. In Jesus Christ God took the whole human experience into his life. The Christian must be concerned about *whole* human beings and the effect that the *whole* of life in this world has upon them. Our generation has suffered much from too rigid specialisation. We cannot pick and choose aspects of concern for the human race. It is true that there must be specialisation in particular disciplines, but the world badly needs those who are concerned to see the *whole* picture of life.

Nowhere is this more true than with regard to urban life. Its complexity frustrates those who want a simple answer to solve all its problems. They would like to be able to say – and some do in fact say – that 'the solution lies in housing' or 'education is what really matters'. The hurts which afflict people in big cities stem from a confusing interlocking of all these great issues. But the point we would wish to make is that our concern with these matters is directly related to the incarnation. It is precisely because we are Christians that we are roused to what we regard as righteous indignation when we witness injustices and see some of the features of the hurt city today.

Our experience is that whole groups of urban dwellers believe that their opinions count with no one. If they are never able to make choices or have a real share in making decisions which affect their own or anyone else's destiny, they feel powerless. Their being made in the image and likeness of God is being trampled on.

Whole areas lack the normal resources which most parts of a wealthy country like Britain take for granted. In such areas normal services like insurance, bank loans, hire purchase, even television rentals, are denied because of the address from which the application is made. Youngsters applying for jobs often try to disguise their home address for the same reason. The way in which large cities have developed housing quarters, segregated by social class, means that many people who live in Urban Priority Areas never meet those who make the decisions which radically affect their lives and their relationship with other citizens. The base for charitable giving and support to community and voluntary bodies has dwindled to a significant degree. Those dedicated people who carry heavy burdens in such vital work for the community now have to bear the additional stress of seeking new means of financial support. This is often erratic and dependent upon chancy political favour. Here is but one example of how God-given abilities are wasted.

The connections between the secular and the sacred are much closer than many of our critics care to acknowledge. At the base of Christian faith is the belief that there is a good, loving and purposeful Creator and Sustainer at the heart of the universe. This faith is sorely tested in the face of such hurts as we have indicated. A black church warden of an inner-city parish said not so long ago: 'People around here are so full of despair at being helpless that they believe that God has deserted them.' The people of God, be they bishops, clergy or laity, cannot turn their eyes away from such hurtful secular realities on the score that they are too busy with matters sacred.

GOSPEL-INSPIRED LAITY

Our two Churches are inclined to use the words 'evangelism' and 'evangelisation' in rather different ways. It is an important distinction to appreciate if a balance is to be preserved between the rightful sharing of the laity in the preaching and worship of the Church (the sacred) and their particular responsibility in working to bring Christian principles to bear in the social order (the secular). In either case the motivation is the gospel.

Anglicans tend to use the word *evangelism* to speak of the proclamation of the evangel or the good news. They see it as naming the name of Christ, so that people may understand and make their personal response to him. On the other hand they use the word *mission* to describe the broad task of all that God sends us to do and to be in his world. In this broader sense Roman Catholics are inclined to use the word *evangelisation*, including both the meanings expressed by Anglicans. This evangelisation is living and speaking and working in such a way that the light of the gospel is shed into every aspect of life.

In his Apostolic Letter, following the 1974 Synod of Bishops on Evangelisation, Pope Paul VI spoke of the primary field of evangelisation for lay people. His words show the breadth of this concept:

> Their own field of evangelising activity is the vast and complicated world of politics, society and economics, but also the world of culture, of the sciences and arts, of international life, of the mass media. It also includes realities which are open to evangelisation, such as human love, the family, the education of children and adolescents, professional work, suffering.
>
> (*Evangelii Nuntiandi*, n. 70)

Even though *evangelisation* can be used in this broad sense, there are many who tend to clericalise the picture of the evangelist in exactly the same way as they clericalise the notion of *ministry*. This restrictive custom is not confined to Britain. The Roman Catholic Archdiocese of Liverpool has a missionary project in Latin America. One priest goes each year to Peru, Ecuador or Bolivia to serve a six-year stint in a local diocese. This evangelising work is carried out in the name of the whole archdiocese, so it was not long before some of the laity asked to serve the project personally and actively rather than just by the provision of finance. Eventually the first layman went out to join the priests. He is a qualified and professional youth worker and, after four months in language school, was assigned to work in a shanty-town district outside Lima. When querulous Peruvian Christians asked him what he hoped to teach the young people – football, drama, even mountaineering? – he replied: 'I hope in time to know their situation well enough to be able to help them to relate their Christian faith to their daily lives.' 'But how?' they asked. 'Are you a teacher?' 'No, I am an evangelist.' 'Ah, you must be *seminarista*,' they said, as light seemed to dawn on them. They were unprepared for the confident reply: 'No, *laico*.'

In days gone by, the laity were described even by socially-minded popes as 'lay auxiliaries of the hierarchy'. It was Pope Paul

VI, in his letter on evangelisation, who referred to 'gospel-inspired lay people'. Here in Merseyside, we frequently see lay men and women in the front line in the caring professions, in teaching, in business life, in trade unions, in the Town Hall, and we appreciate what a difference 'gospel-inspired lay people' can make. This can apply to positions of major responsibility. It is equally true of those on the factory-floor, in offices and shops.

Nowadays witness is given as often by example as by word. On more than one occasion we have been on the receiving end. Some years ago when we were struggling to prevent or ameliorate the closure of a long-established industrial concern in Liverpool, we were called to meet the chairman of the company in a vast multi-storeyed office in London. For a long time we sat in the foyer below, awaiting our summons. At last our turn came and without much hope we moved to the elevator to go up into the presence. As we passed the reception desk the girl inside leant out. 'Excuse me,' she said. 'I too am a Christian and would like you to know that while you are doing your stuff up there, I will be praying for both of you.' At that moment such lay Christian witness meant much.

Examples tend to glamorise. In many difficult situations the Christian voice is often silent, not because no Christians are present but because they feel alone, unsupported and unprepared. It does not follow that because someone is a devout, worshipping Christian, he or she is able alone to think through the complex issues which modern urban life poses. It can make a great difference when people of this kind can meet together, perhaps on an ecumenical basis, to share their dilemmas and experience. In village life, where at least in the past people often worked in sight of their own home, it was relatively simple for the parochial clergyman to understand the problems afflicting his charges and support them with advice or by encouraging them to face these issues together. The anonymity of modern urban life renders the development of any such approach difficult, if not impossible. This applies to the whole range of issues which confront Christians today in the world of work and of leisure.

There are at least two considerations which fall within our responsibility. One is the order of priorities observed by the Church in facing today's challenge. The other is the formation or education provided for adult Christians to enable them to make their intervention positive and relevant in contemporary circumstances.

Churches are tempted to swallow up the time of their most devoted and loyal lay people in church activities and structures.

Sometimes it seems that the usefulness of involvement in secular life is measured only in accordance with how many extra members result in the Sunday congregation. That cannot be the only criterion by which the efforts of Christian laity are judged. One layman from a Toxteth parish attended a meeting to launch a community group. He was the only person present from his parish congregation, though the meeting was held just across the road from the parish church. He found himself elected chairman of the new community group to which he had to give a considerable amount of time. While certain members of the congregation expressed some interest in his work and asked him from time to time how it was all going, almost inevitably they would also enquire whether he had seen any conversions among the members of the group and whether it had led to new attendances at church.

That man was there because he believed that God the Creator cared about the quality of life for all people in that district. He saw this new task as a form of ministry to which he had been called and which reflected the care of the Creator. No doubt there are occasionally connections between the commitment of Church people to the service of the community and the subsequent understanding of others that there is a place for them in the worship and membership of the Church. Making such connections can take many years to establish. It is essentially God's business, the work of the Spirit.

The second hard truth to be faced, if Christian laity are to play an active role in the secular world, is that even for most churchgoers education in their faith ceased either in their confirmation class or when they left school. It is not easy to suggest to people that to play their part in the mission of the Church today they have need of continuing or adult Christian education. It can happen that occasionally the obstacle lies with the vicar or parish priest who is content enough with his own sermons and does not see why his people should be exposed to other teaching. No doubt many people are deterred by fear of some academic course of instruction beyond their capacity or interest. Experience suggests that parish-based programmes, in which parents and other parishioners are involved in the preparation of young people for baptism, Holy Communion, confirmation and eventually màrriage, produce a surprising degree of commitment from a large number of parishioners. Drawn into the life and teaching of the Church in this way, a number discover the further mission of the Church in trying to meet the needs of the wider community.

There is now much experience to be shared ecumenically. There is also a great deal to be gained if such continuing instruction can be shared between people with different forms of ministry, ordained and lay. We learn from each other's difficulties as well as from shared experience and the pooling of assets, spiritual, intellectual, practical and material. This is yet another example of a Church with one mission and a variety of ministries. Spelt out in this way it can provide reassurance for those deterred by the word 'formation', which will in any case vary considerably in accord with local circumstances and needs.

The Archbishop of Canterbury's Commission on Urban Priority Areas, in its report *Faith in the City* (Church House Publishing, 1985), felt it useful to recommend the adoption at parish level of an 'Audit for the Local Church'. The audit should not be regarded as another form to be filled in, 'but as a means of enabling local Churches to undertake, in a fairly consistent way, an outward-looking review of the needs of their area and the role of the Church in responding to those needs'. A suggested basis for such an audit was provided. It aimed at providing an analysis of the locality and the Church, including the people and their needs and how they felt about the Church. It suggested methods for achieving a plan for concerted action. In many ways it reflected the See–Judge–Act technique of the Young Christian Workers and similar lay organisations.

There are many ways in which lay people may be helped to achieve the commitment and competence needed if they are to play their full part in the life and mission of the Church. A handbook is not enough. Practical experience and collaboration are also needed. In Liverpool the Roman Catholic Archdiocesan Pastoral Council, made up of representatives, clerical and lay, from all the thirty-two deaneries of the archdiocese, gave several months of study to the role of the laity in the Church and the world, before engaging in a two-day conference on the subject. They decided to take the model of the parish audit, given in *Faith in the City*, and worked out a detailed introduction and plan for use in all their parishes during the following twelve months. A decision was taken that all or part of the proposed audit should be carried out ecumenically, in collaboration with other congregations in their area. We believe that assets as well as problems should be shared.

Before taking stock of the life of the parish congregation, the first task in the audit was to draw up a profile of the local community. A cross-section of that whole community was to be asked what they felt about their own district. They should list ten things about it which they disliked and ten which they valued – 'ten for sorrow, ten for joy'. They should try to discover the real issues which influence people's lives. What are the causes of conflict in the area (young/old, newcomers/established residents, working class/middle class)? Who makes the decisions which affect the local community? From all this they would be asked to try to deduce the priorities in the mission of the Church in that particular parish.

Simultaneously the same style of parish audit is being used by the Anglican parishes in the diocese of Liverpool, which are putting forward lay ministry teams for courses with the Group for Urban Ministry and Leadership. This is in step with the recommendation in the report *Faith in the City* for a Church Leadership Development Programme. It is a feature of these courses that encouragement and support are to be given to the exercise of leadership and ministry in the local community, as much as to activity in church affairs. It is hoped that in this way the Servant Church will fulfil its role in the city through gospel-inspired and informed Christian laity.

THE MINISTRY OF THE CLERGY

We are not here attempting a full treatise on holy orders. Rather we wish to suggest the particular role of the clergy in the Servant Church and how that role is to be seen within the Church's total ministry in our kind of society today. For there is a specific ministry to be carried out, distinct from that of the laity we have described. Writing to the early Christians at Ephesus, St Paul wrote more precisely of the 'variety of gifts' which he had outlined to the Corinthians: 'And to some, his "gift" was that they should be apostles; to some, prophets; to some, evangelists; to some, pastors and teachers; to knit God's holy people together for the work of service to build up the Body of Christ' (Eph. 4:11,12 NJB).

In understanding the total mission of the Church, we have often to remind ourselves of these distinct ministries or tasks. There is always the danger that the clergy may be tempted to keep all the work in God's service in their own hands and to arrogate all the 'gifts' to themselves. This in the past helped to create the clericalism which contributed to the feeling of so many laity that they could leave the work of the Church to the full-time professionals.

Much has been written in recent years about the specific character of the priesthood and about the role of the clergy. We would want to argue against what we understand as exclusive and monopolising clericalism but in favour of the clergy appreciating fully their specific vocation and ministry, seen within the context of the whole life of the Church. In this their relationship with the laity, and especially their role with regard to the ministry of lay people, is of the greatest importance. Paternalism has to be avoided, though not encouragement and concern. On the other hand, there is often the temptation for concerned clergy so to identify with the people they serve that they may seem almost to play down their own priestly ministry. But we need still to be on our guard against the clericalisation of the laity and the efforts of some laity to keep the clergy quite plainly on ecclesiastical pedestals, well above the water-line of real life.

The clergy have – as part of their proclamation of the gospel – the specific task of calling lay people to an awareness of their responsibility as Christians to share in the life and mission of the Church. The call has increasingly to be specific and help must be given to enable the laity to see just how this responsibility may be exercised. For this the clergy have a second role which is at least to help with equipping the laity who have responded to the call. Sometimes it means ensuring that adequate means of formation are available. It is true that much of the formation of lay people must come from other lay people. But the clergy also should often have some part in it.

Work in the Lord's service in the secular world means that the persons concerned need to be equipped spiritually, doctrinally (in the sense that they must have some knowledge of the teachings of their Church), and with a general understanding of the principles of social justice. This perhaps sounds more formidable than it needs to do. If one adds the requirement of professional training, it is no more than to acknowledge that lay people need to be able to learn how their efforts and witness may be most effective.

To the clergy's role as animators and trainers must be added the task of sustaining the laity in what we have already acknowledged can be a very isolated and at times vulnerable situation. Nor should clergy overlook the heavy burdens many lay people already bear in their secular life. To say that there must be appropriate support can sound too impersonal. It tends to obscure the fact that we are dealing with people; and people need the help and the understanding of other people. Often the clergy will have to take the initiative in setting up family support groups and occasional meetings, even weekend conferences. The co-ordination of lay activity often needs to include the affirmation by the clergy of the effort and sacrifice of those individuals who have answered the call to the Lord's service in the witness of their daily life.

Clergy must also be sensitive to cries for help. They may need to draw together those faced with similar difficulties, but it will sometimes be important for them to use their contacts and position in the community to secure the experience and skills of 'resource people' to advise and help the new group to get under way and be effective. Undoubtedly at times it will be theological skill which is required. Often the need will be for practical 'know how'. Even though some of the clergy may well be best placed to unlock the problems of the locality, they must be very careful not to dominate the scene. It is not an easy balance. The clergy must know sufficient of the situation to recognise their real role and want to fulfil it. On the other hand there are plenty of lay people who hold that the Church has nothing to say about their real problems. This enables some of the clergy to retreat behind the inexperience and reluctance they often feel. With the many demands on their time, younger clergy especially are apt to feel that there is no point in their attending a meeting of a family or Christian social group discussing problems of which they have no direct experience. In fact their presence is seldom sought to secure technical advice, though they must do their best to be acquainted with the problems and challenges of those they serve. Their presence is a sign of the concern of the loving Creator for the quality of life of all his people. It is also a sign of the Church's desire to understand and share the burdens of its members. It is a matter of 'being there' to help to place the problems which are raised within the light of the gospel.

The active concern of clergy for such matters cannot be limited to committed, if puzzled, Christians. To reach out beyond Church circles is not to be restricted to clergy who specialise in the gift of being evangelists. What of those five special gifts mentioned to the Ephesians? Are clergy justified in moving straight to the task of being 'pastors and teachers', leaving the evangelisation of the secular world to the 'non-clerics'? Surely to be 'apostles, prophets and evangelists' will normally mean taking the good news outside the Church community. We cannot overlook those often referred to as the 'un-churched'. In a simple, non-technical sense, to be an apostle means being sent by God to be present. The apostle Paul had a burning desire to preach the gospel where it had not been heard before. No bishop, priest or deacon can decline such a task. To proclaim God's Word is an essential part of his ministry. It means by example as well as by word. He must reach out even to those who do not recognise their need for his ministry.

'To be there' is a very important part of the ministry of the clergy in a situation of hurt or deprivation. It can often be misunderstood.

'*Every Good Friday we have made a point of meeting to meditate on the cross*' (p 62). For the dedication of the first shared Anglican/Roman Catholic Church built by our two dioceses, St Basil's/All Saints, Hough Green, we presented a crucifix, carved and tinted by Stephen Foster.

'Being there': David and Grace Sheppard visit Archbishop Blanch School, Liverpool.

Derek Worlock with children at St Monica's School, Bootle.

(Above) *'If the church leaders had wanted to turn back, they couldn't have'* (p 95). Methodist Norwyn Denny, Salvation Army Douglas Rayner, United Reformed Church John Williamson and Baptist Trevor Hubbard join the bishops in going forward to sign the Covenant, Pentecost 1985.

(Left) *Hands Across Britain:* Free Church Moderator, John Williamson, and the two bishops join in a demonstration for the unemployed in 1987.

(Below) Newly appointed Free Church Moderator, John Newton, and the two bishops wave back to crowded Hope Street, Pentecost 1987.

The pain of protest... Archbishop Robert Runcie's sermon in Liverpool Parish Church is stopped by extremist Protestant demonstrators: he kneels at the altar, while the shouting and jeering continues.

... and the joy of reconciliation. Pope John Paul II is welcomed in the Anglican Cathedral: *'The explosion of pent-up emotions, released at that moment in a great roar of joy, relief and thanksgiving that such an event had proved possible'* (pp 237-8).

The Pope comes to *Liverpool 1982*. Derek Worlock greets him at Speke Airport.

Farewell greetings to David Sheppard following the Mass in the Roman Catholic Cathedral.

'One million people on the streets of Liverpool
to welcome or at least take a look at
Pope John Paul II'
(p 237).

Along Hope Street by Pope-mobile:
'Ecumenism is not only of the intellect. It is also
of the affections'
(p 238).

The Queen meets the City Centre Ecumenical Team in the Roman Catholic Parish Church, St Mary's, Highfield Street. The Rector of the Anglican Liverpool Parish Church, Donald Gray, explains the work of the Team in the shops and offices of Liverpool. Father Anthony Hitchen, Parish Priest of St Mary's, joins us in welcoming the Queen.

She had earlier been present in the Anglican Cathedral when the Archbishop of York, Stuart Blanch, dedicated the final bay of the completed Cathedral which had been building continuously from 1904 to 1978.

Young people, the Church of today . . .
The Archbishop leading a group journeying to
Iona and its ancient Abbey.

*. . . and the hope of tomorrow 'But, Lord, we
found that people like us, who do not share our
beliefs, share our love of you'* (p 268).

'What were you doing, when they closed Dunlop's?' Norwyn Denny and the two bishops join MPs and Trade Unionists in protesting at the loss of 5,000 jobs (p 140).

'Incarnation... included earning a living.' A buggy is needed to visit those who work on the production track at Ford's Halewood (p 122).

The Michaelmas Group *'... endeavouring through personal contact to penetrate the barrier created by what its members regard as a false image of Merseyside'* (p161).

(Far left) *The sorrow of the City...* The Mass on the day after the Heysel Stadium tragedy is attended by great crowds, including quite young children clad in their Liverpool Football Club strip.

(Inset) For hours before and after the service a week later in the Anglican Cathedral, ordinary people queue to sign the Book of Condolence to associate themselves with sorrow for what happened (p 245).

(Left)... *conveyed to Turin.* Hugh Dalton, Chairman of the City Council, with leading Councillors John Hamilton, Derek Hatton, and Tony Mulhearn lead a delegation from Liverpool Football Club and all parties and interests in Liverpool.

(Below) Cardinal Anastasio Ballestrero invited us to join him in blessing the congregation of two thousand at the Shrine of *La Consolata* in Turin.

After the Toxteth Riots. *'In a tense atmosphere of confrontation, a protest march was organised by the Liverpool Trades' Council and the City's black organisations' (p163).*

The Liverpool 8 Law Centre. *'Some people have for the very first time come to realise that the law can be a friend rather than a threat' (p186).*

'The dream of new housing in green field estates was soon shattered. A resident of Kirkby remarked that people live here in a ghastly mistake.'

'We did it better together.' 'As their dreams took shape, they were able to point to plans and explain just who would live in each unit and why' – the Eldonians Housing Co-operative (p 208).

'The affections can also be stirred by the steady round of engagements in which we are seen together' (p 249). Grace comes to football with us.

Time to return to the city.

Certainly such presence has to be there for some time before it is understood as the affirmation, inspiration and sharing it is intended to be. It can lead someone into a situation not altogether of his own choosing but where just being there is a sign of values connected with Christ and his Kingdom. At times such an 'apostle' must pause to ask himself why he is in that particular situation, what purpose is served? His being there may be a reminder to others of forgotten standards, a mirror to others so that they may see how they are treating each other. Josef Cardijn used to stress the importance of the mission of like to like. Sometimes the clergy too must move into the secular situation to remind the lay 'apostles' of that mission.

To ask the question, 'What are they to be a sign of?' risks a theological lecture. Perhaps that is what this book is about. The short answer might well be 'a sign of Christ's suffering, death and resurrection'. But for the clergy working in a hurt city, it may help to translate that theological truth into a list of headings which cannot pretend to be complete. The presence and concern of the clergy in a difficult situation can be a sign of many things: the power and goodness of God being greater than the forces and challenges we meet in daily life; the value of all people; God's concern for the whole of his creation; reconciliation in a divided world; love which is willing to make the first move; love which is compassion, a sharing of hardship; love which refuses to give up; and the way of the Servant.

THE ROLE OF THE BISHOP

It is in the context of the nature, mission and image of the Church and the ministry of its members that we come finally to consider the role of the bishop. The people of God are called to be a sign in the world and to take the way of the Servant. Yet many people associate bishops with power and a triumphalist picture of the Church. We may assign all this to history, to different days and different ways; but we cannot ignore it. The association at least is there. If a small schoolboy is asked to draw a picture of a bishop, he will concentrate on the bishop's 'helmet' (or mitre) rather than upon his staff. So each of us has to deal with himself before God. Real temptations exist around the habit of power.

DAVID SHEPPARD: In my first year as Bishop of Liverpool I went on a course for Church leaders. I mentioned the serious doubts I had felt about my wearing a mitre – not because of old Protestant/Catholic arguments but because of fear of triumphalism. The then Abbot of Ampleforth, Basil Hume, was also on the course. He said to me: 'If you really wanted to wear a mitre, you probably ought not to have been made a bishop.' Shortly before the end of the course he disappeared somewhat mysteriously. A day or two later we all heard that he had been called away to learn that he too must become the reluctant wearer of a mitre and before long the recipient of a cardinal's hat.

The way of the Servant must mean the rejection by the bishop of the love of status, or name-dropping, or the pulling of rank to force those without power to give in to his wishes. Power and powerlessness are today issues for the Church as well as for the State. But this must not be confused with the abdication of leadership which involves the prophetic role of trying to point the way. The true prophet must himself try to follow the way of the Servant. Trying to do this cannot lead him to shrink from bearing responsibility or from the apostolic calling to lead the Church in serving the world in the manner of Christ.

DEREK WORLOCK: When I was consecrated a bishop in 1965 I found that for many this meant that my task would be to preside at great liturgical celebrations. I quoted Vatican II as saying that 'Amongst the principal duties of bishops, the preaching of the gospel occupies an eminent place.' It is after proclaiming the good news of salvation that the bishop gathers the people together in worship; and he also has the responsibility of trying to co-ordinate their efforts to give expression to the gospel in the most effective way. But I soon found that in following Pope Paul's injunction 'to love man in order to love God' was to invite the charge of humanism. People had very fixed ideas about a bishop's role and it had mostly to do with externals which others challenged as irrelevant pomp. In my defence I again quoted the Council Fathers:

> *Bishops should present Christian doctrine in a manner adapted to the needs of the times: that is to say, in a manner corresponding to the difficulties and problems by which people are most burdened and troubled . . . In exercising his office of father and pastor, a bishop should stand in the midst of his people as one who serves.*
>
> *(Decree on the Bishop's Pastoral Office)*

Under normal circumstances a bishop has an excellent opportunity of gaining a wide picture of the life of the community. It would be difficult to spend ten years in Merseyside and region without visiting almost every institution in the area. Josef Cardijn's principle of the mission of like to like suggests that a bishop has good reason to give time to others who hold responsibility for at least part of the whole community, whether in the public or private sector. These leaders in the community often bear very heavy burdens. They often seem to value greatly the opportunity to open their hearts to someone who has comparable burdens but who is used to keeping secrets. This has led to many private conversations in which the two of us – and more recently with the Free Church Moderator as well – have met with managing directors, trade union officials, local government leaders and officers, government ministers and leaders in other political parties.

All this could be very flattering. It might lead us to believe that we have great influence. Perhaps we have been a 'safe place' where people have felt able to express their problems and try out their solutions on those who have some knowledge of how the whole community is likely to react. There was one public figure whom we came to know between ourselves as 'Nicodemus', since he always made his visits under cover of darkness. We have usually taken the line that the fact of such meetings must be open to public knowledge but the content of our discussions must be confidential unless otherwise agreed. Sometimes when particular groups have been unwilling or unable to meet, we have attempted to interpret one to the other, but always as communicators rather than as negotiators. In this way we have tried to walk the difficult tightrope over the chasm of party politics.

The fact that we are usually together on such occasions has made it plain that we are speaking for the whole community and not for sectional interests. The first government minister we met after the publication of the Inner Areas Study relaxed visibly when he realised that we were not there to defend the place of our Church schools, but to make a case for the needs of all inner-city people. Working together in this way has also made it much more possible to listen to all sides in the community, especially as there can be a marked difference in the 'social mix' of the different denominations.

Meeting those in very senior positions can carry its own seductiveness. It can lead us to believe that God takes the powers, values and structures of the world at their face value. Corridors of power may be important places for Christians to tread, but not by these paths alone is society to be changed. Those with whom the incarnate Christ seems to have concerned himself were mostly far from being top people. The first were to be last and the last first. Today those of his choice would include many who have never set foot in the so-called corridors of power.

For us, as bishops, it means taking very deliberate steps to make ourselves available to those who do not have access to such places. Understandably it takes considerable time to acquire their trust. Sadly there are many who feel that the Church and its leaders have not always been serious allies when the going has been rough. When the process has been reversed, there have inevitably been others to complain, 'They are too busy to come to our dinners.'

The Servant Church is called to care about the quality of life of all people, to be concerned for the whole nation, indeed the whole world. Sometimes definable groups can be seen to be excluded from the good opportunities of God's world, to be shut out from the benefits of particular affluent nations. When that is apparent, the Church must make clear where it stands. There is need for responsible intervention in favour of the disadvantaged, for a willingness, if necessary, to give public expression in favour of a voice which otherwise cannot make itself heard. But if that intervention is truly to reflect the needs of the disadvantaged, there must be some genuine listening. At times that can be difficult, if it is to be carried out personally by the bishop. Both in listening and in reaching his judgment, he will need the help of reliable and devoted clergy and lay people whose ears in certain circumstances are likely to be closer to the ground. But there are times when the voice of the bishop may help to make the problems of the disadvantaged both coherent and heard. How often in the last few years have we been approached by frustrated servants of the community who have sought our intervention because of what they have described as our 'clout'!

This concern for the disadvantaged has at times come under attack when expressed as 'bias to the poor'. Attempts are made to translate it as 'neglect of the better off'. No one argues against having a bias to the frail and elderly, widows and orphans, the physically and mentally handicapped. Such bias is not translated as 'neglect of healthy youth'. Yet there is sensitivity on this point. This bias or option is now widely accepted but in the past it could not always be taken for granted. There have been societies in ancient and modern history which have been based on survival of the fittest. The great prophets of the Old Testament, like Isaiah, Amos, Micah and Jeremiah, went further and spoke about the character of God and his indignation at whole groups of people becoming poor and oppressed as a result of injustice.

The Hebrew word *tsedeq* is translated 'righteousness' or 'justice'. The most recent revision of the Jerusalem Bible translates the word, whenever it appears in the Prophets, as 'saving justice'. This saving justice 'topples over on behalf of those in direst need' (Norman Snaith, *Distinctive Ideas of the Old Testament*, London, 1944, pp. 76ff.). This is not the same thing as fairness, for it cannot be assumed that everyone begins from the same starting line. Classical Greece gave us the picture of the blind-eyed goddess of justice. She does not have to look to see if the plaintiff or the defendant is in the greater need. She dispenses even-handed justice, assuming that she is settling a dispute between equals. In the Bible, on the other hand, the God of saving justice is not blind. His eyes are wide open. He sees the need of widows, orphans, foreigners and the oppressed, and he intervenes. He saves. As a leader among God's people, it is the role of the bishop to show that wide-eyed concern. If we are to reflect the character of the God of saving justice, our task is not that of umpires but is to argue unashamedly for a bias to the poor.

'Bias to the poor' means more to us than just the title of a book (David Sheppard, *Bias to the Poor*, Hodder & Stoughton 1983). It is at the heart of what we believe is our calling to give an apostolic lead. In this four motives are uppermost in our minds:

The first motive is the credibility of the Church's message among the poor. It can be shown that the visible response to all Churches is dramatically smaller in urban working-class areas than in suburbs, towns or villages. For too long those at a disadvantage in our cities have felt that the Christ whom the Churches proclaim by our life is not for them. It is not so much a matter of doctrine as of people feeling excluded and protesting to the Church: 'I can't hear what you are saying. What you are doing is speaking too loudly.' There is need for an apostolic lead to change certain attitudes and priorities in the Church.

The second motive is the compulsion we feel to pass on to others what we ourselves have seen and heard. Whether it is through the North/South divide, or between suburbs and council estates, socially Britain is segregated to a very serious degree. Many people are unaware of the experiences of life which are faced by those who live only a mile or two away from them. Some are incredulous about the facts when these are presented. Others are apologetic and express themselves helpless about the gap they recognise but feel unable to bridge. There is a need for those who have that knowledge or experience to 'tell it how it is', so that the whole Church and the whole nation may be moved to fresh action.

The third motive arises from our belief that the Church is called to reflect the character of the God whom we worship. Whether it makes for popularity or not, we are to reflect God's love for mercy, justice and truth, his opposition to oppression and greed. Just as the Son of God took on our human condition, so the Church must be prepared to risk losing its false 'innocence' by becoming involved as a servant in the corporate life of cities like Liverpool. For the sake of justice we must be willing to declare ourselves plainly and seem to take sides, even at the risk of personal unpopularity or misunderstanding among those from whom support might normally be expected.

The fourth motive is to show how false it is to suggest, as is so often done, that two genuine Christian callings can be opposed to one another: to suggest that either you are for changing individual hearts and minds, or you are for changing the structures of society. *Faith in the City* raised the issue of what sort of aid Christians should try to bring to the disadvantaged:

> The question at issue is whether the acknowledged Christian duty 'to remember the poor' should be confined to personal charity, service and evangelism directed towards individuals, or whether it can legitimately take the form of social and political action aimed at altering the circumstances, which appear to cause poverty and distress. We shall argue that these are false alternatives: a Christian is committed to a form of action which embraces both (p. 48).

These four motives add up to what for us is a call. We are not to shrink from the prophetic role of pointing the way in the life of the Church and, where possible, the nation. To be other than reluctant prophets is to risk the charge of arrogance. But we prefer this biblically based concept of our role to the more customary demand made of bishops to 'give us a lead'. We must be sensitive to warnings that 'a leader can sometimes go too far ahead of his troops to keep them together'. This is a point of great importance for a bishop who is required to be a focus for unity. But if he has to secure in advance the total agreement of all those for whom he has responsibility, he will rapidly become the mute leader of a Church of Silence. This may be a profitable witness in time of persecution but cannot be the ordinary expression of the deep feelings he has for the needs of the people he must serve.

In the service for the consecration of a bishop in the Church of England, it is said of the bishop's task that 'he is to have a special care for the outcast and needy'. In the Roman Catholic rite the bishop-elect is required to undertake 'to show kindness and compassion in the name of the Lord to the poor and to the strangers and to all who are in need'. The gospel leaves its hearers in little doubt about what the Latin American bishops, in their famous declaration at Puebla in 1979, called 'a preferential option for the poor'.

The gospel of the Servant Church in a hurt city begins with people coming to realise that they have true worth, that they are valued, and that someone wants to know them and understand their needs. Christ repeatedly makes the first move towards sinful people and accepts them. This leads to a movement in them which is in some measure a response from the heart. Knowing that they are valued in themselves produces stirrings of self-confidence, and as this grows there begins to emerge a willingness to take responsibility. Christian worship sets up a chain reaction. We focus on Christ's love which makes the first move and refuses to give up even where the human heart remains cold for a while. Gradually the thaw takes place and makes way for a response in love and eventually generous commitment.

The focus of unity, which the bishop is called to be, will be stronger, not weaker, if it includes that preferential option for the poor, who have too often been excluded from a real share in the life and mission of the Church. Ultimately that means their recognising Christ in the very circumstances of their own lives. For that the whole Church – bishops, priests, laity – must constantly face Christ's question about the way in which they should carry out their ministry. Christ the Servant of the Lord took a towel and washed his disciples' feet. 'Do you understand', he asked, 'what I have done to you?' (John 13:12 NJB).

7 'GIZZA JOB' – THE INDIGNITY OF UNEMPLOYMENT

Merseyside has suffered a net loss of ten thousand jobs each year, save one, of our time here. Over many of those years its unemployment figures have been double the national average. We have already referred to the fact that over a considerable period the majority of head offices of large companies were transferred from Liverpool. This left their Merseyside operations highly vulnerable in a time of recession. We were to witness a series of closures, with the departure of great names like British Leyland, Dunlop, Tate and Lyle, United Biscuits – each closure removing several thousand jobs. People came to dread 'black Fridays', when the announcement of pending closures or extensive redundancies was made. It was relatively good news if perhaps a proportion of the jobs were to be saved: if, for example, there was to be reinvestment in new technology, which might mean halving the large labour force but at least ensuring the continuing presence of a major employer – such as Lucas Aerospace, British American Tobacco, Pilkington, BICC, Nabisco. Meantime there was increasing help and enthusiasm for small businesses. But it was evident that, although the establishment of each new venture was hailed as a triumph, it would take many thousands of such small businesses to replace job losses on the scale needed to compensate for the closure of the larger firms which had dominated the Merseyside scene for so long.

To try to create an awareness of the extent of what was happening, we convened during our first years a number of weekend conferences under the title 'Work – or what?' There was an obvious initial reluctance to face the disappearance of any pretence of the return to full employment, yet it was abundantly clear from these gatherings that unemployment in Merseyside was not cyclical but chronic. In the North-West dips in the economy showed their first impact in Merseyside, which also took longer than other parts of the region to pull out of recessions. At the time it was argued and widely accepted that there was room for the slimming down of work forces. This could lead to more profitable businesses, with more money available for alternative patterns of work. The Manpower Services Commission was just appearing on the scene. We were becoming used to speaking of job creation and STEP (Special Temporary Employment Programme). There was hope around that imaginative schemes of work creation need not be only temporary. But the likely consequences of the introduction of advanced technology into industry, so far as semi-skilled and unskilled labour was concerned, were not widely appreciated. A few knowledgeable characters spoke of 'silicon valleys' as if they would appear wherever heavy industry had existed in the past. There was still the widespread belief that anyone with a skill and a will to work could find a job. To question this ran the risk of becoming a prophet of gloom.

Some critics insisted that all our problems had 'Made in Merseyside' stamped on them, rather like a trademark. They blamed trade union power and militant attitudes for the unwillingness of firms to reinvest. Bernard Levin alleged that the Transport and General Workers' Union had become all-powerful and that its elite members were the dockers. This was a surprising claim when it is appreciated that the number of dockers in the Port of Liverpool has fallen from forty-five thousand in 1939 to a mere two thousand today. Often the capacity of an unofficial strike committee to say 'No' was the only power ranged against the great impersonal forces of management. In practice diminishing trade gave little opportunity for dockers to have any real share in positive action.

It is undoubtedly true that some disputes produced self-inflicted wounds. Sometimes the troubles had been inspired and fostered by those who wished to smash the system. The managing director of a large firm which was closing on Merseyside admitted to us privately that the workforce as a whole had been most cooperative. But he claimed that they were at the time being led by the nose by a handful of men with other ideas. We felt obliged to ask him about the seed-bed in which such ideas could flourish. Mounting unemployment meant that there were no other jobs to go to. It was not just a matter of an individual losing a particular job. In 'father-and-son' industries like the docks, the basis of life upon which a whole community had depended was being removed. We do not easily forget the words of one of the speakers at Pier Head at the conclusion of a march to protest against the threatened closure of Dunlop's. He raised the whole crowd with the emotive question: 'What will you say to your son in twenty years' time when he asks you what you were doing when they closed Dunlop's?'

DEREK WORLOCK: That protest march at the time of the Dunlop closure marked a new development for Merseyside's Church leaders. When British Leyland closed their Speke factory in 1978, I had been asked by local radio to comment and I had referred to the hopelessness of the men's negotiating power as they were engaged in some token strike at the time. The local shop stewards' broadcast reply was 'What does His Holiness know about it?' A year later when Dunlop was threatened, the workers' representatives arrived at my house well after dark to ask for help. The management had refused to meet them to discuss the matter. The men were proposing a march the following Saturday. I agreed in the name of the other Church leaders to march with them. It seemed right that we should be there as part of the community to demand that the men's representatives and their proposals be heard by management.

Norwyn Denny, the Methodist Chairman, agreed immediately. It was more difficult for David Sheppard, as it meant his leaving his diocesan synod before a vote was taken over an important post he was strongly supporting. He agreed that the march was the priority and joined us. The vote at his synod was narrowly lost, perhaps influenced to some extent by feelings that the bishop had no business to be joining such a demonstration, instead of attending to church affairs. But the press, radio and photographers gave great publicity to the march and to our presence at its head. Two days later the management received the workers' representatives, though no more was eventually achieved than improved arrangements for those made redundant.

SHARED CONCERN AMIDST RECESSION

Gradually we sensed a new kind of trust from trade unionists. They did not expect us to support them regardless of the right or wrong of each issue. But they understood the significance of our readiness to drop other commitments in order to take up human issues which so deeply affected the lives of people. They came to know that we were sometimes able to open doors, at least for consultation. We were invited to meet shop stewards in factory visits or occasionally at union branch meetings. We talked with different groups of Christian trade unionists of all denominations. We discussed wage restraint, work sharing, the likelihood that there would not be in the foreseeable future a return to full employment of the conventional pattern. In all these discussions there would arise the issue of control, or of having a real share in decision-making affecting their future. Perhaps the most disappointing feature of those discussions in the 1970s was finding the proposals in the Bullock Report on industrial participation dismissed by the trade union side. When they said that they would rather stay on their side of the table, reserving their bargaining position in preference to sharing in decision-making, it seemed that they were settling for a world of confrontation and disputes.

During the 'winter of discontent' in 1978/9 we received many requests for guidance concerning the wave of industrial disputes. It is perhaps worth setting out now at some length what we had to say in that period *before* Mrs Thatcher was elected to power: the more so as it is often suggested that our public statements have always been directed 'against the Thatcher government'.

We expressed much sympathy with the claims of the lower-paid public workers. Powerful groups in management and in the strongest unions seemed to have assumed that the Government's pay guidelines should be binding for everyone else except themselves. All who had, whether quietly or aggressively, broken through the levels of these guidelines, were as responsible as those 'in the picket lines for the damage to industry and the distress of individuals which the disputes of the day were causing.

We made clear our desire to dissuade workers from the long strikes which were hurting the elderly, sick patients, the bereaved and the clients of social workers. We argued that one of the dangers of corporate action was to grow callous about what such decisions did to the most vulnerable. However, if ambulance drivers were expected to agree never to strike, they should be offered the same guarantee, pegged to the cost of living, as was received by the police and firemen.

We pressed the powerful unions to ask themselves the traditional trade union questions about brotherhood. 'Free collective bargaining is the customary language of the free market, not of trade unions. It is no use saying that unbridled capitalism is the law of the jungle, if powerful unions follow the same law.' A more corporate and planned approach must involve the acceptance of limitations to freedom in the market by both employers and trade unions. We claimed that there should not be hostility to proposals for statutory cooling-off periods and for secret ballots before strikes could be called.

'It is the proud boast of the unions', reads our joint statement of February 1979, 'to have concern for the poor and the low paid. The poor include those who are not sitting at the bargaining table at all, because they are unemployed.' We said that if all who had the muscle to do so pushed their wage claims far beyond the government guidelines, inevitably the Government would reduce the money supply. This would mean more unemployment in every sector. There had to be that discipline and restraint which followed from genuine concern for others and for the well-being of the whole, including the disadvantaged.

Those who claimed to follow Jesus Christ must, like him, work for the interests of the poor and the deprived. In a country with limited resources this would often mean self-sacrifice on the part of the strong for the sake of those who were weak. 'At the heart of the Christian gospel is the cross,' we wrote. 'It stands for the exact opposite of the "free for all", "smash and grab" approach to life.' The Christian calling was to act as 'members one of another', with concern for those who had less in our own country and in the developing world. We should not be constantly concerned merely with the restoration of differentials or with just trying to secure the best possible deal for ourselves and those we represented. There were times when in the cause of Christian justice we should exercise restraint. Acting as members one of another had to mean accepting some sort of pay and incomes policy. We had not learnt at that time to speak of a 'planned economy'.

A TIME FOR CLOSURE

Within a few months an altogether different approach to the economy swept in with Margaret Thatcher's Government. Now the language was of 'slimming down', a shake-out of over-manning, making Britain 'competitive in the marketplace'. 'Lame ducks' would not in future be helped out by the government. Regional policies in favour of areas where the economy was weaker became, as the jargon had it, 'less overt'.

So far as Merseyside was concerned, the process of slimming down was already very familiar. In fact, as we became increasingly involved in detailed discussions about industrial closures, we often discovered that decisions not to reinvest, made as much as ten years before, had come to be regarded as irreversible. In the new political and economic climate of the nation, firms which had just about held on during a difficult period, now felt that they had the opportunity to close their Merseyside operation and leave for the South, where not infrequently investment in new technology had already taken place. The pace of redundancies increased. It was then that the saga of 'black Fridays' took hold. By making the announcement of closure at midday on Friday, the management were able to ensure minimal treatment by the press the following day. Sports coverage would fill the pages of the newspapers and there could be a natural weekend period of cooling off for those likely to be involved.

Often we received information some days in advance of the formal announcement. It might come from the management, anxious to explain the inevitability of the pressure of market forces, and to stress the so-called generosity of proposed redundancy settlements. Or it would reach us from the shop stewards' committee, anxious for our intervention in trying to save as many jobs as possible. It was always a particularly bitter blow if the firm in question was part of the fabric of local communities and family life. Tate and Lyle's, United Biscuits and British American Tobacco all drew most of their workers from a handful of parishes – and had done for several generations. When, in response to pressing invitations, we visited the threatened factories, more to show sympathy and to raise morale than in any realistic hope of changing decisions already taken, we would meet brothers, sisters, brothers- and sisters-in-law, mothers, sons and daughters – five from one family in one afternoon visit. Nearly a quarter of Tate and Lyle's production workers walked to work from the Vauxhall area, where even before that closure unemployment was already forty-six per cent. We agreed to go as part of a united delegation from every part of Liverpool's life to see the Minister of Agriculture about sugar quotas – but unsuccessfully.

This was the first time we had made such a move at the direct request of all parties in the City Council. Afterwards they expressed regret that the initiative for which they had first invited our presence was an unsuccessful mission. We both felt that in many ways it was better to have begun a venture doomed to failure than to seem to clamber on the back of possible success. There is little doubt about which has been the more typical experience over our years in Liverpool. To be close to people must include sharing moments of disappointment and apparent failure.

In all these three Liverpool-rooted factories which we have mentioned, the management assured us that there was a most co-operative workforce. We were seeing one of the results of the introduction of new technology. In the tobacco factory we saw two machines producing cigarettes under the supervision of one white-coated technician. Each machine had replaced twenty-five factory workers operating the older methods and machines. 'Where did the machines come from?' we asked. 'Germany.' 'How much did they cost?' 'Rather more than half a million pounds each.' The story was much the same at the biscuit factory. The factory floor was full of women from Liverpool rendered redundant and uneconomic through the installation of new technology in another factory of the same firm operating in North London.

On these visits the workforce greeted us very kindly. For the most part there was no sign of bitterness. They had seen their fate coming for some time, and were almost as sad at the realisation that the factory, so big a part in local life, would close, as that they themselves faced a hopeless task in looking for alternative work. Many put the blame not on the Government but on the 'chip'. Most took little notice of those who came to talk to them about the mobility of labour. Community and family loyalties rated very highly in their scale of values. They knew that the redundancy money would not last long enough to see them into another job. Some hastened the process by giving the family a last good holiday before settling down to join their neighbours and relatives among the unemployed. We were told that in Speke all the redundancy money ran out in about eighteen months. Then the 'small shop on the corner' closed for lack of business. The side effects of the closure of one large factory were always more extensive than the loss of jobs of those directly involved.

The chairmen of companies announcing redundancies or closure frequently offered to see the pair of us to explain their positions. Having gritted their teeth to make unwelcome decisions, they were rarely in a position to discuss a change of plan. They would stress the generosity of their redundancy settlements, and it was some years before the early easy acceptance of such provision by those dis-employed gave way to the realisation that the 'generous' terms of some seven figures were financial 'peanuts' in comparison with the firm's overall profits for that same year. Of course we acknowledged that no one company could solve such problems by itself. But we pressed on them the issue of social responsibility towards those who had helped to create the wealth of former and better days, and the effect of their decisions on families and the community.

We became well used to the slogan, 'new technology creates new jobs', and sometimes we asked these captains of industry, just as we did government ministers, to suggest just where the new jobs would come from. We would be treated to talk about 'spin-off' industries, but these were difficult to pin-point and provided little opportunity for those who were semi-skilled or unskilled. One industrialist conjured up a vision of a 'silicon valley' in Cambridge. A senior government figure, consistently confident in public about economic developments, grew silent before our questioning and could only say, 'Well, I despair.' Over the years we came to appreciate that there are public and private voices, as well as public and private faces.

Inevitably we have often been asked how successful we have been in our protests against this relentless closure of firms in Merseyside. Rather more crudely, we are challenged as to whether we have ever been responsible for creating one single job. We readily admit that we have been very unsuccessful in halting closures or reversing decisions, but it can perhaps be argued that lively protests about the effect of a closure on the community may well have influenced other firms to stay in the area. We could also base our defence on our work with the Area Manpower Board and the Merseyside Enterprise Forum, but there is little chance of convincing those who make such a charge. Suffice it to say that we have been told that many who feel powerless in face of the juggernaut of widespread long-term unemployment, have drawn some strength and encouragement from their feeling that the Church has been standing with them; indeed, from the very fact that we have been involved with them in times of threat and of failure.

HUMAN HURT

The burden of unemployment in a nation like Britain does not fall evenly. It falls on predictable areas and on particular groups. In all parts of the country, for example, black people have poorer opportunities for jobs than the rest of the community. In the same way, Merseyside is always up near the top of any table of figures of unemployment or other forms of deprivation. In this it is not alone. Similar burdens fall on other cities. Liverpool has many comparable problems with Glasgow and Belfast. Together they form what we call the North-West Triangle.

Even within these areas – and this is particularly true of Merseyside – unemployment hits some social classes much more drastically than others. Recent figures showed that for every professional or managerial vacancy eighteen people were available. For every vacancy for general labourers, over one thousand were available. In April 1985 sixty-nine per cent of sixteen to nineteen year olds in Liverpool were unemployed or on temporary schemes (*Liverpool City Planning Officer's Report, November 1985*: notes, table 1). In 1986 over fifty-three per cent of Liverpool's unemployed had been jobless for more than twelve months.

There have of course been those who have said that the unemployment figures were not nearly as serious or damaging as might at first appear, because many unemployed persons have been earning money in what is known as the 'informal economy' – more popularly known as 'moonlighting'. *The Times* published a leading article claiming that we all knew unemployed people who were doing rather well in this way. Subsequently, a well-known industrialist, Sir Michael Edwardes, went further and put a figure not only on how much money was being earned in the informal economy – which was fair – but also on how many unemployed people were engaged in this practice – which was not fair. Together with the Free Church Moderator, the pair of us wrote to *The Times* to challenge this slur on unemployed people. We acknowledged that much money could well be being earned in the informal economy. But we pointed out that to produce substantial earnings, it was necessary to possess a van or a set of tools, the very things to which the unemployed do not have access. Such studies as have been carried out show that it is not the unemployed but 'moonlighters' with one job already, who are much more likely to be earning substantial sums in the informal economy. The letter was printed but there was no come-back.

Statistics in themselves cannot adequately tell the story of the human hurt which results from unemployment, or indicate the nature of the poverty which goes with it. When the Archbishop of Canterbury's Commission on Urban Priority Areas visited Merseyside in 1984, one of its meetings was held in Kirkby, best known of Liverpool's overspill settlements. There the people told us in no uncertain terms what long-term unemployment does to individuals and to family life. A wife and mother told members of the Commission: 'I have lived with unemployment for ten years. My husband's pride is now at rock-bottom. He is forty-two and feels that he is on the scrap heap. He's very talented but he can't use most of his talents, because they cost money. As a wife and mother of five kids, I'm driven desperate trying to sustain our family.'

The Commission was told that long-term unemployment hit Kirkby in a big way when the Labour Government introduced Selective Employment Tax in the 1960s. Immediately newly-arrived firms shook out all their surplus labour and hundreds of teenagers became unemployed. Those teenagers are now parents of the present generation of unemployed young people. In other words, many of those parents have never had the opportunity of regular work. Poverty goes hand in hand with unemployment, bearing with it all the obvious mental strains. 'I worry from Friday to Tuesday (Child Allowance day) that I'll run out of money,' we were told by one housewife. 'We have to spend so much time going to see officials, to the Social Security and Housing, asking for advice, it's degrading. They ask you the same questions over and over again. We feel ashamed, so low, as if we are beggars.'

Alan Bleasdale, the Liverpool born and bred playwright, caught the atmosphere of the social security office with telling force, both from the claimant's point of view and from that of the officials, in his series of television plays entitled *Boys from the Blackstuff*. (In Liverpool itself the words used by one of the characters, Yosser Hughes, to describe his desperation in face of unemployment became a catch-phrase used by young and old alike. We have felt justified in using it as the title of this chapter.) Many people from outside Merseyside believed that Bleasdale must be exaggerating. But those living in urban priority areas said quite simply, 'He's got us right.' Here was a latter-day Charles Dickens enabling those with eyes to see to enter into the subterfuges which the system drove people to adopt, the fear of snoopers, the escapism of the redundancy celebration or party, married couples taking it out on one another.

For the most part married life has followed very traditional patterns in areas of this kind. The psychology of the individual who finds his job disappear is well-established. In his evidence to the Merseyside Enterprise Forum, which established a panel to examine the social implications of advancing technology in industry, Father John Fitzsimons, a priest-sociologist with many years of experience of Liverpool life, described the effects of the husband's long-term unemployment on a marriage relationship. For the first three months or so the man, who had never before experienced unemployment, regarded the situation as transitory and was kept going by energetic hope. The next six to nine months brought increasing despair, which eventually gave way to lethargy and a feeling of rejection. Much depended upon his marriage relationship as to how far family life would be affected. The man had traditionally been the bread-winner, absent from home for the greater part of the day. Now he was home nearly all the time. Unless there was a great deal of understanding, with plenty of give and take, the strain could reach breaking-point. Often the man could feel rejection by his wife and family as well as by the rest of society which held no job for him. 'There's nothing down for me,' was Alan Bleasdale's phrase.

'The unease, short temper and frustration', Father Fitzsimons was quoted as saying in the report *Chips with Everything*, 'overflows into relations with the children. If they are young, they are pushed out on the streets for longer periods; if they are adolescent, there will be confrontations, verbal and at times even violent. Where there has been no true partnership before, this too will be the occasion of further difference with the wife' (p. 15). His views were echoed to us by a local member of an ecumenical project looking at a no-work situation in a perimeter estate: 'You can see real live tension on the streets here as a result of unemployment.' The widespread depression which comes with long-term unemployment often works itself out in the growing recourse to alcohol and to drugs, in violence and even in suicide (cf. Julian Charley, *Pastoral Support for the Unemployed*, Grove Booklet 19. Statement from Merseyside Churches Unemployment Committee 1986).

No Christian can be indifferent to these human hurts stemming from unemployment. Addressing the Industrial Christian Fellowship, Ruth Etchells said:

> Attaching to questions of work and the generation of wealth are a whole bundle of feelings and senses which have to do with status and consequence. And attaching to the changefulness of work and unemployment patterns in our society, and the sense of transience and vulnerability which go with these, are another bundle of questions which have their deepest root in our fear of impermanence, of humanity itself as being transient, and, deepest of all, fear of that ultimate transience, death itself, from which all the other fears flow.
>
> (Ruth Etchells, quoted by Peter Brain in
> *Options for the Long-Term Unemployed*, May 1986.
> Liverpool City Ministry of the United Reformed Church.)

We often hear people speaking of the situation today as that of 'relative poverty'. The term is used in comparison with conditions in certain parts of the Third World, or when today's circumstances are set against the 'absolute' poverty and hunger experienced in this country in the 1930s. To compare the lot of the unemployed receiving the dole in this country with that of those abroad, whose loss of job means no relief for loss of income, is scant comfort for those facing long-term unemployment here. We have found that those who speak of the grave hardships faced by their parents in the Depression of the 1930s, often come from the ranks of those who have climbed out of the urban priority areas. Those whose parents were not so successful recognise a remarkable continuity in their situation. Succeeding generations bear the same scars. In an age when television portrays the standards of the more fortunate, poverty, even if only relative, still hurts human dignity when the sharpest pangs of hunger have been assuaged.

LOW ACHIEVERS

We are not speaking just of the middle-aged for whom unemployment may seem degrading. The effect on young people of large-scale, long-term unemployment is very far-reaching. The report *Faith in the City* stressed that this was the biggest single problem facing most schools today. The 1985 Government White Paper *Better Schools* claimed that it was vital that schools remember that one of their principal functions was to prepare young people for working life. The truth of the matter was reflected to us by the Principal Careers Officer of the Borough of Knowsley, who told us that only six per cent of local school leavers went into jobs during the twelve months after they left school.

The collapse of employment for young people inevitably poses the question, 'What are we educating young people for?' British Industry Year in 1986 repeated the challenge to schools to attach higher value to jobs in industry and to develop lifestyles which would help Britain to survive in a highly competitive world through the increased efficiency of its industry and commerce. It was a healthy challenge, but if it failed to take a grip on teachers and pupils alike, it was not just a reaction of cynicism. It needed to be accompanied by the recognition that excellence and achievement are not to be recognised only on a single ladder of academic ability. There is a series of ladders we climb, indicating a variety of talents and skills, as well as different kinds of intelligence. Education must not be restricted to a narrow system of training for jobs, which the pupils already know may well not be there when their schooling ceases.

There is no doubt that the lack of job prospects has had a damaging effect on both teacher and pupil morale. The most alarming aspect is when this situation is so chronic as to be taken for granted. Nowadays we hear rather more about training in life-skills. For young people a full life must not depend upon waiting for a job. They must be trained and prepared for taking some initiatives personally and together with others. Recognition of skills on any of these ladders of ability has the effect of starting to build self-confidence. The Youth Training Scheme has revealed something that many teachers already knew, namely, that what many 'low achievers' lack first and foremost is self-confidence. A personnel director of a large firm in Liverpool told us on one occasion that by their old criteria his company would not have considered employing many of the young people who came to him through the Youth Training Scheme. But in practice, despite a lack of academic qualifications, the great majority had blossomed and developed into excellent work people.

INVOLVEMENT BY THE CHURCH

We have already referred to the question we often face personally about whether we have actually created any jobs ourselves, as distinct from fighting to prevent factory closures. A wider question on the same lines is often addressed to the Churches in general: 'What are the Churches *doing* about unemployment?' To start making distinctions between the personal involvement of Church leaders and the grass-roots work of the rank and file is usually dismissed as hedging. Yet it is a factor. A great number of very committed Christian men and women work hard to ease present problems, whether in management, on the shop floor, or in an official capacity in a Job Centre or some community scheme. We claim no proprietary interest in trying to meet today's scourge of unemployment. As members of the community, church people play their part in local initiatives, often in a quite hidden capacity. In addition, through our then Ecumenical Council of Churches (now MARCEA) we set up in 1984 the Merseyside Churches' Unemployment Committee. This brings together a strong group of persons involved in private and public sectors of employment, Manpower Services Commission schemes and education.

In 1985 MCUC (as it is inevitably styled) commissioned a survey of what Churches in Merseyside were doing at that time about unemployment. Some fifty churches replied to a questionnaire. While a fair number reported regular prayer for unemployed people and support for the jobless among their parish congregations, others spoke of discussion groups set up to see where effective help could be given. A number of churches had arranged informal schemes for unemployed people without outside funding and using their own church premises for support-group meetings, for lunch clubs for the unemployed, 'drop in' centres and clubs for young people, open throughout the day, not just on certain evenings.

The response to the questionnaire reported one hundred church-sponsored schemes in Merseyside, mostly funded by the Manpower Services Commission, frequently through the Community Programme. These schemes employed at the time of the survey 273 full-time workers, 1,123 part-time and 457 voluntary. The Anglican diocese had established its Care and Repair Association. The Roman Catholics had their Church Community Project.

Both were sponsoring agencies supporting many of these schemes. Each had upwards of five hundred taking part, with numbers growing each year. The Church Community Project is based in Liverpool and sprang from a still larger project set up in Skelmersdale called 'Tomorrow's People Today'. The Liverpool operation is matched by the Community Services Agency, sponsoring projects in the new town and elsewhere in West Lancs.

These schemes include a wide range of community care work, ranging from furniture repair and environmental tasks, like clearing up churchyards, to security tasks and work for the elderly. The key to a good scheme and to valuable training lies in the quality of the supervisors, some of whom are persons made redundant in their fifties, but concerned to share their experience and life-skills with young people. A fair proportion of these schemes exist on an ecumenical basis, sponsored by local groups or councils of Churches.

There have been some quite sharp criticisms of Churches becoming apparently dependent upon government-funded schemes: for example, the quality of youth work has been questioned where new youth schemes have been established, which are dependent on untrained leaders who are likely to move on at the end of a year. This can produce hostility at a time when local authorities are cutting back on posts for qualified youth workers. The larger agencies have made great efforts to provide appropriate training. But the twelve months rule for those on a scheme has restricted the quality of community care projects more acutely than it has affected, for example, environmental schemes.

It was interesting that the MCUC Survey concluded that in spite of these difficulties many of the workers did find job satisfaction in what was arranged for them and they did succeed in increasing their range of skills. The schemes have proved valuable to the community to an impressive and wide-ranging degree. But the rule that no one could stay on for more than twelve months and the low pay offered produced dissatisfaction for many. A frequent answer to the questions, 'Are you in work? Have you a job?' is, 'No, I'm on a scheme' – a distinction not adequately reflected in the official unemployment figures. Clearly such schemes do not solve the problem of widespread unemployment. But they seem to us to be an important part of any strategy to develop skills and prevent the most vulnerable from feeling that they are on the scrap-heap.

DAVID SHEPPARD: Church-sponsored projects are typical of the many voluntary-sponsored and community-based schemes in

Merseyside which have played a much larger part in MSC programmes in Merseyside than in most other parts of Britain. For seven years I served as Chairman of the Area Manpower Board of the MSC for Merseyside. This covered a period of great expansion for the MSC. The Area Board included employers, trade union leaders, representatives of local authorities, the voluntary movement and ethnic minorities, together with careers officers and MSC staff. As we were asked and expected to provide more and more places, it often seemed like trying to get a runaway bus into gear, especially as one set of rules and initials gave way to another: JCP to YOP, to YTS; STEP to CEP and then to CP.

Norman Tebbit, who was Secretary of State for Employment when the Community Programme was first introduced, spoke of the measure as his 'Liverpool Scheme'. He had accepted our invitation, originally addressed to James Prior, to talk with a group of very committed Christians in Liverpool about unemployment. Sadly what is remembered today is that after an extremely well-informed debate he told his audience, 'You have not told me anything.' To put it mildly there was great affront. With Norwyn Denny, the Methodist Chairman, we took him out to dinner afterwards and told him frankly that if he had learnt nothing, he could not have been listening. As the evening drew on, he became somewhat more responsive to what we had to say about the effects of long-term unemployment on the individual, who could not be regarded as a wastrel. At one stage he thumped the table and explained that the depths of his feelings made him speak 'with passion'. This led to a discussion about what *compassion* really meant, especially in light of the situation developing in Merseyside.

Some weeks later, while Sir Geoffrey Howe, then Chancellor of the Exchequer, was introducing his budget, Norman Tebbit came on the phone to both of us to explain that he had won additional money in the budget for what was to become the Community Programme. 'I wanted to tell you', he said, 'because what you said about the indignity of unemployment got through to me. What is being announced is your Liverpool scheme, but you will have to give us all the help you can to persuade the unions to let it work.'

Earlier in that same visit to Liverpool when he had crossed swords with the Churches, Norman Tebbit had met with the Area Manpower Services Board. He made it plain that his emphasis in the new Youth Training Scheme (YTS) was that it should be 'employer-led' and that he wanted to persuade 'blue chip' companies to play a part. We warmly agreed that it was desirable to draw major companies into the scheme in as large a way as possible. But for years the Board had faced the challenge of running a quality training scheme in parts of Merseyside which to a great extent were an industrial desert. There were simply not enough companies in the area to provide an adequate and sufficiently varied supply of training places. In Liverpool itself the vast majority of employer-led schemes offered only clerical or administrative training places. For manual skills we had to turn to local authority, voluntary and community projects. We fought our corner as vigorously as possible, later taking a small delegation to London to see Norman Tebbit's successor as Secretary of State for Employment, Tom King. We argued that a sufficiently balanced programme needed these other schemes for 'low achievers', in addition to what employers would offer to those youngsters whom they regarded as the most promising. But we failed to convince him in face of the argument about the relative cost of each place.

The Merseyside Area Manpower Board had consistently seen in the Youth Training Scheme a challenge to offer something better to low achievers. We had no wish to carry forward into YTS all the advantages and disadvantages which had already been established at school. This was the chance to change the pecking order. So we repeatedly asked questions about opportunities for black young people, many of whom were not taking up places in the scheme. We argued with government ministers that it was not unreasonable to expect good training to cost more for those who had not had a positive experience at school, and who therefore would not receive the much larger grants which were eligible for those moving on to higher education. Much very good training was being offered in YTS, but regrettably the more recent rules about funding and the emphasis on employer-led schemes restricted the major contribution made by voluntary sponsors. Among these have been a number of church sponsors. A notable example, to which we have already referred, was 'Tomorrow's People Today' in the new town of Skelmersdale. Providing places for some five hundred young people each year, at one time it lost seventy per cent of its places overnight through a change in regulations governing MSC schemes.

Sponsoring one-year or two-year schemes can make a significant contribution at formative moments in life, for both school-leavers and those who have become trapped in long-term unemployment. Such schemes may seem to be only short-term answers, but they can help young people achieve the experience of work as well as serving to break the habit of unemployment. It is easy to criticise these schemes for their limited length, but in spite of that, if taken positively, they can do much to instil competence and restore confidence and self-respect.

CHANGING PATTERNS OF EMPLOYMENT

Against the background of job loss and restricted job opportunities in industries of decreasing importance or badly placed for new markets, there have been frequent efforts to encourage outside investment in Merseyside, especially the opening of new factories by large firms well-established elsewhere. The frustration and disappointment of persuading managing directors to take the plunge, only to see them dissuaded by their younger advisers – 'anywhere except Merseyside' – have nevertheless led to local efforts to produce new schemes and projects for which private-sector investment has been sought, aided in time by government grant. No one can pretend that it has been easy, especially in face of the image of Liverpool and its City Council; but it must be acknowledged that the area has never lacked committed enthusiasts to keep on trying.

DEREK WORLOCK: In 1978 the Merseyside County Council established an Enterprise Forum, consisting for the most part of leaders of industry and commerce, public services, the trade unions and for good measure the university and the Churches. It was all-party rather than one-party and it had the resources of the County Council to implement its proposals. Broadly speaking, the Forum's task was to produce ideas for the industrial regeneration of Merseyside. All services were given voluntarily and, with Bishop David then newly committed to the Area Board of Manpower Services, I agreed to be the sacrificial offering for membership of the Forum. I soon found that I was expected to be the voice of the community and opportunity was not long lacking for me to find expression for that role. Very early on, these far-seeing leaders of industry and the business world decided that a campaign should be launched to promote 'micro-awareness'. Somewhat cautiously I asked whether thought was being given to possible consequences of the 'chip' on human relationships, and promptly found myself appointed chairman of a panel to study and make recommendations about the social implications of the introduction of advancing technology into Merseyside. My panel included a leading industrialist from Pilkingtons, a senior trade union official, and the Director of Planning on the County Council. Our first report, Chips with Everything *(1980), took us some eighteen months and contained a number of recommendations, all of which were accepted by the County Council. At the latter's request we produced a follow-up report nearly four years later entitled* More than Bread and Circuses *(1984). I discovered that a special role for the Church was to write a report of a highly technical problem in a non-specialist style so that the ordinary reader might understand what was involved. It was a useful lesson for someone customarily trying to convey theological truths.*

The panel's first report dealt with the impact of technological development upon employment and examined some of the effects of long-term unemployment upon family life. The panel concluded that the two groups most likely to feel the immediate impact of the introduction of information and control technologies were the intermediate or more junior non-manual workers, and unskilled manual workers. The panel was brave enough to try to quantify likely job changes and in 1980 forecast that in the larger industrial categories (employing ten thousand or more workers) in Merseyside, the job losses in the following five to seven years would be 7,500 in manufacturing industry and 19,800 in services. The point was conceded that with the introduction of new products and processes some new jobs would be created, but that these would not keep pace with the likely redundancies or be within the capacity of many of those rendered redundant. At the same time it was acknowledged that it was impossible to estimate the number of job losses likely, if the same firms went to the wall by failing to introduce these technological developments.

When that first report was published in 1980, the figures achieved some publicity. Although the panel had listed the companies in Merseyside likely to be affected, the figures were never seriously challenged, save when the Parliamentary Select Committee on Employment visited Liverpool. We were both invited to give evidence and called attention to the significance of the figures projected in the report which had just been published. One of the MPs quickly interrupted with, 'Archbishop, surely you must realise that new technology always produces new jobs. You've got it all wrong.' When in 1984 the same panel produced its further report, *More than Bread and Circuses, a Second Look at the Chip*, it was shown that in fact the estimates of 1980 were an underestimate of what had occurred.

DAVID SHEPPARD: I remember a good example of all this at a public meeting at Kirkby, when the Archbishop of Canterbury's Commission came to Merseyside. A speaker from the floor said: 'Lots of people

*come up here and give us advice. What I want to know is "Are you going
to advise Maggie to invest in Merseyside?" Yes or no?' A senior local
industrialist, serving on the commission, asked to reply. 'I have got some
good news and some bad news for you,' he said. 'The good news is that
over the next five years we shall probably invest more than £100 million
in the North-West. The bad news is that in order to remain competitive
we shall also make redundant two thousand of our employees.'*

Both of us have repeatedly said that for at least the foreseeable
future the employment market, as we know it, will not require the
whole labour force. The establishment of the Community Programme, with its large element of part-time work, was tacit acknowledgment of this claim. In 1986 the House of Commons Select
Committee on Employment proposed a guaranteed job for the
long-term unemployed. This was to be achieved by extending the
Community Programme. But clearly a balanced economy of industrial operations is as desirable as it seems difficult to achieve.
Chips with Everything had argued the need to develop, alongside
the large capital-intensive industries, a fair leavening of smaller
industries of a more labour-intensive and usually less mechanised
nature. We are also on record as having urged an extensive
programme of public works, renewing old cities, and the imaginative development of much-needed services to the community.

Simply to speak of learning to use leisure creatively may conceiv-
ably be very fulfilling for those who have experienced higher
education. But it is those who are least recognised in other spheres
of life, and who have few skills to offer in the marketplace, who feel
devalued by not having 'a proper job'. Communities need that
balanced economy of industrial operations. It means that if there is
to be adequate fulfilment and the avoidance of the human wastage
created by redundancy, there must be widespread training and
re-training for new skills.

We shall develop more fully elsewhere our views about the
reality of the North/South divide. Here we would wish to stress
that many of the information technology developments and
government-supported research and development activities could
well be located in the North. Distance from the capital and general
location are of no consequence to their purpose, yet almost invariably they are established in the more prosperous regions in the
South-East, South-West and East Anglia. The report *More than
Bread and Circuses* recorded in those regions a massive concentra-
tion of publicly supported research and development agencies. By
way of illustration, the Medical Research Council has thirty-seven

establishments located south-east of a line drawn from the River Severn to the Humber, with only seven such establishments north of that line. Similarly with the Agricultural Research Council, there are twenty-six establishments to the south-east of that line, and to the north-west none in England and just one in Wales. The report went on – and it was our voice also – to plead that the Government should consider a progressive programme for relocating some of these activities in areas where the need for employment opportunity is highest.

We are not arguing against the introduction of advancing technologies into industry. But if the consequences are not to be highly damaging to whole areas of the country, then care must be taken to share the benefits across the nation's community at large. If there is not to be polarisation, there must be concerted efforts to develop partnership, not just between employer and employed but between the various regions which make up our 'one nation'.

Slogans need to be questioned. The Christian presence not infrequently challenges the received wisdom of one political approach or another. 'New technology always produces new jobs' was a good example of the need to say, 'What do you mean?' Slogans become catch-phrases which can be as wrong as images can be. Merseyside suffers from an image of being a strike-torn hot-bed of industrial unrest. But the most recent study of strikes on Merseyside, covering the years 1974/83, shows that what strikes there have been have been concentrated in a small number of industries. Docks, ship-building and car manufacture provided less than seven per cent of employment, but over the period as a whole accounted for two-thirds of the days lost. On the other hand half the industries on Merseyside have a better strike record than the national average for their industries. Forty-four per cent of all industries in the area were completely free of strikes (cf. Ron Bean and Peter Stoney, 'Strikes on Merseyside. A Regional Analysis', *The Industrial Relations Journal*, Spring 1986).

Much of the image was established in years when fears about the loss of trade and jobs were high, when trade unions were in a much more powerful position than they are today, and when maximum publicity was given to every Liverpool dispute. In the years 1968/73 Merseyside lost two and a half times the national average of working days through strikes. But in the years since then there has been a radical change in strike patterns. In the docks the negotiation of a two-year pay and productivity deal in 1983 has contributed much stability to the port. It was in fact the good record in the Liverpool docks in 1983/4 which helped to win from the Government the much sought-after facility of a 'Freeport'. Similarly it was the good record of productivity of the Halewood car factory which led Ford to make a considerable investment in their works there, contributing greatly to improved industrial relationships and confidence. But in both cases we had to make some effort to ensure that the true facts and figures were brought to the attention of the Prime Minister and other government ministers concerned.

DEREK WORLOCK: Our efforts to correct a false image have not always gone unchallenged. There was the occasion when the Prime Minister, Mrs Thatcher, made a visit to Liverpool to open a high-technology plant. To a strictly limited audience she expressed her regret at a recent national dock-strike, adding: 'How sad I was to find the Liverpool dockers the first to come out on strike, the last to go back.' The Chairman of the Dock and Harbour Company, seated near me, indicated dissent and afterwards came to Bishop David and myself to plead with us to ask the Prime Minister to withdraw the allegation which he insisted was untrue. He added that if it appeared in the press, it would be gravely damaging to the mission to Hong Kong for which he was about to leave to seek business for the Freeport.

The opportunity came at lunch when the same remark was repeated. Somewhat rashly I jumped in to make a correction: 'No, they were the first out all right, but they were also the first back. As soon as a national settlement was reached, they immediately responded to the union leadership and returned to work.' The Prime Minister listened as I went on to explain that often what appeared to be industrial militancy was an expression of worker solidarity, bred of decades of hardship. Recently the Chairman had congratulated the men on their sense of union discipline. Mrs Thatcher appeared to be unimpressed but once again there was evidence that points made are heeded, if not always accepted. The original unfavourable comment on the record of the Liverpool dockers never appeared in the press.

THE BURDEN OF MANAGEMENT

We often meet senior businessmen who know from experience that it is possible to make a good living in Merseyside. Some say, 'There is more hassle here, but if there is good management there can be a very co-operative workforce.' We have found that many are quite ready to recommend investment and reinvestment in Merseyside. But the bad image which undoubtedly exists, reinforced by confrontations between the City Council and central government over the rates, continues sadly to provide apparently prudent reasons for expanding businesses to stay away. One major company claims to have become aware that applicants for senior posts in their Merseyside enterprise are prepared to go through lengthy interviews, only to refuse the offer of the post at the last moment. They concluded that it is man and wife making that decision, because of the bad image of the area. The company's response now is to invite applicants and their partners to come to stay for forty-eight hours in Merseyside at the beginning of the process of selection, to enable the couple to see that it is a very good place to live. The company's experience, like our own, is that 'once people have come, seen for themselves and experienced the atmosphere here, they never want to move away'.

Other factors, which are not 'made on Merseyside', can contribute to the unwillingness of people from both private and public sectors to move to Liverpool. There is the fear of home owners that they will lose their equity. If they sell a house in the South of England for £150,000, they may well be able to buy the equivalent for half that price in a very 'desirable' part of Merseyside. The fear is that the gap in value will widen and that they will never be able to move back to the South, should that become necessary.

The 'image' of Merseyside elsewhere is a matter of major concern to business people and to those anxious to attract private-sector investment into the area, especially from the city of London. It was at one time suggested to us that we should use some of our southern contacts to put Merseyside businessmen, with ideas for new projects, in touch with those in London who might be willing to provide some measure of financial backing for worthwhile schemes. Accordingly we invited a hand-picked group of those in senior management and with a known commitment to Merseyside, to discuss this proposal and to see what projects needed such backing. We met at Archbishop's House on 29 September 1984, and thus was born the Michaelmas Group. Although after a series of meetings the group decided not to act as entrepreneurs for new projects, it was thought worthwhile to share what contacts we all had to help in an 'enabling' role with projects calculated to improve the economic, commercial and social prosperity of Merseyside. Though the group remains restricted to twenty persons under our chairmanship, we have found that the only practical time for such busy people to meet is before the day's business has begun. The Michaelmas Group holds monthly breakfast-time meetings, and fulfils a different purpose from the Enterprise Forum in the exchange of information and ideas, endeavouring through personal contact to penetrate the barrier created by what its members regard as the false image of Merseyside.

We are very conscious of the heavy burden of management that falls on those who feel the responsibility to help the whole nation to flourish, and not simply those parts of the country which are already more affluent. This is where the image of Merseyside is of such great consequence. One senior director in a major company shared with us his experience of long battles with his board of directors to maintain investment in Merseyside, while many of his colleagues were aspiring to move away. He insisted that the decision to stay should and could be based on sound commercial judgment. He refused to appeal to charitable generosity, important though that might be. There is a moral challenge not to walk away from the great cities which market forces brought into being and once needed so badly. If this point is pressed too hard, the accusation is quickly advanced that the locals are claiming that 'the world owes Liverpool a living'. Appeals are made for prudence in the cause of justice to investors and shareholders. But it is short-term prudence which would allow whole cities to become dependent on welfare and government programmes.

It has become clear that public funding is necessary in order to attract or encourage private-sector investment. At times it has seemed that the reverse procedure is true. This serves to indicate the importance of partnership if the good of the community and the prosperity of industry is to be secure. On one occasion we asked a visiting politician his views on how to treat an area which had in the past depended upon one industry that had since died. We had in mind some of the mining areas whose very existence was threatened by pit-closures. 'Fund it,' he replied without hesitation. That was fine for a village or small town, we agreed, but what about a large city, such as Liverpool, much of the traditional industry and purpose of which appeared to be dying? With still less hesitation, a two-word response flashed back: 'Bigger funds,' he added. Would that it were as simple as that! We talk nowadays about the need to renew the city's assets, but for this public monies are required as well as private sector support.

In 1986, following his resignation from the Government, another well-known politician, Michael Heseltine, returned to the theme he had put forward vigorously while he was the original Minister for Merseyside in 1981–82. The scale of reinvestment needed in the old cities – even assuming continued reduction of population – was far beyond the scope of private business alone. A substantial injection of public funds was needed to produce the confidence necessary to attract private investment. A good example of this has been the rehabilitation of the Albert Dock in Liverpool. The investment of government money, through the Development Corporation, has made the conditions right for private companies to join in the major development which the reconstruction of the old buildings has made possible. But generally the dream of inner-city partnership in Liverpool, arising from the Government White Paper of 1977, has not been fulfilled because of the breakdown of relations between central government and city council, with dire consequences to such bodies as voluntary organisations. Inner-city partnership is not so much a basis of claims upon central grants of money, but also a way of working together for the good of the community. Sadly this relationship has virtually been destroyed through the heat of political confrontation.

The economic regeneration of old cities would inevitably be costly. All governments have shrunk from the scale of investment needed to have a serious chance of turning round the decline. Perhaps it is necessary, in calculating the expense to the exchequer of such a vast undertaking, to take into account the enormous cost of mass unemployment. The cost is not simply that of Unemployment Benefit and Supplementary Benefit – just short of £200m for Merseyside in 1986. Thought must also be given to the fact that people who are not employed do not under normal circumstances pay tax. Calculations based on those figures, including lost taxes, suggest that the cost to the nation would be perhaps three times the visible total of benefits paid out. Even then the calculation is not complete. Unhappily unemployment also produces increased costs of policing, probation work and – because of mental stress, alcoholism, etc. – in the Health Service. Such a calculation is not easy. When wages and salaries are reduced in an area, there is less money in circulation. Economic activity diminishes. A careful study carried out in 1986 suggests that in financial terms alone the cost of unemployment in Merseyside might be as much as £1bn, four or five times the outlay on benefits (Peter Brain, *Options for the Long-Term Unemployed*, May 1986. Liverpool City Ministry of the United Reformed Church).

Alan Bleasdale's saga of *Boys from the Blackstuff* reminded us that the calculation could not be merely or even primarily financial. The indignity of unemployment inflicts a cost in human terms which must be unacceptable to Christians and indeed to all citizens who uphold the theory of one nation.

8   'A TIME FOR HEALING'

In July 1981 the Liverpool 8 or Toxteth district of our city exploded into several nights of rioting. Large buildings were burnt to the ground, shops were looted and lines of police were attacked with bricks, petrol bombs and iron railings. By 1 a.m. on the second night, according to the Chief Constable's Report, the police had 'been subjected to three hours of attack of a scale and ferocity, which, I believe, was unprecedented'. At that moment the Chief Constable decided to order the use of CS gas for the first time on the mainland of Britain. Gradually the disturbances were brought under control, but continued in Toxteth and in several outlying estates over a period of some six weeks. In all 781 police officers were injured and 214 police vehicles were damaged (cf. *Public Disorder on Merseyside, July–August 1981. Chief Constable's Report to Merseyside Police Committee 1981*). Injuries were of course also sustained by some of the rioters, though for obvious reasons these were seldom brought to official medical attention. But one evening, when police vehicles were used to disperse groups of rioters, one young man was knocked down and killed. Subsequently, in a tense atmosphere of confrontation, a protest march was organised by the Liverpool Trades' Council and the city's black organisations, calling for the dismissal of the Chief Constable. The scars which Liverpool 8 bears to this time as a result of those nights of conflict are by no means restricted to burnt-out buildings.

THE TOXTETH RIOTS

The 1981 riots began with an incident which proved to be a flash point for igniting the tinder of accumulated discontent and anger. A young man was arrested for allegedly taking a motorcycle without consent. He shouted for help and a number of local black youths rallied to him and attacked the police. In Lord Scarman's report on the disturbances in Brixton earlier that summer, there was included additional but shorter evidence about what happened in Toxteth.

Many felt that the learned judge's analysis of the riots in Brixton would not have made a misleading account of events in Toxteth.

'The disorders', reported Lord Scarman, 'were communal disturbances arising from a complex political social and economic situation . . . The riots were neither pre-meditated nor planned. Each was the spontaneous reaction of angry young men, most of whom were black, against what they saw as a hostile police force.' On the second night, however, 'outsiders did participate in the rioting. They were attracted into the action by the publicity given to the events' of the previous night. 'These people (some of whom were clearly identified as whites) played a significant part in intensifying the disorder by making and distributing petrol bombs.' There was also an element of 'elation felt by many youngsters at their success, as they saw it, in defying the police with such dramatic results' (*The Brixton Disorders: Report of an Inquiry by Lord Scarman*, HMSO 1981, p. 45).

There was a remarkable parallel between the Brixton disorders and what happened in Toxteth three months later. The Toxteth riots began with a spontaneous eruption of anger, mainly from black young people. The longer the rioting lasted, the younger and whiter those taking part appeared to be.

On the third evening in Toxteth, the pair of us went out together. After the horror of the previous night, we had spent much of the day trying to persuade the Deputy Chief Constable to ring the area with his men, but not to move into it or snatch any of the would-be rioters unless it became absolutely necessary. We also suggested to the black community leaders that, if at all possible, they should encourage local people to stay at home and keep clear of trouble. Clearly no hard undertakings could be given by either side, but the point was taken. The hour before darkness is always the danger-point, when tension mixes with the excitement of those gathering in the streets to see if there is going to be trouble. True enough, that night the police ringed the area and virtually sealed it off. We waited together anxiously at the perimeter, watching to see if there were any signs that the crowds which, despite weariness from the previous night, had gathered in Upper Parliament Street, would disperse and return to their homes. We could see large numbers of black youngsters, restless, excited, ready for action in the event of an incident. The police, under the direction of Mr Peter Wright, the Deputy Chief Constable, held back. We knew that the leaders in the community were quietly moving among the crowds, trying to defuse the situation; but no one shifted.

We decided to go to the offices of the Merseyside Community

Relations Council to see if there was any way in which we could help. Just as we arrived, a young black lad ran in with a message from one of the leaders of the black community. He and his colleagues inside the ring could not make themselves heard. Could anyone get hold of two megaphones for them? Such things are not easy to locate at 10 p.m. It was agreed that the only immediate source seemed to be the police. But it was also clear that the police would not be willing to hand over megaphones to a black young-ster that night. So we offered to go with the boy to the local police headquarters and to make the request ourselves. Outside the police station a number of press reporters were waiting; but we managed to enter without them. We explained our request to the duty officer. What did we want them for? To help the leaders of the black community address the crowds inside the ringed area. We received an old-fashioned look. Who would take them? Our young messenger disappeared at once. We would take them. Could we guarantee their safe return? No, only their safe delivery. The duty officer disappeared upstairs and we waited. When at last he reappeared, official regulations had triumphed. It would be all right if we were prepared to sign the book for the two megaphones. No problem.

Those signatures doubtless survive in the Merseyside Police records. With the megaphones under our jackets we made our way out of the police station, through the unobservant press reporters and back to the perimeter ring of police. We talked our way through the lines and headed for Upper Parliament Street. We were stopped by a couple of black middle-aged somewhat aggress-ive men who did not recognise us and told us to get out. It turned out afterwards that they were visitors from Manchester who had come over to join in any trouble which might be going. We managed to press on until we were in sight of the particular community leader who had sent the request. We decided that it might not make life easier for him if at that point he was seen with us. We gave the megaphones to two small boys and asked them to take our valuable cargo to the leader. There was something almost biblical about the scene as they ran off on this precious errand. A few moments later we heard his advice carrying across the waste ground to the crowds gathered about him. 'Go home,' he called. 'Go home. You will be better there. There is no need for you to be out tonight.'

As the crowds slowly dispersed, we made our way to another sector of the area where with one of the local clergy we walked the streets for the next three hours. Several large fires were burning and we sat with one of the priests in his house as he waited to see if the fire would be brought under control before it reached his church. It was a vigil which for several weeks became for us a nightly patrol: trying to sustain local clergy and parishioners, seeking to calm things down just by being seen on the streets each night, and to win the confidence of both the local community and the police. The task was made no easier by the presence of the 'visitors' from other places who desired no peaceful solution, and by the importation of additional police from other forces throughout the country. The latter were quite unprepared for Liverpool folk who appeared hostile at one moment and brought them out cups of tea the next.

WHY DID IT HAPPEN?

Various interpretations were offered to explain the cause of the riots. At the time many commentators, national and local, expressed surprise at the eruption of feeling and the violence with which it was expressed. There were some who were quick to allege that agitators took advantage of the genuine grievances of unemployed youngsters. But the local people replied wryly: 'We have had unemployment so long, why riot about that now?' To youth unemployment, some commentators added abysmally poor housing, disillusion with local government, and despair. Certainly the people on the spot had little hope of ever having a real say about their future. Asked what they wanted, they would reply more often that they wanted to be listened to, than that they wanted any specific reforms.

DEREK WORLOCK: *On the day after the episode with the megaphones,* The Times *pressed me urgently for my opinion as to what response the riot called for. I pointed out that there was evidence that, despite some efforts by community workers and by the police themselves, there had been long-term mistrust between the black community and the police. I added:*

The problems are at least complex. They add up to explosive frustration. No one is looking for a quick solution. Political slogans and moralising do not satisfy. But no one here is looking for another social study of a city that has probably suffered more social surveys than any other part of the country. Action will be necessary. This long-term tackling of our problems will have to include a lot of listening. For this is not a community upon which a solution can be imposed. Just at the moment, against the racket of riots, it would be difficult to hear what the genuine local voice of Toxteth is trying to say, but it wants and needs to be heard. Perhaps that is one of the more hopeful signs of these last hours. The black community in our city has its own leaders. They have their own views, their own way of expressing them and their own methods of communication. There are signs that they are being listened to at last, at least in certain quarters . . . Like the rest of those seeking to serve the community, they are to a great extent powerless in face of an invasion of hooligans and sightseers from outside . . .

(The Times, 8 July 1981).

There was widespread rejection by the local people of anything which smacked of the establishment or institution. Much of the anger of July 1981 was focused on the police. Under ordinary circumstances they were the only representatives whom Liverpool black people would meet of the society which kept them excluded from its normal life and opportunities. So they were the natural target.

DAVID SHEPPARD: Dick Crawshaw, MP for Toxteth at that time, told me subsequently that he had been to see the Home Secretary several months before the riots to warn him that an explosion would take place unless policies were changed. After the riots Dick said, 'I believe that these events came about because, rightly or wrongly, there is a genuine belief, not only in the black community but also among white people, that in that area the enforcement of law and order is not even-handed.'

There was anger too against the political parties. The people of Toxteth felt that each party tried to make political capital out of the riots. Generally, the feeling was firmly against 'them' in the Town Hall. This was nothing new. It had been common enough in the past, whoever was in power. There was a feeling of powerlessness, of having no say in the way in which their lives were run. Walking through Toxteth immediately after the riots, we were disturbed at the extent of the damage. Yet there was also the strange feeling that even now it was not so very different from how it had been before. Half-completed demolition and rubbish skips, which had proved a plentiful ammunition dump for the brick-throwers, gave the impression that authority did not care much about the neighbourhood. Requests for housing repairs were frequently not dealt with inside a year.

Even though a substantial black community had lived in the city for at least one hundred years, of the twenty-six thousand

169

employees of Liverpool City Council, only 169 were black. In his wisdom Lord Scarman recognised that there were certain lessons which the police needed to learn. However, he rightly commented: 'Whilst good policing can help diminish tension and avoid disorder, it cannot remove causes of social stress where these are to be found, deeply embedded in fundamental economic and social conditions' (*Scarman Report*, p. 100).

We must also admit that, although in this case 'anger' may be too strong a word, there was also alienation from the Churches. Institutional religion was seen in the same connection as all the other institutions of society. Organised religion did not appear to have any place in such a hurt community. Its members would tell you plainly that they saw few if any black people in positions of leadership in the Churches. Yet remarkably there remained a wistful feeling that the God of Jesus Christ cared about the quality of life which they experienced.

THE WORK OF RECONCILIATION

The word 'reconciliation', with its counterpart 'alienation', became a regular part of our vocabulary soon after the outbreak of the riots. It was following the worst night of the fighting, while the smoke was still rising from burnt-out streets and vehicles, that Brian Redhead, from the BBC's *Today* studio, put the direct question: 'What is the Church's role in all this?' In replying with the one word 'reconciliation', we were setting ourselves a role for the years ahead which has been at least as difficult as it has been important.

'Reconciliation' is one of the great words of the New Testament. It is often dismissed as a 'soft' word: suggestive of encouraging clergy to avoid conflict, pouring oil on troubled waters, pretending that both sides can be equally right, or that two parties to an argument both really think the same thing. A popular dictionary suggests that the word means 'making friends again after estrangement'. That sounds nice, but we have not always found that it is a word which is easily understood. There are those who think of reconciling accounts, of balancing books, and even of wiping out differences which may contain important distinctions.

The Christian holds that by ourselves we human beings are incapable of reconciling ourselves with the Creator whom we have offended by our sin. Here the action of God is both primary and decisive. 'It was God who reconciled us to himself through Christ and gave us the work of handing on this reconciliation' (2 Cor. 5:18

JB). At one of our clergy seminars Professor C. F. D. Moule led us into St Paul's thinking about reconciliation. For every human reconciliation to take place, there has to be a first move from the person who has been offended or estranged. Generally this will require a costly act of self-giving. This in turn calls forth from the offender a response which involves a change of heart. This too can be costly and difficult because it requires an admission of being wrong and a surrender of pride. Professor Moule spoke of this process of reconciliation as involving a 'pooling of energy' which not only made possible the repair of a broken relationship but also rendered it out of the question to go back to how things were before.

So it is with the sacrifice of Christ on the cross. His sacrifice, involving the supreme giving of himself, calls forth repentance and a change of heart. It enables us to go forward to a new relationship with God, rather than going back to how things were before. God's action is, in the words of St Paul, rather like 'a new creation' (2 Cor. 5:17 NJB). Reconciliation implies renewal. Those reconciled are called to be 'ambassadors for Christ' (2 Cor. 5:20 NJB), charged with 'the ministry of reconciliation' (2 Cor. 5:18 NJB). Such thinking has its relevance to what is needed today for the reconciliation of conflicts in the inner city: energy which draws forth energy from the other person, making the first move, staying with the conflict, possibilities for new relationships, not going back to the way things used to be.

To try to take on the role of a reconciler has sometimes proved exceedingly difficult. By night we might walk in the middle of the road to give some reassurance to those watching from their windows or doorways. Yet by day it could also mean being a target from both sides and from one moment to the next. Throughout the worst of the 1981 riots we managed to maintain close contact with Peter Wright, the Deputy Chief Constable, who himself retained throughout the respect of most of the leaders of the black community. Often it was possible for us to communicate feelings and suggestions between those for whom direct contact was impossible. Inevitably it left one open to criticism and vulnerable to the danger of being disowned by those for whom one had carried out this service.

DEREK WORLOCK: *Two weeks after the worst of the riots, the Chief Constable and his Deputy called on me to ask me to take the chair at a public meeting designed to promote reconciliation between the local community and the police authority. Eventually I agreed on the understanding that my doing so would have the agreement of the other Church leaders and that my services would be acceptable to the police themselves, to the chairperson of the Police Committee, Mrs Margaret Simey, and to such leaders of the black community as I would be able to consult. It took some days to achieve this assurance. The Chief Constable, Kenneth Oxford, wrote to the officers of all the ethnic groups making up the black community of Liverpool 8, the Police Committee, and county and city councillors, inviting them to a meeting at the university, under my chairmanship, and offering a free and frank exchange in the hope of restoring broken relationships.*

After some indecision, with each group watching the reaction of others, all was finally set. Unhappily towards the end of July, a few days before the meeting was due, there were further disturbances in which mobile patrols were employed by the police in response to stone-throwing, and a young man received injuries from which he died. Once more the situation became electric. Several groups announced that they would boycott any meeting at which the Chief Constable was present. After consulting my colleagues, I suggested to Mr Oxford that the time for such a meeting was not ripe and advised that the meeting be postponed. This he declined to do on the score that he could not yield to what he saw as a threat. After some agonising I decided that I must stand by my publicised commitment. For the only time in my life I had to walk through a picket, strengthened for the occasion by outsiders. When I heard someone scream 'racist', I turned to face my accuser. She was white and, to the best of my knowledge, not from Merseyside.

The meeting itself was reasonably attended. Undoubtedly some local people were deterred, not unreasonably, by the picket. There were a few prepared statements, some allegations made, some answers given. In such a charged atmosphere the best I could hope for was an agreement to examine the accusations and to meet again. This was achieved just before darkness fell and Peter Wright, reporting that a crowd was gathering outside, suggested that we depart in daylight. Kenneth Oxford was set upon as he left, and had to be protected by a police guard as he made his way to his car. From my point of view this proved a distraction which enabled me to leave unmolested. Several months passed before the meeting was re-convened. By then certain representatives of the black community agreed to be present to put their case. Local community meetings were arranged. The Scarman Report recommendations were undertaken and my invidious task was over. But in the meantime we had come under attack from some police officers and from a spokesman of the Police Federation.

DAVID SHEPPARD: In July 1981, when the riots took place, I was in the strange position of being away on sabbatical leave. I returned to

Liverpool at two key junctures. Derek Worlock and my colleague Michael Henshall, the Bishop of Warrington, kept me informed by telephone each day. Eventually I felt that I could not stay away, cut the sabbatical short by a fortnight and came home to Liverpool. That gave me a fortnight in which I was totally free to move around and ask a wide range of people for their account of what had happened and to seek their comments. In light of the attack which was to come, this was just as well.

LIVERPOOL 8 DEFENCE COMMITTEE AND SUBURBAN ANGER

In late August there arose for us a new crisis which for a short time left the Church in danger of tearing itself apart. In the days following the worst of the rioting, a Liverpool 8 Defence Committee had been established by some of the black community leaders. It was often portrayed by the press as a sinister revolutionary group. In its early days it was concerned mostly with trying to provide transport for families wishing to visit people, held on remand after the riots, in Risley Remand Centre, near Warrington. It was at best a loose-knit organisation. Some of its members were housewives, some community workers. It was never sufficiently developed to appoint particular spokespersons, so that remarks attributed to the committee were often the personal comments of self-appointed representatives, addressing the media without the agreement of the committee as such. It was a situation ripe for confusion and misrepresentation.

In late August it suddenly became known that a grant of £500 was to be made to the Defence Committee by the British Council of Churches, through its Community and Race Relations Unit. In point of fact we ourselves had never been consulted about the proposal. But the press branded the donation as the gift of the Churches, and in a matter of hours it had become either our direct gift or at least made at the recommendation of the Liverpool Church leaders. A definite attempt was made to drive a wedge between us on this issue, and politicians, bruised by their experience of a few weeks earlier, were quick to find a new scapegoat. There was a double danger for us: either to seem to have acted irresponsibly and insensitively, as alleged by some, or, had we disowned any part in the grant to the committee, to appear to have abandoned the efforts of the black community leaders to look after their own people.

To remain silent amidst the furore was impossible. We kept very

173

close to each other and to other colleagues among the Church leaders. Together with Norwyn Denny we made a public statement. We pointed out that the British Council of Churches did not have to ask our consent to make such a grant. We commented that the path of Christian justice often meant picking one's way through a minefield of misinterpretation. Then we added:

In trying to fulfil our difficult role of reconciliation, we ask understanding for this gesture of help towards those who have felt alienated from the rest of the community. It is our earnest belief that Liverpool 8 should be enabled to help itself to stand up after years of massive deprivation. That means that on occasion support must be given to groups, already established in that community, which are an authentic expression of some strongly held feelings.

Our statement continued:

As Christians we also believe that some, who have at times found themselves in conflict with society, do make a new start. To help draw together different sections of the community, we should be willing to offer them realistic co-operation and friendship. In reaffirming our condemnation of violence, we wish to make it plain that we can have no part in the continuing campaign against the Chief Constable and the police. We regret the Liverpool 8 Defence Committee's boycott of discussions to improve police and community relations. Our hope is that, as groups like the Defence Committee receive co-operation from others, so they will feel encouraged to work together for the removal of long-term mistrust, and to build more positive relationships for the future.

Carefully as we had tried to set out principles while we walked the knife-edge of reconciliation, this statement was represented in the press as direct identification with the gift to the Defence Committee and with the activities of the Defence Committee against the police. Many senior police officers chose to ignore our clear dissociation from the campaign against the police and treated us to sharp criticism in public and even stronger words in correspondence. Every letter was answered, no answer was acknowledged. It reached a climax in November when a senior officer of the Police Federation criticised us publicly in the presence of the press, even alleging that we had ourselves given money to those who had attacked the police. As at that time we were being pressed by the Chief Constable and the Police Committee to chair the next meeting to promote police and community reconciliation, we had to insist that they both dissociate themselves from these charges against us. This eventually they did and the meeting took place in early December.

DEREK WORLOCK: The main object of this meeting was to prepare the way for regular community/police meetings on a much smaller, more local basis. This was agreed. After it was over I received the following letter from Mrs Simey, chairperson of the Police Committee:

> *I expect Mr Oxford will be sending our official thanks to you, but may I add this word of gratitude. Quite apart from this week's difficult meeting, your comprehension of our difficulties was a tremendous help. To be understood is a wonderful solace to a battered spirit! A long slow plod lies ahead of us but for the first time I have a sense of the tide turning. For all you have done to bring that about, my very best thanks.*

It had been a long and at times even dangerous haul. David and I attended the Chief Constable's Christmas party and I spent most of Christmas afternoon visiting police stations. Actions speak louder than words.

DAVID SHEPPARD: I also received some fiercely critical letters from police officers and from suburban churches, as well as from the shires. On the other hand, there were also letters, for example, from an outer estate parish, speaking of ministering to a police-officer member of the parish who had been injured in the riots, but at the same time being thankful that Church leaders were trying to stand behind those who had been so deprived. There could be no doubt that Christians found themselves deeply divided about this grant, feeling the pain which arose from the fact that some quite close to one another and to us expressed opposite points of view. Grace and I spent an evening about a month after the riots with a group of such friends. One clergy couple lived close to the scene of the rioting. They saw matters very much through the eyes of inner-city people whom they felt the police had picked on over the years. Another clergy couple then told us their son in the police force had had his face permanently scarred by a brick thrown on the first night of the riots. We were rightly and uncomfortably feeling torn in half between two groups of people, knowing that we belonged to both.

After the publication of Lord Scarman's report, the police made vigorous attempts to recruit, to train and in practice to develop right relationships with a view to giving better service to inner-city communities. In Liverpool 8, a fresh police station was opened in Hope Street to serve the area within 'the Chief Constable's box' of named streets. Community liaison meetings were part of a determined effort to help community and police to understand each other. Foot patrols were continued, often with considerable bravery, when attacks were being made on police officers. Arrests were sometimes made in the early morning rather than when a suspected person was surrounded by a group of friends. On one occasion a large-scale raid to search for hard drugs was accompanied by a senior police officer, standing outside to explain to neighbours and those who had gathered just what was being done and why. The 'bobby on the beat' has become in many areas a known character of value and acceptance. A difficulty still lies in the fact that in times of tension other special riot units have to be drafted into an area where they are not known nor know the leaders of the local community.

FURTHER DISTURBANCE IN 1985

There have continued to be times of great tension, for the underlying experience of people in Liverpool 8 has not significantly changed. Four years after the rioting in 1981 there were further eruptions of anger and violence in Bristol, in Brixton, in Handsworth and in Tottenham. At such times one watches anxiously for 'copy-cat' riots. Often the effect is that the fuse is shortened and an incident which might otherwise be tolerated fires off a more serious explosion. On 1 October 1985 there was an incident in Liverpool which might easily have developed into a full-scale riot. It was damaging enough as it was. It began with frustration and indignation over delays and confusion in the hearing of a charge of affray against several members of the black community. When it was discovered the men charged had been removed unseen to Risley Remand Centre, those who had been waiting in the court for the hearing raced back to Toxteth in a state of great indignation. Bricks were thrown at police vehicles, and some private cars were stopped, occupants pulled out and the cars wrecked or burnt. The police moved quickly and in massive force to contain the disturbance. They succeeded in denying access to the area around Granby Street – towards which we had seen a considerable movement of people. This quick action by the police undoubtedly reduced the number of those involved in the subsequent disturbances.

At about 8.30 p.m. we received a phone call asking us to go to the Liverpool 8 Law Centre. We checked this with Mr John Burrow, by then Deputy Chief Constable, who agreed that such a visit might be useful. We walked the streets for more than an hour and were told that there had been some disturbances but that the very large police presence had brought it under control. However, there was considerable anger among both black and white residents at the strength and intensity of the continuing police presence. We witnessed a number of police vehicles moving fast through the streets, with lights flashing and sirens wailing. This heightened the tension, especially when the vehicles mounted the pavements. We again telephoned the Deputy Chief Constable who was in operational control. He assured us that he was endeavouring to withdraw the vehicles and return to foot patrols at the earliest opportunity. We passed on this message to the community leaders, who used it to try to reassure local people.

At 10.30 p.m. we received further calls, asking us to return to the Law Centre and to witness what was happening. We were taken by local black community leaders to the main area of disturbance in Granby Street. One said: 'This is about territory. Granby Street is the heart of our territory.' Every good policeman dreads being put in the position of appearing as part of an army of occupation. Just then the rows of police vehicles, filled with police officers in riot gear, seemed horribly like that. In practice there were not more than 150 persons out in Granby Street, mostly local residents, the largest group numbering no more than thirty or forty. We walked together in the middle of the road to be clearly identified, and made our way to the next street to speak with the police inspector in charge. We asked if, in light of what the Deputy Chief Constable had told us, it would now be possible to withdraw the vehicles and especially to stay out of Granby Street. He assured us that it was his intention to do just that. Evidently the vehicles drawn up behind him were under different radio direction. At that moment, they turned on their headlights, 'revved' their engines, drove straight through our group, and with sirens blaring raced into Granby Street, to the obvious chagrin of the inspector.

We walked back there at once to try to help calm things down. While at least ten police vans were parked in the street, two Land Rovers, with strong spot-lights and sirens going, swept on and off the pavements to scatter those still gathered there. At one stage we both had to flatten ourselves against the wall, as a Land Rover came on to the pavement between a lamp-post and the wall of a house. One of its side-mirrors passed just beneath our faces. Eventually most people were persuaded to go inside or leave Granby Street. We returned to the Law Centre and again telephoned the Deputy Chief to report what had happened. The community leaders, reluctant to pass on police reassurances a second time as their credibility was at stake, nevertheless continued to act as a restraining influence and dispersed some youngsters who were trying to set fire to a property. Fire engines were now able to come in without difficulty and the police pulled back from the immediate area soon after 1 a.m. The next day we did a complete debriefing session with John Burrow, who publicly expressed his thanks to the Law Centre and the community leaders for what they had achieved. By next evening all was relatively calm and the police vehicles waited discreetly and at a distance in a side street.

In setting out an account of this one incident, we would stress that we are fully aware of the pressures on the police. Some shopkeepers complained that, if there were not sufficient protection, they would have to remove their business from the area. Yet black people in the community were frustrated because they felt that their descriptions of police action were not believed. We ourselves felt it necessary to speak up for them, as did the local clergy, who are often turned to as the only professional people left living in certain inner-city areas. At the same time we have tried to continue visits to police headquarters and to the individual police stations to show our concern for them in the very difficult situation in which they can be placed. Sadly this has on occasion meant visits to hospitals to see some of those injured in the course of their duty.

A MINISTER FOR MERSEYSIDE

Soon after the outbreak of rioting in July 1981, the city received a visit from the then Home Secretary, Mr William Whitelaw. Both to him and some days later to the Prime Minister, when she herself came to Liverpool, we tried to give some picture of the degree of alienation felt in Toxteth and other deprived parts of the city. We explained the feeling that London did not know, let alone understand, some of the social problems facing Liverpool. We asked that a minister of Cabinet rank be appointed, who would be seen regularly in the area and through whom local people might have confidence that their true needs were being brought to the attention of the Government. It was difficult to make headway in trying to deal with all the various government departments which might be involved in such a complex situation. We asked for a minister with acknowledged special responsibility for Merseyside, someone who would come and listen to a not always coherent voice, but who would be seen to share the people's concern.

Mrs Thatcher gave us the undertaking for which we had asked and soon afterwards Michael Heseltine, as Secretary of State for the Environment, was given this special responsibility as Minister for Merseyside. He immediately spent fourteen days in the area, listening and seeing for himself. His genuine personal shock at seeing some of the worst examples of urban dereliction – in the outer estate of Croxteth as much as in the more publicised inner city area of Toxteth – led him to ask the Cabinet for a major expansion of public expenditure. When this proposal was defeated by the Treasury ministers, he threw himself wholeheartedly behind a strategy which attempted to bring together interests concerned with the regeneration of Merseyside but which promised very little fresh money. He established a Task Force, an outposting of civil servants with some people seconded from private industry and commerce. Its original task was to work with local authorities and the private sector to achieve the best use of current government expenditure. It was to make suggestions for modifying the policies of government departments or for switching resources between them. Above all it was to examine how additional resources might be used to reduce unemployment and to improve the social and economic life of big cities (cf. 'The Government's Response to Inner City Riots: the Minister for Merseyside and the Task Force.' Michael Parkinson and James Duffy in *Parliamentary Affairs*, Winter 1984, Vol. 37, no. 1). Michael Heseltine himself said later that his answer to Liverpool's problems was 'to make things happen . . . to work through existing organisations to achieve examples of how programmes could be better carried out to cope specifically with the problems that confronted us . . . so that the pattern might be repeated on a wider scale' (Michael Heseltine, 'Merseyside One Year On', speech in Liverpool, 17 December 1982).

The poor opportunities which black people faced were too deep-set to be shifted by modest short-term projects. The black community claims that nothing much has changed. A good instance of this may be found in a Manpower Services Commission study of the problems faced by ethnic minorities in Liverpool in their search for work. This study showed that in 1985 black people continued to be at a disadvantage compared with inner-city white people when it came to a job. On average black people need to go after twenty-five vacancies before securing a job, compared with white people in the same area having to pursue fifteen vacancies before achieving success ('Ethnic Minorities in Liverpool.' Report by Merseyside Area Manpower Board, Ethnic Minorities Sub-Group, December 1985). In addition, subtle forms of racism continue to limit what even well-disposed teachers or employers expect black people to be able to achieve. Black young people say plainly that they have been steered away from academic subjects towards music and athletics. The stereotype points that way.

Even so, we would argue that Michael Heseltine brought much new hope to the city, and it was very damaging to morale when he was moved to the Ministry of Defence less than eighteen months later. In the four years which have followed, four more Secretaries of State for the Environment have been appointed, each in turn giving steadily less priority to special responsibility for Merseyside. Much of the effectiveness of the Task Force has depended upon the importance attached to those responsibilities by the Secretary of State. The situation has deteriorated since the confrontational tactics of the Militant-led City Council resulted in Government ministers staying away from the area.

Michael Heseltine was a dynamic, sympathetic and impassioned advocate, and since his departure the city has increasingly lacked having a friend at court. He managed to convince almost everyone he met of his sincere commitment to relieving the plight of the under-privileged. He set out to break the 'culture of failure' which has been so damaging to the whole image of Liverpool. It was equally important to show others living outside the city that the cycle of failure *could* be broken. He was eager to produce visible signs of success: for example, the Albert Dock, the International Garden Festival, the Anglican Cathedral precinct site, Minster Court, Stockbridge Village, and refurbishing Lime Street Station. All these proved to be examples of good development in Merseyside and had the effect of encouraging the private and the public sector to place confidence in the city's capacity for renewal. When in 1986 Michael Heseltine resigned from the Cabinet over the Westland affair, he returned to the expression of his concern for Merseyside and for urban priority areas nationally. He made it clear that the private sector alone would never be able to find the necessary resources. He urged that there needed to be a major injection of public money before there would be any hope of attracting the necessary involvement of the private sector.

The Church leaders discussed with Michael Heseltine, during his first Merseyside walkabout, the importance of recognising and preserving local expressions of community life. In our opinion there was need for the encouragement of affirmation, validation and investment if such instances were to be developed. He agreed. We asked him if he was willing to risk giving money to projects in deeply hurt areas, where perhaps as much as fifty per cent of the finance offered might be wasted. He said that he was willing to take just such a risk, provided that the press did not make the position impossible.

STEPS TOWARDS HEALING

These first steps towards reconciliation and healing remain crucial for both Government and the Church. Somehow we have to try to bridge these wide gaps between economic and spiritual ideals and the harshness of reality. Reconciliation will not come about unless the people concerned can genuinely believe that they can have a say in their destiny, and that it is worth their while to try to play their part in the life of the community. There is no quick way forward in trying to secure the responsible participation of people who have for so long felt totally alienated from the conduct of their affairs. Where people have grown altogether distrustful of 'them' in the Town Hall, no matter what their party political complexion, the 'system' itself becomes suspect. Bitter experience has so alienated such people from the accepted way of the established authority that they no longer feel it worthwhile to respond to even genuine attempts to consult and involve. It is frustrating and sad when those anxious to tackle the problem discover that what they regard as their most rewarding offers are quite unacceptable because the whole system has lost credibility and even respectability.

The problem is not confined to relations with the Town Hall and all its works. There is a real lesson here for the Churches also. We must remember that many of these alienated people do not see any connection between the lifestyle, language and worship of the Churches and the frequently traumatic and anxious conditions in which they themselves live. For the institutional Church the first steps towards reconciliation must involve 'being there', close enough to where the troubles are to be sensitive to people's experiences and feelings. It means 'being there' in a listening kind of way, rather than standing back with all the answers. It means entering into an ongoing conversation and relationship, standing with people in causes which matter deeply to them.

BEING THERE

'Being there' in such a sensitive way must include respect for the experience and culture of the people of that neighbourhood. The truth is that sometimes in such areas the voice which is heard is that of men and women who have emigrated to other cultures, but who travel back to worship and sit on church or parish councils without having much empathy for the ways of the majority groups who have remained. We salute those Christian lay people who have determined to remain in an area of deprivation, and who desire that their witness be that of a Servant Church in a hurt city. We salute the increasing number of Religious sisters who are discovering new ministry as they abandon their large 'safe' institutions to share the life of the poor and the powerless in urban priority area parishes. We salute clergy whose quiet, persevering presence in those urban priority areas often provides the light of hope needed to recognise Christ in the life-and-death situations faced by ordinary folk. These heroes have learnt *how* to be present in areas of high risk as a source of strength and consolation to those who are in great, if unspectacular, need. It can mean 'being there' when secular issues are under discussion, attending endless meetings about community projects, being available to give advice, but more commonly just showing support. Experience, holiness and commitment have helped these men to understand the needs of those to whom their presence brings consolation and encouragement: being there with a family trying to respond to the arrival of a baby born out of wedlock; the sudden discovery that a teenager is hooked on heroin; the death of an old lady whose mourning descendants scarcely include one churchgoer. Such clergy know how to sit through the night, hearing confessions upstairs in a bedroom, as the conviviality of the wake continues downstairs. They even know how to prepare themselves to welcome all the family and friends to the church next day, conscious that they are unlikely to be there again until the next funeral.

Whether we call this phenomenon an unconscious faith or a feeling after God, a rumour of God or an echo of his voice, there seems little doubt that some toe-hold of faith and Christian values remains. The Church is very blind if it dismisses all this as mere superstitious 'folk religion'. In many deprived areas, shared hardships and discrimination can produce a remarkable degree of solidarity. Being 'members one of another' becomes a living reality in such circumstances. The people know how to respond together to injustice, grief and joy. In face of a crisis, especially where a child is concerned, their generosity and mutual support are immediate. Yet such people are often not on parish electoral rolls or visiting lists. They will often be hesitant, if not actually reluctant, to admit to having a faith. Somehow they see little connection between their faithful ways and what they understand as the formal teaching or disciplines of the institutional Church.

The difficulty is not all one way. Sometimes clergy may be troubled in conscience about what may be reasonably required of the 'unchurched'. There can be a real problem about having to ask for a commitment which seems beyond the capacity of such people, or at least beyond what may be reasonably expected of them. One must not ignore the movement of grace, but it can be difficult to achieve the right balance between upholding reasonable requirements and being sensitive to the circumstances which have led to an almost unconscious alienation from what churchpeople take for granted. This situation can arise, for example, over the requirement of solemn promises at baptism. No longer is a church ceremony regarded as almost necessary for respectability. The same situation is increasingly apparent with regard to marriage. Generation after generation has in the past been led to expect the Church to meet its needs by a celebration of the great events of birth, marriage and death. But now, *not* to seek the blessing of the Church can for some people be almost a matter of integrity. For the clergy to take a hard line with regard to the future commitment of such people may be to fly in the face of contemporary opinion.

No priest wishes to lead people into meaningless mockery. A great deal of patience is required in helping young people especially to face their burdens of responsibility. It is particularly sad when, in the current atmosphere of instability, those who judge themselves failures in today's highly organised league of success see the Church as yet one more authoritarian organisation, insisting upon their filling in the right form or repeating the right formula. It is an area of high sensitivity, if not exactly a new situation. One is tempted to wonder whether St Joseph made a good job of the census forms at Bethlehem when Mary was caught away from home as her baby became due.

These real-life situations can be an opportunity to close the gap, or they can be the occasion for deepening the wound. Surely our task is to 'be there' for the healing, trying as far as possible to be close enough to share the common experiences of ordinary daily life, helping people to recognise the language and manner in which Christ speaks to them in their human, family and community relationships. We do not have to take Christ into such circumstances, as if this was to him enemy territory. He has been present there from the beginning, beckoning to his closest followers to come and join him. In our listening role we can discover new truths about what he stands for in such situations. But the gap between religion and life, between the institution and the 'unchurched' will not be closed until the estranged and alienated are able to recognise Christ in the circumstances, joyful or sad, of their daily lives.

Whether the alienation be from the Government or the Church, save for a miracle there will be no instantaneous healing. There has to be a continuing relationship, with on-going conversation. The professionals need to join in authentic dialogue. They need to be challenged and at times to make clear their own deep feelings on the matter in question. The Church, in its calling to be a priestly people, needs to create the context in which different groups of people can speak freely, even if it takes a long time for those who feel themselves powerless to begin to find their voices. It is not always an easy or comfortable process. Professional people, politicians and priests must be prepared for the fact that they are likely at first to hear angry words.

We not only salute such clergy (and laity – for they are also involved in this process) for being there and staying there. We readily acknowledge how we ourselves have leaned greatly upon them for their advice, their insights and the contacts they have painstakingly built up over the years.

BLACK PEOPLE IN DECISION-MAKING

The report *Faith in the City* dealt specifically with the sense of estrangement felt by so many.

> This sense of alienation provides a social context in which the preaching of the gospel becomes urgent and relevant. Those who are alienated can identify with the forsakenness of Christ on the cross, and may the more easily come to believe that this same Christ now assures us of direct access to God and eternal life with him, if, stripped of our own power, status and pretensions, we come to him in penitence, faith and love. But this gospel is also one which must be witnessed to by the corporate life of the Church.
>
> (*Faith in the City*, p. 59ff.)

The Church must show in its confession of the faith, in the language of the liturgy and in the way it celebrates the liturgy, in the process by which it takes decisions, in its ordained ministry, in its involvement in social and political issues, that it stands for a gospel of righteousness and love. So, for example, women must not feel excluded by a language which alienates in the confession of faith; black people must not feel excluded from ministry or decision-making; the poor must know that the Church is on their side by the way the Church lives and acts in society. If the gospel is to be seen as a gospel of reconciliation, this must be proclaimed in every aspect of the Church's life.

Our insistence on the need to be close to people in their ordinary lives is often mistaken as playing down the importance of good liturgy. This is far from the truth, as should be evident from our two cathedrals. Worship in inner-city communities should be an inspiration. It should underwrite spiritual commitment and help to bring reality to dreams and ideals. But if it says nothing about the domestic violence or the leaking roof to which many will go home, it can leave people with a sense of inferiority. The harsh realities of life, and the people who do something to remove them, need to be recognised in prayers, sermons or notices. Forgotten or excluded, they will not be shared. Alienation is carried a stage further if people feel that they must hide from the clergy and the local church their crises, their debts, their court cases, the troubles in their marriages, their fears for their children in trouble.

DAVID SHEPPARD: When Faith in the City *was published, many black Christians watched with great interest to see if the Church of England would carry through the recommendations contained in the report. They felt deeply hurt when the Standing Committee of the General Synod, while bringing forward several recommendations, explicitly said that they did not at present support the proposal to establish a Standing Committee for Black Anglican Concerns. The Archbishop's Commission had proposed the setting up of a standing committee, with a majority of black members, accountable to the black Christian community and with power to question all the work of the different boards in Church House, Westminster. For many members of the General Synod it was the first time they had faced such a proposal. The advice of the standing committee was carried by a narrow majority. The pain felt by the black community at this reverse communicated itself to members of the General Synod. This and the consequent confusion proved highly educational. Many discussions followed in which members from 'comfortable Britain' had for the first time to ask themselves what our Church looked like to black Christians, who wanted to belong to it. Nine months later a modified proposal was carried by 360 votes to 39.*

Black people have often felt that they are tolerated in church life only up to certain ratios and certain levels. As they see black people elected or appointed to council or office in parish, diocese or nationally in the Church, they begin to believe that we genuinely want to make space for them so that we may receive the gifts they have to bring. The same is true with regard to candidates for the priesthood and the episcopate.

DEREK WORLOCK: In the Roman Catholic Archdiocese we have a trickle of vocations from Liverpool's black community. But I have still to look forward to ordaining a black Liverpudlian. The course of training is long and none has yet found his way into the forty per cent of the starters who eventually reach ordination. Should the training be different? Is there a danger that this would merely be seen as lowering standards? It is not an easy question. At the international level the whole picture has changed in the years in which I have been a bishop. As exemplified in the International Synod of Bishops, the face of the Roman Catholic Church, which was in the past overwhelmingly European, is now no longer so, any more than is the case with the United Nations.

The suspicion with which Liverpool black people regard local politicians goes back a long way. When in 1980 all parties agreed to adopt an equal opportunities policy, it seemed that at last persistent campaigning had borne fruit. A Liaison Committee was set up, comprising nine councillors, officers of the City Council and twelve representatives of black organisations. For the first time it was possible for Liverpool black people to have access to the decision-making processes of the Council. The chief executive came to meetings and encouraged other senior officers to be present. In the private sector determined attempts were made after 1981 to make sure that jobs were available in stores, offices, manufacturing and service industries. We believe that in most instances their efforts were genuine. In fact many expressed their disappointment that black people did not immediately respond. The uncomfortable truth is that suspicion, based on long-term exclusion, dies hard. Both in secular and church life there has to be consistent intervention, together with careful monitoring, to see that opportunities are genuinely available and actually taken up.

At its first meeting in January 1986, the Merseyside and Region Churches Ecumenical Assembly passed a resolution calling for the appointment of two officers in the field of community and race relations. The main thrust was to be in an educational programme, to try to change attitudes in the largely white parts of the Church.

Plainly there would be difficulties in raising the money and in helping white members of the Churches to begin to acknowledge that they *themselves* have a problem, but that they have more power than they think to improve opportunities for black people. We soon discovered through a working party that there were difficulties also among the black people of Liverpool 8, who were very suspicious of a project which seemed to be coming from outside their area. We had to heed once more those truths about listening and being seen to listen, about entering into an on-going conversation and offering to black people a real share in decision-making. But relationship implies both sides. At the same time we had from the early stages to find ways of ensuring adequate representation from those white areas which might in due time receive such an educational programme.

THE LAW CENTRE

Soon after the 1981 riots, community leaders from Liverpool 8 approached us for help in setting up a centre where potentially explosive issues might be defused and where legal advice might be available. Even though it would not necessarily have been our priority, it seemed important that we respond positively. Accordingly, we began a whole series of meetings at which the Church leaders of five denominations sat across a table, not knowing from one meeting to the next which of the black community representatives they were to meet. It was evident that the community leaders were anxious about the issue of control. We made it clear that we hoped that control and management would be in the hands of a body elected from an annual meeting of people from the neighbourhood. For our part we undertook to help to raise the money. When this had been done, we would not walk away. We would try to act responsibly in partnership with them. Gradually suspicion gave way to increasing trust. At one meeting, two members of the Liverpool 8 Defence Committee described how hurt they had been by the crude attacks made upon them in certain sections of the popular press. Then they remembered and, looking across the table at us, added, 'And you took some flak too.'

Eventually a constitution was worked out by which an elected management committee of some twenty members would include three nominated by the Churches, with one representative from the Liverpool Law Society. We accepted the more detailed recommendations of a joint working party and in due time suitable premises were found. All this meant for the pair of us two substantial sets of meetings: one route took us to government ministers, trusts and companies to help us raise the money needed to launch and maintain the Centre; the other route took us to meet a wide range of people in Westminster and Liverpool so that, before the public launch, we might explain what we hoped the Law Centre would do. When at last the launch took place in the spring of the following year, it was heartening to hear the appointed chairman say that he 'wished to thank the Church leaders for the respect they have shown for the community'.

In the years which have followed, the Liverpool 8 Law Centre has faced many difficulties and anxieties, not least about adequate funding. Its committee has been plagued by long delays and indecision about grants. It has had to face changes in government policies, as have all the fifty-five Law Centres in Britain. At times the Law Centre has stumbled, but on balance it has meant that some people have for the very first time come to realise that the law can be a friend rather than a threat. One young Liverpool-born black man worked hard in the establishment of the Law Centre on a voluntary basis. Then he was not to be seen for quite a long time. At last, one of us met him and asked what he was doing. 'My work at the Law Centre made me realise that I needed an education,' he replied. 'I am on an access course now and hope that I may get a place at university.'

The solicitors at the Law Centre have had heavy work-loads. This, and the fact that many cases have been referred to local solicitors, has shown how great is the need. It has emphasised the importance of making legal services available more widely than is customary. But the Law Centre has also served as a place where justice in small matters as well as in large is taken seriously, and where it has proved possible to begin a more normal negotiation and relationship with the community police. It was an encouragement to both of us, after our experience in the disturbances of 1985, to hear the Deputy Chief Constable say how much he valued the presence of the Law Centre as a meeting-point where contact could be made with responsible representatives of the community. Our own experience that night, described earlier in this chapter, underlined the point.

MILITANTS AND THE BLACK CAUCUS

When the City Council established its Liaison Committee in 1980, the Community Relations Council duly organised meetings at which the twelve representatives of minority ethnic groups were elected by those organisations which had made the submission for the equal opportunities policy. It was agreed that these representatives would report back regularly to the wider group which had elected them. Because they also met together, they quickly became known as the Black Caucus. Further elections took place in 1983 when over seventy race-relations groups and local black organisations were invited. Authentic representation was being taken very seriously. Of the seventeen members of the Liaison Committee as a whole, nine were Liverpool-born black people, three Africans, two Asians, two Chinese and one Jew. There were seven women and ten men.

The Liaison Committee soon ran into other conflicts. For nine months a typists' strike prevented any letters being sent out from the Municipal Offices, so there were no meetings convened. Under the Liberal leadership economies were made which meant that several posts involving the black organisations were 'frozen'. The Liberal leader of the Council proposed that the Liaison Committee should examine ways by which the number of black people employed by the City Council would be steadily increased to reflect the percentage of black people living in the city. This was challenged by the Labour group, with Derek Hatton speaking of the need to increase job opportunities for both white and black people. The ideological views of the Militant Tendency became the dominant factor in the race-relations policy of the District Labour Party. They opposed affirmative actions which set out to redress the disadvantage of particular groups. They insisted that all deprivation stemmed from class divisions, claiming that all positive discrimination or affirmative action for black people would merely divert attention from the class struggle.

When Labour won a clear majority on the City Council in 1983, the Militant Derek Hatton became chairman of the Liaison Committee. The following year the Commission for Racial Equality published a report on race and housing in Liverpool, showing that black people were receiving a significantly smaller share of the better grade council housing in South Liverpool, where most of them live. Careful monitoring of housing lettings was recommended as the most vital link in achieving an effective change. Even before the press launch of this report, to which we contributed a foreword, the Council declared its opposition to monitoring. They claimed that their policies were fair and would remove any discrimination.

The most bitter struggle lay ahead. In October 1984 the Council agreed to implement the proposal, for long advanced by the Liverpool black organisations, that a Central Race Relations Unit be established, with a Principal Race Relations Adviser. Three Black Caucus members were included in the appointing group, together with the NALGO trade union adviser, six Labour councillors and one Liberal councillor. The Labour councillors alone voted for Sampson Bond, who had a post in the Surveyor's Department of Brent Council but who had no previous experience in race-relations work. It became known that he was a member of Militant Tendency. He was chosen by the Labour group in preference to applicants from the Liverpool black community. Derek Hatton claimed that the major issue was to appoint someone who would support Council policy and that this could not be said of the candidate from Liverpool. The three Black Caucus members and the trade union adviser walked out of the meeting. Next day, Derek Hatton's office was occupied by black protestors and he signed a statement agreeing to reverse the appointment. The following evening the District Labour Party meeting abrogated this, claiming that the signature was given under duress. The appointment of Sampson Bond stood.

Now the battle lines were drawn. Members of the black organis-ations refused to attend any meeting at which Bond was present. The councillors refused to meet them without him. Deadlock ensued. Quite early on we had asked to meet the leadership of the Council to plead the case with them. Derek Hatton and Tony Mulhearn met us together with the leader of the Council, Council-lor John Hamilton. We asked that the post be re-advertised but our plea was politely but firmly turned down. Months later, as the bitter struggle continued, it was suggested that we put our 'two honest brokers' reputation to the test. Both sides agreed to meet informally under our chairmanship for 'talks about talks'. We had several meetings but in the end it was clear that the councillors were under instructions not to move on the question of Sampson Bond. We saw first hand the tools of political power, with patron-age and grant being used to promote the Militant cause. We were both present when the offer was made of three additional posts, with the necessary finance, for the Merseyside Community Re-lations Council in return for the recognition of Sampson Bond. That such an offer was firmly rejected showed both the strength of feeling and also the solidarity of the Liverpool black community on this issue.

The price was high. Government resources, which the city urgently needed, were not taken up. No official money for minority ethnic groups' projects came into Liverpool for more than two years. On several occasions we found that grants from different bodies were being held back from black organisations. When we pressed for reasons, we were told horrific stories of the record and character of some of those supporting the particular project. We insisted on names being named and specific allegations. We then made enquiries and found that the deliberate 'smears' were untrue. On one occasion we found that the Merseyside Action Group had warned the leadership of the Merseyside County Council against making a grant to the Law Centre. No one then knew who the Merseyside Action Group was. Later it turned out to be made up largely of black Militant Tendency supporters, imported from outside the area.

The stereotype that black people are immigrants and therefore young, has meant that 'colour-blind' policies have missed the elderly black population, long present in Liverpool. We meet black people whose grandparents came to the city in the 1890s or before. Yet the records of the Liverpool City Council Social Services for 1983 show that only seven elderly black people were to be found in 1,143 units of accommodation for the elderly; only nine were receiving 'meals on wheels' out of a total of 4,553; six out of 1,038 in day-care facilities, and eight in residential homes out of a total of 1,391. The true proportion should have been in the region of seven per cent. One last example: the Home Office had agreed to find seventy-five per cent, through Section 11 funding, for some eighteen posts in the field of race relations. All were frozen through the action of Militants on the City Council (cf. *The Racial Policies of Militant in Liverpool*, Runnymede Trust, 1986).

ALIENATION OF OTHER URBAN GROUPS

We have concentrated on the particular story of Liverpool's black people, for their sense of alienation and rejection by the powers that be is very clear. But the truth is that there are also large groups of white people, both in the inner city and (twice as many) in the outer estates, who have a comparable experience, even though their anger is not so explicit. Without doubt they know a real degree of poverty, and have a sense of powerlessness, exclusion and humiliation.

People in 'comfortable Britain' are apt to argue, 'Why cannot *they* do something about it themselves? *They* need to work harder. I have done so. Why can't *they*?' These people find it difficult to acknowledge that there is poverty in our country. Of course it is not the starvation poverty of the Third World. But we have created patterns of living where gadgets, which were once luxuries, have become necessities. These are the pressure points in many areas today. If we take an outer housing estate as an example, here we see a neighbourhood created with the shops so far away that a refrigerator in the home becomes necessary. Otherwise people are at the mercy of the mobile shops which come around selling at cruelly high prices. A neighbourhood has been created where a washing-machine and dryer are needed because it is unsafe to hang out the laundry, and there is no private garden or yard; where a car is needed or the use of taxis, because the bus service is rare and expensive; and where there are only the most expensive forms of central heating, with the unemployed staying indoors much of the time.

In these outer estates are large numbers of families who feel powerless to make decisions which seriously affect their own lives. Unemployment excludes them from the normal world of work and they often become dependent on officials at the Supplementary Benefit Office of the Department of Health and Social Security. Their very honesty appears suspect. In the office, chairs are screwed to the floor; leaflets and notices are behind a sheet of perspex nailed to the wall; the staff are separated from the clients by screens of steel and glass. The whole setting seems to proclaim that this is a place of mistrust for second-class citizens.

All this adds up to a strong sense of alienation from the mainstream of British life. This is made plain by vandalism and graffiti which are destructive of pride in the area. Many of the elderly reach the stage when they are scared to go out because of the hateful attacks made on them and the violence which is all too common. Where attacks on persons or property are concerned, the police are only able to proceed if witnesses will come forward. Sadly individuals are often unwilling to do this; and in the newer estates there is not even the support of neighbourly solidarity, because people do not know each other in the same way.

Drug addiction has added dramatically to these fears. Desperation for a 'fix' often leads to robbery. The number of heroin addicts passing through the hands of the police rose between 1982 and 1984 to two thousand in a year. At that stage the Mersey Regional Health Authority asked us to take the initiative in calling together in a forum the various organisations and support groups trying to work in this very tragic sphere. Now a Standing Committee on Anti-Drug Abuse meets regularly and there are signs that the number of new cases may be falling slightly. But from our contacts with parent support groups, it seems evident that, while there is success in helping dependants to come off drugs, it is still very difficult to prevent their return to them, often because of the desperate situation in which so many of them appear to exist.

This general picture of alienation is widespread and varied. For the Church especially there is the particular role of healing. But for this to be effective we have constantly to be seeking new ways to ensure that alienated and hurt people may have an effective voice and share in making decisions which affect their future and that of their neighbours. Both Church and secular bodies must be willing to make space for unaccustomed and unexpected groups to have their say, even if at least initially the voice is an angry one and unused to having an opportunity to express itself freely in our company.

9 HOUSING IS FOR PEOPLE

On their drive into Liverpool for the celebration of the Queen's Jubilee in 1977, visiting journalists following the Royal party spotted relatively few signs of celebration. The people were out in the streets in fair number, but the bunting and the street parties had been much more in evidence in the Lancashire towns. But there was something to celebrate in Liverpool, and signs of it, if you knew where to look. In Upper Parliament Street in Toxteth housing associations had put up their notices, promising to rehabilitate the crumbling elegance of the Georgian houses which had long since been split up into flats, flatlets and single rooms.

THE HOLE-IN-THE-HEART CITY

At that time rehabilitation rather than demolition was the order of the day. The bulldozer, preparing the way for a road to the now under-used docks, had created a hole-in-the-heart city. The dispersal of the former dockside communities to green-field estates had left behind a disproportionate number of old people and disadvantaged families unkindly labelled 'inadequate'. But now something was to be done. Shelter Neighbourhood Action Plan (SNAP) in Liverpool had been nationally acclaimed. It argued that the decay which led to demolition could be turned around. The old landmarks could be preserved and neighbourhood communities revived. National policies made it possible to declare housing action areas in which extensive modernisation and repairs could be funded.

When we arrived in Liverpool, the hole-in-the-heart legacy was all too apparent and the dreams of a better way of life in the outer estates showed little sign of fulfilment. We began to suggest that the limbs of the body would never be healthy until the hole-in-the-heart had been attended to. Everyone had agreed that the appalling slum conditions needed to be vigorously tackled. In what was called a 'crusade', thirty-three thousand dwellings, declared by the

Medical Officer of Health to be unfit for human habitation, were demolished between 1966 and 1973. The pressure to shift the huge waiting-lists ran into the equally tough pressure of financial yardsticks. There was perhaps an unspoken view that a lower standard of housing would be tolerated by those who desperately wanted a move from their current deplorable accommodation. Between the two pressures some undoubtedly closed their minds to the need for quality in building and for the provision of all-round facilities for community living. If something had to be sacrificed in the bid to move people out of the slums, then standards of construction and variety of design might have to give way to speed and volume. Up went the monster blocks to replace what was remembered as the overcrowded homeliness of the back-to-backs. There were the usual problems of the lifts in the high-rise blocks, but it was not just a housing problem. The new constructions appeared to have forgotten local culture: the need for ease of communication between people whose strength had been neighbourliness and mutual concern. Now there were signs that the people who had been left behind were suffering from what some Americans call 'the hedgehog syndrome'. Stacked one above another, their need to communicate was severely thwarted. The higher the high-rise, generally speaking, the less the communication. However dramatic or skilful the design was, the sheer scale was inhuman. Housing policies are not simply arguments between one ideology and another. Housing is for people.

DEREK WORLOCK: As I visited the parishes, trying to learn Liverpool and its people, I used to ask the local parishioners to take me around to visit their sick and their very high proportion of geriatric housebound neighbours. One Sunday afternoon in the south docks area an elderly man – a proud member of St Malachy's parish, where the survivors call themselves Malachites to distinguish themselves from their fellow Catholics in St Finbar's and St Pat's – was showing me around what was left of his parish, where once there had been disgraceful overcrowding but real community life.

He was leading me past acres of rubble and tip from buildings pulled down to build the new Jerusalem, which at least at that stage had not materialised: later the Garden Festival and the Albert Dock were to add lustre to the surrounding parishes. Suddenly he stopped and pointed to a heap of broken bricks. 'That was us,' he said, 'that was where we were before we were demolished.' Perhaps if something of communal benefit had stood where the demolition had taken place, he could have understood and accepted the sacrifice which had been asked of him. But no, his past, his memories of home life, no doubt coloured over the arches of the years, lay in a meaningless heap before him. No matter how disgraceful the conditions in which he had had to live, for him that demolition was still desecration. The demolition of a family home more often than not leaves behind a human wound. Surgery leaves a scar. Its purpose and the need for it must be explained to the patient.

It was a sign of the times in Liverpool that we should have looked for hope to the voluntary movement in the form of housing associations. Receiving public money through the Housing Corporation, they were able to act without taking funds from the local authority. At that stage there was no council housing building programme in Liverpool. The private sector felt unable to help very much, save in the more favoured suburbs, and mortgages were exceedingly difficult to obtain. With the City Council's lending resources cut back by more than half, in the year 1975/6 more than four hundred applications for corporation mortgages were redirected to building societies. Three-quarters of those applications were rejected. In some cases the condition of the property was the reason, but more usually the reason was the location of the house.

For most of the years between 1973 and 1983, a Liberal–Conservative coalition was in power in Liverpool City Council. To encourage businesses to remain in the area, the Council's policy was to keep rates as low as possible. In fact, to the subsequent detriment of the rate support grant, the City Council's expenditure on local services at that time was substantially lower than the Government's guideline figures for all local authorities. When the Inner City Partnership arrangement offered more resources to the city, the decision was taken to direct as much as possible to building advance factories and to improving the environment. When, during what was called the Heseltine Arborification of Merseyside, a large number of new trees was planted, and improved lighting was provided, there was criticism that so many housing repairs had been left undone, and that local residents had not been consulted about their order of priorities.

During that same period the Liverpool Liberals encouraged private developers to build some 'first-buy' estates in Liverpool. They also encouraged the development of housing co-operatives and tried to work in close co-operation with housing associations. The three largest such housing associations were Co-operative Development Services, Liverpool Housing Trust and Merseyside Improved Housing, and by 1985 they had grown steadily to provide between them some 16,500 houses. Each year they were re-housing 1,900 households. A visit we paid to the Liverpool Housing Trust showed that it was possible to rehabilitate whole communities. One whole street had been compulsorily purchased and handed over to the Housing Trust. A very challenging but rewarding task had to be carried out. The houses in that street, by no means the worst of their period, had been built without damp-courses; the bricks had been left in the sun to dry rather than being properly baked; accordingly they were porous. In effect the whole work of rehabilitation involved putting an entire new framework inside the existing walls. The result was that outwardly the street remained as the residents had known it in the past. Once the work was completed the people who had been living in that street previously were able to move back into their own homes.

All these happenings were a source of encouragement. They made a strong contribution to the renewal of the city. The housing co-operatives established in the 1970s had by 1984 provided houses for some two thousand householders. But the truth was that it was not on a large enough scale to keep pace with the steady deterioration of the rest of the public sector housing in the city.

DAVID SHEPPARD: When I made a parish visit to Norris Green, which is made up for the most part of council housing from the 1930s, I was confronted by the question, 'Why cannot local young couples be offered housing within their own district, so that they can bring their own gifts and commitment to the community of which they have been part?' It is always a cause of sadness when marriage and the prospect of a family means that a young couple have to leave the community to which they would be likely to look for support in the early years of their married life. In this particular case the answer of the local authority was that the pressure for good housing in other parts of the city was still so heavy that families with the most 'points' from all over the city must be given priority. In a city the size of Liverpool, even with a fairly sophisticated points system to govern the allocation of accommodation, one comprehensive housing list can be destructive of local community bonds and loyalties.

DISILLUSION IN DREAMLAND

Next door to the Liberal-run Liverpool of that period was Labour-run Knowsley. There the 'Corpy' (Corporation) was no more popular. Labour was blamed for the massive urban renewal of Liverpool and the slum clearance programme of the 1960s. With little consultation with the people concerned, longstanding communities in the inner city had been broken up and sent out to the perimeter estates, some still in the city of Liverpool, more in Knowsley. Even those who had been prepared to 'give it a go', mindful of some of the shocking living conditions in pre-war Liverpool, rapidly became disillusioned. The dream of new housing in green-field estates in healthy surroundings was soon shattered. A resident of Kirkby remarked that 'people live here in a ghastly mistake'. The credibility of politicians and planners alike suffered. The largest and perhaps most telling example of graffiti we have seen was painted one night in mammoth letters down the side of a tower block in an outer estate. It read quite simply: 'To Guy Fawkes, the only man to enter Parliament with honest intent.'

There was none the less great variety in what council housing offered. In one large estate, the flat-dwellers formed a tenants' association separate from that formed by those who lived in houses with their own small gardens. We have visited high-rise blocks of flats where good caretakers have made sure that lifts are clean and in working order, where tenants have put carpet down on the landing, and where neighbourliness has meant that people living there feel safe and supported. On the other hand, a walk through a 1970s estate of small houses, where it should have been easier to create such an atmosphere, could leave the impression that the place had been shot to pieces by vandals.

A local answer to the inevitable question, 'Why?' was that the tenants had simply been gathered together there from the city's comprehensive housing list, with the result that they were all living next to strangers. In strange surroundings they had lost their mutual regard for neighbours – and perhaps, too, that sense of loyalty to locality and to the 'externals' we have mentioned earlier and which were so strong a feature of inner-city life. Too often residents, surrounded by deplorable conditions, only felt able to intervene with a view to correcting things, for example, in giving evidence against vandals, if they were confident that they could trust their neighbours to support them.

Disillusionment with the housing of the 1960s has resulted from poor design, poor repairs, mistaken allocation policies, and uncertain reputation due to the erratic history of the estates in question. The original dream of 'streets in the sky', or of large-scale, well-planned and adequately provided 'country' estates, was based on an idea of self-contained communities, each with its own shops, entertainment, pubs, launderettes and community facilities built into the original design or plan. But constraints on costs meant that local authorities felt obliged to cut such provisions out of their schemes. The private sector not surprisingly often waited to see what market would develop before introducing shops. The vital first years, when the sense of new community needed to develop, were often enough to destroy confidence in the estate.

As we have already indicated, allocating housing on a points system, giving highest priority to low-income families with young children, and drawn from all over the city, often resulted in very unbalanced communities. There was little of the compensating neighbourliness to help sustain the disproportionate number of households facing one difficulty or another. Once an estate has achieved a bad name it is exceedingly difficult to reverse the slide into being regarded as a 'hard to let' area. When that happens, it is all too easy for councillors and officials to start blaming 'problem families' for all that goes wrong. A vicious circle is quickly established, but the problems do not all come from the tenants. More often than not they have been given no opportunity to share in decisions made about their estate, and the process of alienation (of which we wrote in the previous chapter) is set in motion.

Many of the complaints are related to poor maintenance and to a slow response to the obvious and often urgent need of repairs. A fair example of a typical complaint was that the glass front door of a flat was smashed. It was more than twelve months before the glass was replaced and the door mended. Waiting for something to happen presents an additional problem to that of security. The occupant may decide that he can wait no longer and try to carry out his own repairs. He will be sharply criticised by his neighbours, who will claim that the Council should not be let off the hook, nor avoid its responsibilities. In 1984 one estate manager told us that on certain parts of the estate no maintenance had been carried out in the seventeen years since that estate's completion. (Incidentally, headteachers may tell you much the same about repairs and maintenance due in their schools.) In Liverpool the efficiency of the Council's direct labour force is also a factor.

It is not surprising that in certain estates tenants apply to be transferred elsewhere. It is alleged that a high proportion of these applications become 'lost' because of the extreme difficulty in re-letting the vacated unit. We would have to say that throughout our years in Merseyside maintenance and repairs have received too low a priority. Both central and local government are vulnerable to the charge of believing that more votes are to be won by claiming the number of new homes built than by maintaining in good repair those which already exist.

The frustration arising from poor management and undue delays in dealing with applications for a transfer has led to stories of tenants setting fire to their own flats or maisonettes in order to force the Council to rehouse them. For the same motive roofs have been stripped of their tiles. At one time some groups of tenants organised themselves to take the Council to court for failure to carry out repairs. Campaigns were started to demand the demolition of some of the hated blocks of flats. When one of the young priests in the area became involved in such a campaign, some of the councillors in their anger moved a resolution that he be reported to his bishop – all this much to the embarrassment of the leadership of the Council, who came to see the bishop to explain the difficulties they faced. They were most anxious to show that socialism need not mean inefficiency.

Progress was made subsequently in several estates by 'capping' the walk-up blocks: that is, by removing the top two storeys and re-roofing in a more efficient manner. This method has produced some very attractive terraces in Liverpool and Knowsley. 'Safe Neighbourhood' units have shown how estates can be made more secure by closing off walk-ways or side-roads by which thieves and vandals can more easily escape. Some of the large concrete jungles have been divided up into smaller more manageable units, where some form of community existence becomes possible. A few years ago a new word appeared in Liverpool language after some multi-storeyed blocks of flats were sold off to a private building organisation, which decapitated them, refurbished them, changed their name and had little difficulty in selling them to local families. The process became known as 'Barrattisation', but local party-politicians soon developed other ideas about that.

A NEW STRATEGY

When Mrs Margaret Thatcher's Conservative Government came to power in 1979, a very different philosophy set fresh markers in the housing debate. The main plank in the Government's housing strategy was the encouragement of home ownership. To achieve this, council tenants were to be given the 'right to buy'; private developers were encouraged to build for sale to a wider market; and every reasonable financial encouragement was given to increase the possibility of home ownership. At the same time public expenditure on housing sustained larger cuts than any other service.

The 'right to buy' was at first resisted by Knowsley District Council. When it was made clear that the law required the Council to comply, they duly co-operated. Soon they felt able to acknowledge that many council tenants welcomed this opportunity to purchase their own home. In very large estates like Kirkby, the 'right to buy' has changed whole streets. New front doors, bow windows, well-kept gardens, proclaim that their owners have a stake in improving the neighbourhood. The long-term results of a wide-scale response to this policy could be far-reaching. It seems much more likely that a good proportion of young couples, who have achieved well in school, will choose to stay in their own neighbourhood by buying a home there.

A more mixed community will generally be a more healthy community. Yet it must be appreciated that, pushed too far, this policy could add to the divisions in a district unless there is the balance of a corresponding development of good council housing. For predictably it is the best council housing which has been sold into private ownership. As a rule it is almost without exception houses with their own gardens. If the desirable estates with good houses all become owner-occupied, leaving those families who can afford only rented accommodation no choice other than what is left in the less popular estates, then the divisions in the general community will become deeper, and the segregation between ghetto estates more pronounced.

The situation regarding housing co-operatives is also relevant here. They provide an important opportunity for their members to have a stake in their community. But they are not likely to accept a full proportion of families who have rent arrears or who are for one reason or another unpopular. If the councils are left with only the most unpopular tenants to house and only the least desirable housing stock to offer, the problem of ghetto estates will be compounded. The report of the Inquiry into British Housing, which was chaired by the Duke of Edinburgh, gave a number of clear objectives. One was 'to avoid the creation of "ghettos" of poor and disadvantaged people, concentrated on specific estates or in particular areas . . . We believe this division of communities leads to alienation, hostility and resentment, and we see housing policy as fundamental to overcoming it' (*Inquiry into British Housing Report*, National Federation of Housing Associations, 1985, p. 8).

A major part of the initiative of Michael Heseltine, as Minister for Merseyside, was to encourage private sector interests, banks, building societies, developers and builders, to come into urban priority areas. Some took over 'hard to let' blocks, refurbished them, strengthened security, introduced porters and ansaphones, and in this way were able to offer desirable flats for sale. But the largest of his initiatives resulted in Knowsley District Council's selling a large council estate, Cantril Farm, to a private consortium. On-site management of the newly-named Stockbridge Village immediately effected an improvement in repairs and maintenance. Since then, rows of houses and maisonettes have been altered to produce closes in which houses face each other and through which cars cannot be driven. Where previously residents pestered the Council for transfer, many now clearly wish to stay.

It is very important that this experiment should not fail. Five years on, it has needed substantial fresh injections of government money; and the most difficult parts of the estate have not yet been tackled. Proper monitoring of this experiment must include accurate statistics of those who have been decanted from this chosen area to neighbouring council estates. For unless the latter are also improved over the next ten years, Stockbridge Village, instead of helping to raise the quality of life throughout the district, will merely have sharpened the divisions between successful and unpopular estates.

Ian Gow, when Minister of Housing, made a bold claim for the government housing policies in 1983: 'We have opened up choice. And choice is at the centre of liberty.' We are both fully in agreement about the importance of offering choice in housing. But we have to ask how many people are in fact presented with a choice by government policies. Merseyside as a whole has 19·7 per cent unemployment. In each of its urban priority areas the percentage of unemployed people is considerably higher. For a brief period in the early 1980s, there was discussion of the suggestion that someone on supplementary benefit might be able to obtain a mortgage. At that time we met Tom King, who had just been appointed Minister for Merseyside (the second of five Secretaries of State for the Environment between 1981 and 1986). We argued that if home ownership was the key to all housing problems, why not go the whole way and make it possible for unemployed people to own their homes? He immediately made it clear that this was not acceptable, even though he agreed that no stigma should be attached to unemployment. But he saw unemployment as a temporary phenomenon, and feared that offering home ownership to everyone would have the effect of cutting the nerve which makes people seek work.

Our experience is clear that poor people in Merseyside have little or no choice about where they live. Often the situation is that they never wanted to live in their present home, would love to move, but have no choice in the matter. The 'right to buy' council housing, and the development of cheaper housing in the city, certainly help to bring about a more mixed community. But if there is to be any choice for those who cannot afford to buy, there needs to be also a vigorous programme of public sector housing. That must include fresh council house building and the provision of efficient council house repairs. Further possibilities of choice can be offered through grants to housing associations and co-operatives. But for poor people in general freedom of choice over housing is still seriously restricted.

A MORAL ISSUE

In February 1985 the Roman Catholic Bishops' Conference of England and Wales published a report entitled *Housing is a Moral Issue*. It claimed that poor housing conditions affected human dignity as well as health. The rightful privacy and reasonable independence of the family were at stake. Bearing in mind the poor state of the nation's housing stock on the one hand and national resources on the other, the bishops argued that the priority given to housing was a matter of urgent moral concern.

DEREK WORLOCK: After the report had been published I corresponded with Ian Gow, at that time Minister for Housing. In answer to the report he wrote:

> *If housing is a moral issue, then so too are health and personal social services, social security and education, which together take up more than half of public expenditure. Some would add other services, including defence. So I do not think that by describing housing as a moral issue, it means necessarily that it should be given a higher priority.*

> *I replied: 'Given the fundamental nature of housing need, it is necessary to challenge on moral grounds both the high proportion of cut-backs which the housing programme has borne relative to other programmes, and the way in which the cut-back is distributed within the field of housing.' Taking the official figures for the years 1983/4, compared with what was planned for 1987/8, I pointed out that public expenditure on social security was to increase by twenty-five per cent; defence by twenty-two per cent; education by six per cent. By contrast*

public expenditure on housing was to decrease during that same period by nineteen per cent. In the league of expenditure on moral issues, housing seemed scarcely to rank as a high priority.

Ian Gow's answer stressed government support for home ownership. He added that 'more resources could be made available either by increasing the total of public expenditure or by a reallocation within existent public expenditure'. The Government was firmly opposed to increasing the total of public expenditure on housing. 'The long-term interests and well-being of our people would not be served by adding to public expenditure, which could lead to higher inflation and increased pressure on interest rates.' And that was that.

One example on a huge scale of government subsidy for home owners is that of mortgage interest tax relief. Its purpose is to encourage home ownership, but it is evident that it provides most help to those who need it least. For example, the average relief for someone earning £9,000 per year is £430, whereas for someone earning £30,000 the average relief is £1,290. This anomaly was taken up by the Duke of Edinburgh's Inquiry into British Housing, which suggested that the money from some mortgage interest tax relief might be better realigned. It might be used as an allowance to benefit those who could not afford to buy a house of their own. The proposal was not to abolish mortgage interest tax relief, as government spokesmen claimed, but simply to establish a sliding scale of earnings which would remove tax relief from the wealthier and transfer that money to those whose needs were greater. Certainly, no one with earnings below £10,000 per year would have received any less in tax relief.

This proposal from the Duke of Edinburgh's Inquiry was echoed by the Archbishop of Canterbury's Commission on Urban Priority Areas, but there was immediate opposition from the Government. In both cases a raw nerve was touched in the public debate, and it was clear that questions of political power and popularity took precedence over the provision of good housing for those in greatest need. A senior government minister dismissed the questioning of mortgage interest tax relief on the grounds that it had been proved overwhelmingly popular. He did not, however, say that it was more just and equitable; nor did he indicate in which part of the population it was overwhelmingly popular. That needs to be spelt out. The policy is of course popular in marginal constituencies, on which political parties tend to concentrate, and where it is difficult for party politicians to operate purely from considerations of justice. The Labour Party was committed in 1974 to reducing mortage interest tax relief, but backed away from that commitment in the interests of 'political reality'.

It is widely believed that self-reliant home owners buy their houses with no help from the State, and that on the other hand council-house tenants receive vast hand-outs from the welfare state. The truth is the reverse of this picture. Because of the tax allowance, the cost to the nation in lost tax revenue of a private house is now greater than the long-term cost of providing a council house. Given the fundamental nature of housing need, we challenge on moral grounds both the high proportion of cuts which the housing programme has borne relative to other government programmes, and the way in which the cuts have been distributed within the field of housing.

URBAN REGENERATION STRATEGY

In 1983 Labour won the local elections in Liverpool with an outright majority. They determined to make housing and the defence of jobs the absolute priority before which all else must give way. They introduced an Urban Regeneration Strategy in seventeen priority areas of the city. Although as we have seen, central government policy offered councillors reduced spending on council housing, all resources in Liverpool were directed towards a massive house-building programme, together with some sports centres and a major park. They set out to build six thousand homes in three years and, through stimulating the construction industry, to create thousands of jobs.

The architect of the Council's Urban Regeneration Strategy was Councillor Tony Byrne. He always claimed that he was not a member of Militant Tendency. He liked to operate from behind the scenes, chairing the key committee, but he only came into the open as leader of the City Council when Militants like Derek Hatton were expelled from the Labour Party, and the non-Militant John Hamilton was ousted from the leadership by an unexpected manoeuvre. Tony Byrne was single-minded to the point of ruthlessness in his determination to tackle the housing problem. He rejected housing policies held nationally by the Labour Party which favoured the mixed provision of public sector, private sector and third arm housing or co-operatives. He claimed that such a consensus policy had failed. 'I am a socialist,' he declared, 'I believe in public ownership, control and accountability for housing through the elected council. It is the local authority which must satisfy the needs of the working class. Working-class organisation in this city lies in the Labour Party and in the unions, and not in housing associations.'

Such views inevitably led to little or no consultation. Here was a case where consultation, though often professed, proved to be no more than the provision of some information. When the Urban Regeneration Strategy was published it was set forth in an exhibition in the Town Hall. Local meetings, though advertised as for consultation, did no more than announce what had been decided. Questions were barely dealt with, objections were pushed aside. People in West Everton discovered that the plan made provision for the creation of a large park. To make space for this, several unpopular tower blocks were to be demolished, but with them was to go some good modern housing which was fully occupied. A door-to-door canvass was carried out by members of the West Everton Community Council, and this showed an overwhelming majority of residents in favour of being re-housed, but specifically asking that the re-housing should be in their own neighbourhood. But protests and petitions were ignored. The programme was pushed rapidly ahead, and people were dispersed and re-housed in several different parts of the city. Some of the residents resisted all the way. We saw the roofs being ripped off good four-bedroom houses and gave public support to the Langrove Street Action Group, who successfully went to court to obtain an injunction to stay the demolition of their homes which were in good condition. A few weeks later Councillor Byrne and his colleagues were disqualified from local government, and the Liberal interim administration reversed the Council's policy once again.

The insistence of the Labour administration that the answer lay with public ownership had led the Council to purchase a newly built private estate for council housing – even though buyers' deposits had already been accepted. It also led the Council to show dogmatic opposition to housing co-operatives.

DAVID SHEPPARD: Tony Byrne told me in a long discussion that I did not realise the source of policies which supported housing co-operatives. For him it meant the policies of the Liberals, in the Town Hall, who had discontinued council house building programmes. I said that many of us with no party political affiliations, but who were deeply involved in urban life, believed that housing co-operatives were an excellent way of giving local people some stake in their own destiny. He replied that clergy had an outdated and romantic view that parishes were like villages and that we were out of touch with reality. On another occasion Derek Hatton dismissed my argument that local people had made plain what they wanted in plans for a housing co-operative which the city was blocking. His response was, 'All they want is a good house. When we can offer them good housing, all that support for a co-operative will melt away.'

The ideology of the Labour City Council was that the local authority alone had to be seen to satisfy the needs of the working class. There must be no other source of housing provision. The Urban Regeneration Strategy (sometimes incorrectly known as 'Derek Hatton's houses', when in reality they were the brain-child of Tony Byrne) was to be the Militant Council's abiding legacy to the city. No doubt there will be attempts to quote it as a major achievement made in the teeth of the Tory government's hostility. It was certainly recognised that it would provide a continuing political base among grateful tenants. There was always the sense among the leading councillors that they did not expect to remain in office long. During their period of control, everything had to be irreversibly changed. They tore down the bad housing. New starts were made in all the seventeen priority areas. They changed the face of the city, providing well-built brick houses with small gardens. There is no doubt that their single-minded application brought about a remarkable achievement. But it was done at a great price.

The cost to the city financially was enormous. When faced with thirty-four per cent cuts in the government grant for Liverpool's housing for 1985/6, Tony Byrne said, 'We will not reduce our building programme by one single unit.' He had recourse to a variety of ploys in order to keep his extensive programme of municipal housing going ahead at full speed. Reserves were used up, assets sold, large loans obtained from French, Swiss and Japanese banks. To repay them would take up half the allocations of money for capital spending in the city for years ahead, though in all probability he and others entertained the hope that a future Labour Government might make some retrospective grant to help retrieve the situation: and this despite clear declarations from shadow ministers at Westminster that the Labour Party had no such intentions.

Each year, as bankruptcy was forecast, Tony Byrne succeeded in juggling his resources so that somehow an adequate budget would be presented. Subsequently it became clear that the figures hid very considerable reductions in services and in staffing, in spite of repeated assurances that levels of employment and the quality of services were being maintained. Going into any school or educational establishment, we were able to see shortages of textbooks and even exercise books, not to mention a lack of equipment for the courses advertised, and a very serious lack of necessary repairs. Visiting social services teams in deprived areas, we learnt of posts being frozen for six months before they were allowed to be advertised, even though the previous holders of the posts had been carrying a full case-load of individuals and families in great need. In exactly the same way voluntary bodies, customarily in receipt of grants for salaries of workers, found vacant posts frozen. In one year twenty-five projects sponsored by voluntary bodies were refused renewal of grants.

In Britain there had long been an understanding that neither central nor local government would push party differences too far. Even with conflicting party political allegiances, pragmatic deals ensured that resources continued to flow. It is now a matter of debate as to how far the confrontational attitudes of the Militant Labour Council constituted a deliberate and wilful challenge to central government; but there can be no doubt that confrontation was an accepted tactic for some of the Militant councillors. The end result was of course the breakdown of almost all communication between Westminster and Liverpool.

In the following chapter we shall chart some of the events and challenges of those turbulent and to a great extent tragic years. When in April 1987 nearly all the Labour councillors were surcharged by the District Auditor and disqualified from office, we were able to give public recognition to the achievement of the Urban Regeneration Strategy; but we had to maintain that it had only been carried through at an immense cost to other services, and by means of loans which must be an obstacle to the city's economic recovery for a long time to come.

THE SAGA OF THE ELDONIANS

In 1978 a report appeared in the *Liverpool Echo* to the effect that the council flats and tenements in Burlington Street, Eldon Street and Portland Gardens were to be demolished by the Liverpool City Council and the tenants re-housed. The streets in question were in the heart of the Vauxhall district in the northern sector of the inner city, and the residents were for the most part members of a tight-knit community of Roman Catholics, members of Our Lady's

parish in Eldon Street. A meeting was called to oppose the demolition of the property and the dispersal of the residents who saw
themselves almost as a village community surviving in an area of
widespread demolition. At that meeting the Eldonian Community
Association was established and in due time it formed a housing
co-operative which planned a number of building projects to
provide for the local people. When the Militant Labour Council
gained power in 1983, a radical change in policy took place and, as
we have already explained, the housing co-operatives ran into
unexpected opposition. We had done our best to encourage such
co-operatives as a way in which local people might grow to feel
more involved in their decent housing and living circumstances.
One of the great attractions of the housing co-operative movement is that members are able to share in planning their future
homes and to be involved in their subsequent maintenance and
repair. Now it was to be municipal ownership and control, or
nothing.

After the heavy blow of the closure of the Tate and Lyle factory,
the Eldonians, as they came to be known, set their eyes on the site
and began to plan their Eldonian Village. With the help of
architects from Merseyside Improved Housing, who agreed to
design the houses and superintend the building operation, they
prepared plans for 145 dwellings of one or two storeys, with
associated access roads and a limited number of local shops. As
their dreams took shape, they were able to point to plans and
explain just who would live in each unit and why. On the initiative
of the Secretary of State for the Environment, Patrick Jenkin, the
site had been acquired on behalf of the Government in 1982 by
English Industrial Estates. Now the Eldonians took an option on
the site as a location for the co-operative housing scheme, subject
to planning permission being granted. Just as all seemed settled,
and with £4m available from the Housing Corporation, the City
Council refused planning permission in May 1985 on the grounds
that the Eldonians' proposals did not coincide with the Council's
plans for the area, and that the location was a hazard to health. The
Eldonians decided to appeal and, as we had often put their project
on our agenda in meetings with the Secretary of State, they asked
us earnestly for help.

*DEREK WORLOCK: It happened that the public hearing of the
Appeal was held in Liverpool at a time when we had had to declare
ourselves openly against the confrontational tactics of the Militants.
This coincided with Neil Kinnock's public challenge to Derek Hatton*

at the Labour Party Conference in October 1985, so it was at a critical time that I was called to the hearing as a witness. In the temporary courtroom in the City Library, which was filled for the occasion with applauding Eldonians, I assumed the mantle of a prophet as I testified on their behalf: 'I share the view of many that the next decade will see the further development of the riverside area bordering the Mersey. The work of reclamation, begun at the Garden Festival and the Albert Dock, will continue along the waterfront below Vauxhall. It would be an injustice if the present families in the Vauxhall community were to be denied the opportunity to share in the benefits of this facility.'

In the following month the Secretary of State upheld the recommendation of the inspector who had conducted the enquiry, and directed that approval be granted to the project by the local planning authority. There was much rejoicing in Vauxhall, but still further delays occurred as other detailed examinations of the site proceeded. During that time we made several visits to the Department of the Environment and the Merseyside Task Force to try to press the matter forward. Meantime the Council's officers did their best to persuade the families, who were growing increasingly frustrated by these delays, to accept new housing elsewhere in the city. Somehow the people held firm and resisted this tempting bait, designed to achieve their dispersal. It was not until the late autumn of the following year, 1986, that finally clearance was given and the financial allocations confirmed.

One of us was invited to break the ground of the site with a bulldozer, the other to lay the first brick. A great celebration took place in the packed church in Eldon Street in mid-November. Then in pouring rain a procession formed to go, as it were in pilgrimage, to the site which was to be the cherished Eldonian Village. Elderly housebound people were brought in local taxis and vans to witness the scene of their dreams. Schoolchildren lined the route, waving their flags. Perhaps the most remarkable feature of this act of thanksgiving for the success which had marked the solidarity and perseverance of the local people, was the wording of the great banner across the road. In this area in the heart of Scotland Road, where sectarian bitterness was for so many years at its worst, banners across the street and slogans in the windows had always been a familiar sight. The occasion of the breaking of the ground for the Eldonian Housing Co-operative was no exception. But the content of the slogan said much for the different spirit. Across the street, in the windows, on the back of the service booklet, the message was plain: 'Our thanks to Archbishop Derek, to Bishop David and to all our friends. WE DID IT BETTER TOGETHER.'

The context and the wording of the slogan itself seemed to provide us with the right title for this book.

10   TWO NATIONS

The 17.50 train from Euston to Liverpool on Fridays provides a vivid piece of social history in the making. It is a comment on the way in which Merseysiders have been forced by circumstances to respond to the enticements embodied in the policies of 'Get up and go'. It is also a comment on the cost of housing in the South-East which makes it difficult for northerners to be able to afford to set up permanent homes where they have discovered job opportunities. And it is a comment on the family-life background of young Liverpudlians who are anxious not to lose contact with their homes and with the relationships they have known in the past. On the 17.50 each Friday large numbers of them go home for the weekend. So great is the number that the train, now known locally as 'The Tebbit Express', is invariably filled to overcrowding, as is the back-up train which has regularly to be provided. The reverse process is repeated on Sunday night and early Monday morning. It is a phenomenon also to be witnessed on the corresponding long-distance coaches.

SELECTIVE MOBILITY

There are those who argue that such mobility of labour is the main answer to the problems of ageing cities like Liverpool. But in practice this mobility is highly selective. Mobility can be a healthy feature in the life of a community, provided that it is a reasonable cross-section of the community which moves away, and that it is also a reasonable cross-section which remains or moves in. In fact selective mobility, leading away from the city, overwhelmingly takes with it the younger and more self-confident members of the community, often those who have achieved well at school. It includes relatively few family men and women who have been made redundant and who remain behind to join the ranks of the long-term unemployed. Their desire not to endanger the security of their housing and their children's education is a further

213

deterrent. A change in surroundings is seldom welcome to those who already know deprivation. Families which do resolve to give it a try often move in on relatives already established in the South. Young migrants have no alternative but to abandon their grand-parents who have been an accepted element in their upbringing. The social consequences of this selective mobility are far more widespread than its advocates recognise.

In the last thirty-five years the population of Liverpool has dropped by 275,000. Of course this process of reduction includes the 'rippling' out of Liverpool into Merseyside and the surround-ing region. But that is a massive fall for any city. We are neverthe-less ready to acknowledge that the Liverpool of the future may well have to be still smaller. The challenge will be how to resist the polite pessimism of those anxious to wash their hands of the situation by suggesting that, like a dependent geriatric, the place be allowed to grow old gracefully and die. The alternative is to learn how to manage efficiently and humanely a reduced but renewed city. To achieve that there needs to be a reasonably balanced community ready to face the changes required in renewal, and at the same time there must be a good mixture of jobs. For even when a degree of mobility has been given effect, there will still be a substantial population in Merseyside. At present the number is equal to that in Northern Ireland. But, as we have said, to encourage health and resilience and to avoid destructive segregation, enabling a balanced community to emerge, will be crucial.

DAVID SHEPPARD: Early in 1987, in an article on the leader page of the Sunday Times, *Brian Walden offered some advice to Merseyside and to me:*

> *But what are we to say to the Rt Rev. David Sheppard, Bishop of Liverpool, who wants tax cuts withheld so that more money can be spent on the poor of the inner cities? The bishop is a good man and so I am reluctant simply to tell him that sizeable sums have been spent already . . . What is needed to release the bishop's flock from unem-ployment and comparative poverty is mobility . . . Some of Liver-pool's unemployed have jobs waiting for them in the south and east . . . Anyone who tells the bishop that the work can be brought to the people, rather than the people to the work, is deceiving him.*

> *I telephoned the* Sunday Times *to see if they would welcome an article in reply. The acting features editor said that he would be interested to see a piece from me. I asked if it would be worth pushing myself to produce an article in the next couple of days, as I was facing an*

already very demanding week. Clearly he could not promise to publish it unseen, but he thought that it would be worth my while. When he had received the article, he told me on the phone that he liked it very much. Two days later he informed me that at the editorial conference it had been decided that there was no room for it because of immediate major news items.

During the following week we had a further conversation in which we agreed some minor changes. Thereafter silence, save for eventually a phone message to the effect that they would not be using the article. In light of the fact that Brian Walden's original article had explicitly directed some paragraphs at me personally, it was hard to avoid the conclusion that a deliberate decision had been taken at senior level that I was not to be given the right of reply. For some weeks previously the newspaper had been advocating tax cuts and asserting that there was no such thing as the North/South divide.

The media have a heavy responsibility to ensure that both sides of a question are presented, if more than lip-service is to be paid to the ideal of one nation. We have taken seriously the need to advocate the good name of what we see as a disadvantaged North-West, and to defend from misrepresentation those whose voice cannot often or easily be heard. Sadly the right of reply by letter or matching article can no longer be taken for granted. The news editor's power to clip from sound or video-recordings has similarly removed the value of any assurance that a recorded message, interview or comment will be broadcast as given. The pressure on people working in the media is very great and must be acknowledged. When we are challenged over silence or an inadequate answer, it is hard to have to reply that our words were 'lost on the cutting-room floor' and cannot be traced. The exercise on some occasions, especially in newspapers, of what is virtually party political censorship can be both dangerous and unjust.

In this particular context it will be seen that it may be convenient at the present time to portray some of Liverpool's problems today as the inevitable product of the 'loony left'. We also see something of similar problems faced by other cities. Is it seriously suggested that there are jobs waiting in the South-East of England for all the unemployed from places with problems comparable with those of Liverpool? Is mobility to produce full employment for all the unemployed of Glasgow, Belfast, Newcastle, Middlesbrough, Sheffield, Bradford, Leeds, Manchester and the West Midlands, in addition to the allegedly work-shy Merseyside? We would argue that, more than any other factor, selective mobility has made many urban priority areas what they are today. Those who moved away from the inner city, taking with them their skills and resources, and those who removed investments and assets from the cities from which they derived their wealth in the past, have helped to make the inner city what it is today just as much as those who still live there.

Not all have the same starting-line in life. All too often the claims of the more successful that their parents had to 'pull themselves up by their bootstraps' turn out on examination to be at best exaggeration. There is no reason to believe that equality of effort produces equal opportunities and results. Those who are critical today of areas from which their forebears sprang are apt to forget the far-reaching changes which may have taken place since they or their parents moved away from the neighbourhood. The 'upwardly mobile' can entertain all sorts of fanciful ideas about past relationships in areas where in truth they may always have been out of sympathy with the majority in the district. Often one generation emigrates emotionally and spiritually from its own particular community, leaving it to the next generation to make the physical move.

It seems extraordinary to us that, when a government goes out of its way to adopt policies to prevent a 'brain drain' away from this country, its members should actively encourage what is virtually a 'brain drain' away from very large regions within this country.

DIVIDED BRITAIN

The term 'North/South Divide' crept into increasing prominence as a popular way of describing a reality which was widely observed. No one claimed that it was a precise geographical division. Some spoke of a line from the Humber to Bristol. 'North of Watford' was more commonly used, though politically-minded comedians preferred 'north of Finchley'. The general idea was of a divided nation and unequal opportunities. 'Comfortable Britain and the Other Britain' was another way of expressing the same thought. There were dramatic differences to be observed between, for example, house prices, availability of jobs, living standards and wealth, North and South. The divide for us became sharper when it was recognised that the figures for Merseyside showed decisively a greater degree of poverty than was apparent for the rest of the North-West.

The reality of this division became even more apparent in the general election of June 1987, yet the idea that we are a divided nation is not readily acceptable to many for whom the unity of the country is seen as part of the patriotism which has so often saved us in the past. But it is difficult to secure from such patriots in Comfortable Britain an acceptance that the social, economic and industrial problems in the Other Britain are to be regarded as '*our* problems', and as the focus for a determined national programme on a scale sufficient to reverse deprivation and decay. Interest in problems, and the commitment to tackle them, needs to be sustained if they are to remain strong all through the tortuous decision-making process of government, which so often feels the need to claim success for its schemes after only a year or two. It is hard to escape the conclusion that Comfortable Britain lacks the will to mount and sustain a wholehearted war on poverty. (It is not only cynics who would add the words '. . . until the next riot'.)

In his study *Scarman and After*, John Benyon describes a five-year 'issue-attention cycle'. Each stage may vary in length, but the order of events is usually the same:

1. *The pre-problem stage*: Some highly undesirable social condition exists, which may be of concern to experts and specialised groups, but which has received little public attention, e.g. racism or poverty.

2. *Alarmed discovery and enthusiastic pursuit*: The public suddenly becomes aware of and alarmed by the evils of a particular problem, often as a result of dramatic events. Invariably there is enthusiasm about finding a solution to the problem in a short time.

3. *Realising the cost of significant progress*: Gradually it dawns that the cost of solving the problem is very high and may require sacrifices by large numbers of people. The most pressing social problems often involve the exploitation of one group in society by another.

4. *Gradual decline of intense public interest*: The public becomes discouraged, bored or feels threatened. Their desire to keep attention focused on the issue wanes, particularly if another social problem enters stages 1 and 2 above.

5. *The post-problem stage*: The issue enters a twilight period of lesser interest. The public feels sporadically guilty about the problem as it resurfaces. Now policies may have been

established which have some impact on the problem, but the will to solve it has not been sustained.

(John Benyon (ed.), *Scarman and After*, Pergamon Press, 1984, p. 240)

It must be evident how important the news media become in determining how long attention is focused on a problem. As soon as it is felt that emphasis on a particular issue is boring or threatening readers or listeners, focus is shifted to a new issue. The issue-attention cycle suggests that a government can delay action which it dislikes for reason of cost or unpopularity until the issue fades out of the public agenda. How information is presented for popular consumption has a critical effect on the importance with which it is treated for any length of time. But there are so many aspects of the two nations debate that in one form or another it has stayed before the public as an issue for the last few years.

In 1980 the Black Report was published, showing that death and disease strike the poor substantially younger and in higher proportions than is the case with the professional and managerial classes. It stated that 'present social inequalities in health in a country with resources like Britain are unacceptable and deserve to be so declared by every section of public opinion . . . We have no doubt that greater equality of health must remain one of our foremost national objectives.' In the report the population was classified. People in class I live about seven years longer on average than people in class V. The causes are complex, but the dominant factors are the wealth and poverty of those concerned. When incomes grow more equal (as they did during the two world wars), so do the death rates. The Black Report contained a number of important facts, well wrapped up in a vast and dense volume, quite inaccessible to popular readership. Only a very limited number of copies were published and reaction was accordingly limited.

In 1987 a further report on *The Health Divide* underlined these same trends. All the major killer diseases were shown to affect the poorest occupational classes substantially more than the rich. The report claimed that unemployment causes a deterioration in mental health. In support several studies had found a decline in mental health in persons becoming unemployed, and an improvement in their condition following re-employment. Comparable differences were apparent among school-leavers, dependent upon whether they went on the dole or into 'real jobs'. *The Health Divide* report also showed that, in the case of coronary heart disease, not only has the gap between the social classes widened but the rate of mortality in manual workers and their wives has actually increased. The Black Report had emphasised the importance of child nutrition. *The Health Divide* report confirmed the recommendation, with facts linking heart disease with a deprived childhood.

This time the problem of publication was not due to the difficulty of extracting technical information from a poorly presented document. The publication of *The Health Divide* report took place amidst an atmosphere of sharp indignation. At the last moment the press conference to launch the report was cancelled by the chairman of the Health Council, Sir Brian Bailey, on the score that it was 'political dynamite in an election year'. This suppression of information was of course counter-productive and served to create additional interest. More important, it strengthened an uneasy feeling that government departments were not expected to publicise the results of any research they initiated, if their findings were judged likely to bring disadvantage to their political masters.

Only a few weeks earlier, in January 1987, it was evident that government spokesmen and their supporters must have taken the decision that the concept of two nations, and especially of the North/South divide, was damaging to their record. Margaret Thatcher announced that the northern region was a paradox: 'There are areas which are very prosperous . . . you can, income for income, live better on housing and travel costs because you don't have so far to travel.' Norman Tebbit, the chairman of the Conservative Party, was only a few days later asked by a questioner in a group of Merseyside businessmen to comment on the North/South divide. He responded, 'What North/South divide?' This was echoed when the *Sunday Times* published a leader under the caption, 'The nonsense of North/South'. The article which followed spoke of the prosperity of Aberdeen, Edinburgh, Harrogate and north Cheshire. It made quite correctly the point that the economic inequality in Britain was rather more complicated than the simple geographical division suggested, and it went on to speak about inner-city problems.

The division between two nations is not new. It was clear enough in the 1950s and 1960s, and some with longer memories will point to the early 1930s. But it has grown much sharper in recent years. To us the description of the 'North/South divide' is far from being nonsense. It represents a division which is real, deep and extremely damaging. We have already instanced health in relation to poverty. In January 1987, the Department of Employment published its 1984 job census, together with projections based on it for 1986. These showed an overall net loss of 745,000 jobs in Great Britain between June 1979 and June 1986. Excluding the self-employed, the census revealed that ninety-four per cent of the jobs lost were in Scotland, the North, the Midlands, Wales and Northern Ireland. Only six per cent of the jobs lost were in the South-East, South-West and East Anglia. Turning to the pattern of new jobs, the census showed that more than two-thirds of the service-industry jobs created during that same period of seven years were in what may now be called the Southern Triangle.

As with the inequalities shown in *The Health Divide* report, it seems that the publication of the research into unemployment statistics is sometimes undertaken very reluctantly. The release of the information from the census on employment was delayed for many months. Even then, certain figures, broken down into smaller regions, were still not published. Yet the need for such detailed figures to be made known was of particular importance because changes in the definition of 'unemployment' made comparison with earlier unemployment figures unreliable, if not misleading.

A VOICE FOR THOSE UNHEARD

This difficulty in making known what are vital statistics for Britain (whether one nation or two) is a cause of frustration and at times indignation. For Comfortable Britain the picture is complex and confusing. For the Other Britain it gives rise to the justifiable anger which we hear expressed so regularly, but which is only very rarely heard by the nation as a whole. The unemployed and the poor have very little clout or voice when they try to express their sense of real grievance. It is difficult for them to reach the decision-makers. Even when their voice is heard, it is not always heeded, and still less frequently is it understood.

This has been a major reason why we have felt it right to seize opportunities, when they have come our way, to speak up on behalf of groups who have little power or even voice in the nation. It has led to our being accused of being obsessed with the subject of unemployment, the inner city and racial issues. For some years we have both had to ride the taunt of being traitors to our upbringing. To us it has seemed a straightforward obedience to the charge laid on bishops 'to have a special care for the outcast and the needy'; or, to borrow words from John Wesley, who left this among his *Twelve Rules for a Helper* in the Methodist Church, 'Go to those who need you, and especially to those who need you most.'

We have sometimes felt another anxiety: that those on whose behalf we try to speak might turn round and say that they had no wish that we speak for them. In fact, there have been great encouragements from that direction. Both of us have frequently been stopped in the street or on the train by people wishing to say, 'Thanks for that speech for the unemployed' or 'Thanks for what you both do for Liverpool.' But not all approve. We have both appeared on Sir Robin Day's programme *Question Time*. One appearance produced questions on subjects as diverse as unemployment, South Africa and the ordination of women. The next day a vicar asked an elderly parishioner if she had seen the bishop on television. 'Yes,' she replied, 'I agreed with everything he said until he got on to religion!'

There has to be accountability if a bishop's public statements are not to be simply an expression of his private opinions. We are probably more accessible than most public figures to those wishing to voice direct criticism. Two or three times a week we each lead worship in parishes in our dioceses, and afterwards, either at the back of the church seeing the congregation away, or in the church hall over a cup of tea, we are wide open to questions and comments from the laity on what we may have been doing or saying. They seldom miss a chance to question things we have said, but usually do so in a supportive way. Neither of us has ever known people like Merseysiders for possessing their leaders. We are constantly challenged about all events in Church and State which affect people's lives. Happily for us, the bond can be personal. Visiting the sick and housebound in their homes leads months later to an encounter in which an apparent stranger will stop one to pick up a conversation begun in that person's home in the course of a visit to a sick relative. With such an ease of relationship, feed-back on a particular issue is seldom lacking. It is also reflected in the daily bombardment of letters, requiring almost encyclopaedic knowledge about all matters, from unemployment and unilateral disarmament to last Sunday night's television programme and 'our Annie's' matrimonial problems.

We have mentioned earlier our accountability to each other and to our immediate advisers. Clearly we are accountable also to our brother bishops: statements and decisions about diocesan matters frequently have wider consequences. There are continuing debates within the Christian Church in which there are sustained attempts to look in the light of the gospel at complex issues affecting deeply the lives of people. Contemporary bio-ethical developments, for example, raise questions to which the Church does not necessarily claim to have an instant answer.

If, as bishops, we enter the public debate, we do not claim to have a hot-line to God on contentious issues. Some of these matters raise a mixture of social, economic and moral principles, brought into question through the acquisition of new technical knowledge. When called upon to give a lead, at whatever level, we hope to come to the scene well-briefed and with distinctively Christian moral insights. But we have to accept that there may well be disagreement expressed by other sincere and well-informed Christians.

Many people wish that such public disagreement be avoided at all cost. We must have careful regard for the biblical and traditional teaching of the Church, but on many contemporary ethical matters we are being asked to break new ground. In such an issue, as in many matters of social justice, we hope that what we say may contribute to worthwhile debate or to the clarification of some complex question or principle. We may foresee that our views are likely to be unwelcome in certain sectors, so that there will be criticism and contention. We have to be prepared to face this, especially if the alternative is to close our eyes to the harm being caused to communities or individuals.

It is alleged that among the various nick-names attributed to our partnership is 'Fish and Chips' – always together and never out of the newspapers. This has the ring of Liverpudlian humour, even though it is believed to have been thought up by the press. The truth is that access to the media is not only demanding but is generally in the media's own time, at moments when there is media interest in some current public issue. Then for a matter of hours there is pressing demand for church comments. It can mean dropping everything to meet that demand, or the Church remains silent, and more often than not is liable to be criticised for that silence, which itself can be misrepresented. Working together and with the Free Church Moderator we do our best to sift our words to avoid unguarded phrases. Where there is time and opportunity, we will do our best not only to consult together but to consult our own expert advisers in the particular field concerned.

In facing the challenge and demand of modern means of communication, we are concerned both for the spiritual transformations which Christ brings and for God's concern for justice in society. Media reports of what Church leaders have to say on subjects, not always of their own choice, are unlikely to keep that balance. In the nature of things, national newspapers and television companies are unlikely to think it newsworthy to report that a bishop preached on one of the virtues or the power of prayer. Reports which do appear can easily give the impression that matters of justice in corporate life are more important to those Church leaders who speak of such matters than the power of Christ to change people's hearts.

DEREK WORLOCK: We have both suffered in this respect. Some years ago, the Daily Telegraph *included an article by Paul Johnson criticising 'meddling bishops', and me in particular. He wrote:*

> *One of the curious things about our very verbal political bishops is that they appear to have absolutely no sense of Christian priorities. That is, they pronounce constantly on matters which are not really of immediate concern to the episcopate, such as details of economic policy, while remaining totally silent on issues which are, or certainly ought to be, their particular province.*

He went on to say that it was a long time since he had heard a bishop preach a sermon on 'the evils of fornication . . . The deadly sins of the flesh, the sins that lie at the root of the problem of poverty (sic) remain uncastigated . . . I wonder', he concluded in specific reference to me, 'how long it is since His Grace preached a sermon on the virtue of chastity.'

Father Paul Thompson, my press officer, wrote at once to the editor of the paper to point out that I had devoted a recent pastoral letter (read in all the churches in the archdiocese) to the whole question of marital problems and sexual morality; that at every parish visitation (on many Sundays each year) I preach on the virtues of family life; and that only a few days earlier, on the feast of Our Lady of Lourdes, I had preached on chastity to a congregation of two thousand persons in the Metropolitan Cathedral.

To expect an apology or correction might be too much. I had not anticipated the insistence which would be required of us to ensure that the reply would eventually be printed in the letters to the editor. It reminded me of an earlier occasion in Portsmouth when I wrote a pastoral letter on the Blessed Trinity, only to receive from an angry correspondent a complaint that I lacked devotion to the Blessed Virgin Mary, as I had not mentioned her.

DAVID SHEPPARD: The power of the media to call attention to the responsibilities of the Church in the life of the nation is great. This can be used for good or evil. Positively I can recall the opportunity afforded me by the BBC in 1984 to give the Dimbleby Lecture on 'The Other Britain'.

This was watched on a Sunday night by 4.7 million viewers. However, nearly two years later the launch of the report Faith in the City *(mentioned several times already in this book) was pre-empted by a deliberate and hostile leak in the* Sunday Times, *in total breach of the official embargo. The front-page headline proclaimed that this church report was 'Marxist'. A 'senior government figure' was quoted (though never identified) as saying that parts of the report were 'pure Marxist theology'. In light of the carefully prepared launch planned for the report a few days later, my feelings can be imagined as over breakfast I read this newspaper leak, with its many misrepresentations. I had the radio on. As my consciousness slowly emerged from that front page, I became aware that in a broadcast service the Scriptures were being read. The words reaching me were, 'There shall be truth and integrity in the land.' I found myself crying out aloud, 'O Lord, how long?'*

This was a case where an attempt to rubbish a report in advance of publication proved counter-productive. The following day the *Financial Times*, in a leading article, declared that the smear that *Faith in the City* was Marxist was itself rubbish. It said that the report's suggestions were not revolutionary but sober and for the most part within the Government's terms of reference. They deserved a thoughtful hearing. In practice they received much more of a hearing precisely because of the attack by the government spokesman. *Faith in the City* remained a main item of news on television and radio and in the national press for four full days. For a Church report that must be a record.

LIVERPOOL'S RATES CRISIS

Future political historians will have to judge whether the crisis, which led in March 1987 to the disqualification from office of forty-seven of Liverpool's city councillors, was the result of a deliberate policy of confrontation with central government or merely the inevitable result of the reduction of the Rate Support Grant. Whatever the reason, Liverpool was to become the cockpit of confrontation between Margaret Thatcher's Tory Government and the Labour City Council, elected in 1983 with an overall majority but with the Militant Tendency dominating its approach. To understand the whole story fully it is necessary to appreciate some very complex arguments about the methods by which central government makes grants to local government. A lucid account has been given by Michael Parkinson, of Liverpool University, in

Liverpool on the Brink (Policy Journals, 1985) and there is no point in our attempting a detailed analysis here. But certain factors which led to the long-drawn-out political and economic crisis in the city of Liverpool may usefully be recorded.

The Inner Areas Study, set up by the Heath Government in the early 1970s, was concluded under Harold Wilson. In 1977 James Callaghan published the Bill which became the Inner Urban Areas Act 1978. This was affirmed by Margaret Thatcher's Conservative Government which brought the partnership scheme into operation and continued to fund the Urban Programme. The preliminary White Paper had argued that the mainline funding through the Rate Support Grant should be bent in favour of the cities and should be topped up by the Urban Programme. Certainly the Government maintained and at times even increased the Urban Programme: this enabled it to speak often of pouring millions of pounds into the inner city.

We have taken great trouble to discover accurate comparisons. According to figures taken from a government reply to a parliamentary question on 30 June 1987, the payments actually made were as follows: In 1981/82 (the earliest year comparative figures are available) authorities which were either Partnership or Programme Authorities under the urban programme, received £81 million at 1987/88 prices. In 1986/87 these same authorities received £129.2 million, an increase of £48.2 million. Over the same period the same authorities had had a cut in block grant of £146.8 million and a cut in housing subsidy of £179.7 million. This represents a total cut over five years of £326.5 million (all of these in 1987/88 prices) on these two mainstream programmes alone. (Cf. Hansard, col. 64W.)

As the Government came increasingly to mistrust Labour local Councils, it endeavoured to establish other methods by which it could ensure that such resources as it made available for local use were utilised in accord with its own policies. The establishment of Urban Development Corporations was one such method. But it meant that local government had less and less monies available to implement those of its own plans for which it claimed to have been elected to office. This led to frustration, embitterment and ultimately to defiance by the Liverpool City Council, with resultant hardship to many of the citizens. To remove from local government the capacity to do anything other than to implement the harsh cut-backs demanded by central government downgrades the role of local councillors, who feel deprived of the opportunity to prove to the electorate that their ideas are practical. In Liverpool it contributed to the process of pushing voters into the arms of extremists.

For Liverpool the percentage paid by central government as Rate Support Grant fell from sixty-one per cent in 1979/80 to forty-eight in 1985/86. And the total block grant fell in real terms by sixteen per cent. Many people felt that, in the light of the electoral pledge of the Labour councillors that there would be no redundancies and no ('massive') increase in rates, the crisis of confrontation was inevitable. We constantly pleaded and worked for greater flexibility and negotiation. As relationships between the Council and the Government deteriorated, it became increasingly clear that the former at least was set on a collision course, even claiming a mandate from the electorate for this.

The leader of the Labour City Council was John Hamilton, a Quaker schoolmaster, a man of very simple lifestyle. He was of the old school, left-wing Labour, and had survived a coup to unseat him a few years before. The hard left had helped him to regain his leadership then, and he sincerely hoped that his presence as the leader could moderate the policies and practices of the new councillors. Events proved that he was unable to control the tiger he had attempted to ride. Shortly before the mass disqualification of councillors took place, he was manipulated out of the leadership, which was taken over by Councillor Tony Byrne, who had been chairman of the Finance Committee.

However, for the greater part of the time when the Labour Party was in power, it was the deputy leader, Derek Hatton, who, in public at least, called the tune. He had left no one in any doubt about his desire to confront the Government: 'There is no way in which we can fail to have a confrontation with this Tory Government,' he asserted strongly. 'We have chosen the ground on which it will take place – housing and jobs.' Even in the presence of John Hamilton he made himself the spokesman of the Labour group on the Council. For quite a long time he was able to carry a large proportion of the people with him. Most of them were genuinely glad that here at last was someone who was ready to stand up for Liverpool against its critics, not least Margaret Thatcher's Government. When finally he challenged Neil Kinnock and the National Executive of the Labour Party, he was, after various delaying tactics, expelled from the Party itself. The same fate overtook Tony Mulhearn, the Chairman of the District Labour Party. It was at that stage that the real power behind the scenes, Tony Byrne, a close ally but not a member of Militant Tendency, emerged from the background to take over from John Hamilton.

Tony Byrne was a man who lived simply and was utterly dedicated to his cause. He was clever with figures and, having mastered all the details of housing finance, was quite determined to remain in office until the last possible moment to carry through his policy. His overwhelming interest was in housing and in the Urban Regeneration Strategy of which he was in one sense the architect. To forward this he was quite prepared to make cuts in the provision of any other services, and to borrow monies which he believed that others would in due time have to repay. Hostile reaction to such single-mindedness, which was certainly not evident among the occupants of the new houses built, left him quite undeterred. He appeared quite unconcerned about personal popularity, but before long he seemed to lose regard for the views even of those he claimed to be helping. His authoritarianism was most evident in his opposition to housing co-operatives, which he saw as possessing an unacceptable degree of freedom and flexibility.

THE GOVERNMENT AND MILITANT TENDENCY

We have earlier (chapter six) referred to the role of a bishop as a communicator rather than a negotiator. This has special importance, we claimed, when particular groups are unwilling or unable to meet and there is need to interpret the views of one to the other. The deadlock which arose between the Department of the Environment and the Liverpool City Council over the difficulty in setting a legal budget in March 1984, proved a prime example of our need to try to fulfil this aspect of our role. Patrick Jenkin had assured us that his door was always open, and locally we were kept informed of developments so far as the city budget was concerned. We appealed publicly for another way of solving the problem of the rates through negotiation and Tony Byrne invited us to the Town Hall to explain to us the state of the city's finances. There was to be a large demonstration a few days later and he invited us to join the protest. 'If we were in South America,' he said, 'you would be telling your priests to come out on the streets with us.' We replied that we had both been in South America a short time before and had seen what happened next, with the take-over by military governments.

There was certainly a great sense of crisis and even talk that the time for revolution was fast approaching when other cities too would stand up to the Government and refuse to make legal rates. We did not join the demonstration. We called for special prayers that day, 26 March 1984, and both took part in midday services in the heart of the city, at Liverpool Parish Church and at the Blessed Sacrament Shrine. The march and the demonstration were large but not vast. All passed off peacefully and the police throughout kept a low profile.

During the months that followed we made a number of visits to Patrick Jenkin at the Department of the Environment and we were in frequent touch with John Hamilton as leader of the City Council. In one sense Liverpool's case was a strong one. The penalties imposed for overspending were based on limits related to expenditure by the Council in arbitrarily chosen years. It happened that the years in question, 1978/9 and 1981/2, were both years when the previous administration had held back expenditure in order to keep rate increases to a minimum. Liverpool's officers calculated that between those years the city had lost between £26m and £34m in government grant, as a direct result of penalties based on those particular years of expenditure. This enabled the Labour councillors subsequently to claim that the Government had 'stolen' £30m from the city.

The other continuing objection was that the grant system took insufficient note of the city's decline in wealth and population. The level of economic activity had fallen dramatically since the rateable valuation of all properties had last been carried out in 1973. In addition, with a large and rapid reduction in the city's population, the unit costs of providing local services had increased rather than decreased.

The general feeling about the attitude of the Government was exacerbated by the fact that the Secretary of State for the Environment also bore responsibility for the legislation required for the abolition of Metropolitan County Councils. We believed then, as we believe now, that the abolition of the Merseyside County Council was a disaster for the area. Far from being the haunt of extremists, the County Council was the one place where partnership between the political parties, and with central government and the European Economic Community, was actually working. It had initiated a number of new developments and had proved that genuine consultation with the local community was possible and profitable.

Patrick Jenkin faced his responsibility for Merseyside and came regularly to Liverpool to see for himself what was happening. He was prepared to listen to Liverpool's case, but his problem was that to make an exception for either city or county might be quoted as a precedent by other councils. Nevertheless, during the summer months he tried to find ways of helping the city to achieve a legal budget, which had been held back from April until July 1984. His understanding was that the details of the negotiations would remain confidential until the Council had fixed a legal rate. When at last an old-style deal had been worked out, the Liverpool councillors returned home that evening to present the package to the District Labour Party for its endorsement. When the leaders finally emerged from that meeting, television cameras were there to record the shouts of 'Victory', and to film the clenched fists and the crowds chanting the miners' song 'Here we go'. Derek Hatton announced that Margaret Thatcher and Patrick Jenkin had 'bottled out' of the confrontation with Liverpool, adding, 'There is no way even Thatcher can take on the might of the working-class in this city.'

That moment of Derek Hatton's 'dancing on the political grave' of Patrick Jenkin proved the turning point, and brought negotiation and even communication to an end. No other minister was prepared to risk being sucked into deals with such a leadership. The Council leaders themselves believed that they had won by the use of threats of an illegal budget and of the collapse of the city and its services. The following year it seemed that the same policy was to be employed. At first the Labour councillors felt strengthened by the declared intention of more than twenty other Labour councils in various parts of the country to take the Liverpool line of resistance and to set an illegal rate. Central government left them in no doubt about the consequences and, as the months went by, the would-be rebels fell away until only Liverpool and Lambeth stood out. The Government, having once burnt its fingers, stood back. Almost as soon as the legislation abolishing the Metropolitan County Councils was complete, Patrick Jenkin was removed from office, to be succeeded first by Kenneth Baker and subsequently by Nicholas Ridley. For a long time neither they, nor indeed any government minister, came near Liverpool. Official policy was to let Liverpool 'sweat it out' on its own. There were obvious reasons for that. Disappointingly, that same policy continued even when eventually the councillors were barred from office.

In July 1985, when it was clear that the City Council was embarked on a collision course, and the setting of a rate was held to have been 'wilfully' delayed, together with Moderator John Williamson we issued a statement, warning against the policy of confrontation and its likely effect upon the services due to the people. As the autumn drew on, the situation deteriorated. On our return from Assisi at the end of September (Cf. chapter twelve,

p. 287), we were pressed to make an explicit statement of guidance and a clarification of the position of the Churches as the mounting problems came to affect our schools and our social services. The pair of us, therefore, submitted an article to *The Times*, making plain our belief that the Government should have given greater resources to Liverpool, but expressing our strong opposition to the policies of confrontation. We hoped that trade unions might recognise that the reckless courting of bankruptcy for the city would in no way be of benefit to those employed by the Council. But the influence of the union officials was severely restricted by the role given by the Council to a Joint Shop Stewards' Committee, which was also under Militant leadership.

As the Council's finances ran out, the Labour councillors forced through a motion to make redundant all the thirty-one thousand employees of the city. This was to save salaries and wages, while those displaced would at least for some weeks draw social security benefit. It was a desperate move, made in the hope that the threat of so many lost jobs might encourage the Labour Party Annual Conference to help apply pressure on the Government.

The Times printed our article on 2 October, giving it the caption, 'Stand up to Liverpool's Militants.' That same day, at the Party Conference in Bournemouth, Neil Kinnock launched an all-out attack on Derek Hatton and on the irresponsibility of Militant tactics which, he said, had ended up in 'the grotesque chaos of a Labour Council hiring taxis to scuttle round the city, handing out redundancy notices to its own workers'. This was the signal for an all-out challenge to Militant Tendency supporters in Liverpool, a number of whom were subsequently expelled from the Labour Party. Meantime a promise was made that national trade union leaders would visit Liverpool to examine the city's financial position. Their report, when in due time it was published, made plain that there were a number of ways forward which would keep Liverpool solvent. At national level the Labour Party leadership had always discouraged the tactics of confrontation. A local trade union took the Council to court and obtained an injunction against the redundancy notices. The city struggled on uncertainly with many posts unfilled. In effect substantial parts of its services were severely cut back.

By then the law had already entered the scene in a way which was to prove decisive, even though the process seemed to all those involved quite insufferably long-drawn-out. The District Auditor had warned all the councillors personally that they must set a rate no later than 1 June 1985. Tony Byrne declined to do so and set the date for fixing the rate as 14 June. But just before they did eventually meet, the District Auditor wrote again to the councillors, telling them that he must proceed against them for wilfully delaying affairs in such a way that they had lost the interest on the grant they should have received had they acted by the approved date. He would have to surcharge them for the losses incurred by the city through no rate having been made between 1 April and 1 June. John Hamilton subsequently said that the District Auditor had 'shot-gunned' the group into its decision. The reaction of the Labour councillors was 'you might as well be hanged for a sheep as for a lamb'; so they set the rate on 14 June on a nine per cent rate rise. With the penalties incurred, it looked as though this would leave the city short of what it needed that year by no less than £117m.

In the event the city stumbled on for another twenty months, helped by unexpected windfalls, by capitalising some of their assets and by large loans from overseas banks. We began to hear more and more about creative accountancy. The law ground on exceedingly slowly. The councillors' appeal against the District Auditor's penalties was dismissed, as was a further appeal to the House of Lords. What was called the 'day of judgment', when the appeal was ultimately rejected, did not take place till 12 March 1987. By then two of the surcharged councillors had died. The remaining forty-seven of those originally involved were disqualified from office and surcharged personally for the loss of £106,000. Only a limited amount of legal aid money had been judged applicable, so, with legal costs, no less than £500,000 had to be found. Not surprisingly there was talk of personal bankruptcy.

With John Williamson again, we stated publicly that while we stood by our condemnation of the disastrous confrontational tactics, we wished to acknowledge that the solidarity which had held the forty-seven together meant that, with the disqualified Militants, there were other councillors who had for many years given the city distinguished public service. In no way were we defending their breach of the law, but the system of personal surcharge, which seemed unique in our legal system, surely called for review. The statement was open to misrepresentation, so that once again we did not lack critics, mostly by correspondence. But it was good to have kept faith at that moment with 'some very fine public servants', who, though they had for a time fallen for the wiles of the Militants, had 'genuinely sought what they believed was in the best interests of the city', and as a result had now to face a personally tragic conclusion to their service to the community. In subsequent weeks two of the political parties undertook at national level to introduce, if returned to power, legislation to abolish the personal surcharge of individual councillors.

At the same time as we made this statement, we called electors in the city to 'keep in mind the need to choose councillors who, while persevering in their long-term political aspirations, may be willing in the difficult years ahead to co-operate across party barriers for the good of the city as a whole'. It happened that the statutory interval between the disqualification of the forty-seven councillors and the holding of by-elections brought the latter to the exact date when local elections were due, 7 May 1987. With the separation of the law from political considerations, it was a remarkable coincidence. For the interim the Liberal councillors took over the administration of the city, restored the Lord Mayoralty (complete with coach and horses) and endeavoured to dismiss Sampson Bond.

At the local elections and by-elections two months later, a Labour council was returned, avowedly more moderate than its predecessor and with a much reduced majority. For the first time for many years a black woman Labour candidate, Liz Drysdale, was returned as a councillor for the Granby Ward of Toxteth. (Sampson Bond accepted a cash settlement and left both his post and the city; and although the Lord Mayoralty was again dropped, the coach and horses were retained for occasional use by the Council Chairman.) There was talk of co-operation between the parties to secure confidence in the city. It would take some time before it could be known just how influential would be those members of the majority party who were supporters of Militant Tendency and whether their more moderate colleagues could and would stay with them.

PRIVATE CONVERSATIONS

During these extremely anxious years for Liverpool, we have frequently met with senior politicians in both London and Liverpool. Soon after the Toxteth riots one minister said to us in Liverpool that he had been told by Margaret Thatcher to come and see us, to secure the authentic voice of the community. The years of the rates dispute brought frequent journeys to London to meet with the Secretary of State for the Environment and on occasion with other ministers and opposition leaders. In our role as communicators and interpreters, with very rare exceptions, we have been received with courtesy, seriousness and great openness. We have always understood that the fact of our meetings was not secret but that the contents of our discussions were private. We have set out to offer the most accurate account of the situation and of attitudes, as we have understood them, and we have generally been given the assurance that frankness has been appreciated.

We will admit that there have been times when we have asked ourselves in this context whether we have been 'used' by taking part in such open conversations with government ministers. On a number of occasions when leaving a government department we have felt ourselves to be at the end of the road, with no sign that the points we have made at an interview or discussion have been in any way acceptable. Yet often enough, a few weeks later the suggestion, or something recognisably close to it, has appeared to be taken up and before long a further exchange has been required. But not always! There was one occasion when we were very firmly and rather crudely put in our place by a minister we were meeting for the first time. His attitude had been such a clear rejection of all that we stood for that, strangely, we emerged from the encounter reassured by the battering we had received. No one could accuse us of compromising our convictions on that occasion. However, the treatment accorded us that day was exceptional. Perhaps there were times when more vigorous exchanges would have proved a better release for our feelings. But we doubt if it would have served Liverpool so well. Generally speaking, the more frank and good-humoured meetings have allowed trusting relationships to develop to mutual benefit.

At times we have been conscious that we have been breaking new ground, and have truly agonised about the responsibilities we have borne in discussing certain important issues with individuals who were sharply critical of persons and interests we have tried to represent. Perhaps the most acute anxiety was experienced over the issue of whether commissioners might be appointed to run Liverpool if local government finally broke down. There were real doubts in our minds about the degree of co-operation which might reasonably have been expected of us if such appointments had been made. Fortunately it became clear that there was no desire to put in commissioners, save as a very last resort. But we had plenty of time to agonise over just what our position would have been under such circumstances, which might have brought all manner of sinister significance to the 'collaboration' which could have been required.

These meetings with ministers have included at intervals quite lengthy discussions with Mrs Thatcher. At one stage, when the House of Lords' judgment was awaited, the whole future of Liverpool seemed cloaked in uncertainty, should the councillors lose their appeal against surcharge. We discussed with the Prime Minister ways in which some sort of partnership between local government and central government might get on the road again. It became clear that the Government would need to feel confident that there was a stable council in office before any offer of fresh help could be considered. We came away from that meeting with a sense of challenge to do whatever lay in our power to work for more co-operative attitudes, across party barriers, in place of the spirit of confrontation which had proved so disastrous for the image of the city.

We decided to take those feelings to the Michaelmas Group of senior businessmen, whom we had first called together two and a half years earlier (cf. chapter seven, p. 162). One of their chief concerns was with this image of Merseyside. The commonly held picture of a strike-torn, bloody-minded workforce had turned many businesses away. These businessmen knew that the reality is far different in many ways. There is, for example, a proven willingness and loyalty of an office workforce, which can cut costs very considerably from London and the South-East. An interesting example, given to us, was that of a firm of business consultants who looked at a very large office-based operation in Liverpool. Even allowing for London costs being higher, they arrived at a figure at which, they believed, the same operation might be carried out more efficiently and effectively. They offered to implement the change which they assumed would be an economy, only to discover that the highly successful Liverpool company was already working at one third of the consultants' estimate. However, the aggressive and destabilising image projected by the Militant-dominated City Council has not helped, especially when firms, either from Britain or from overseas, have been considering investing in Liverpool. One of Liverpool's most effective business promoters remarked that 'saving Liverpool is not just for the local benefit: it is necessary for the nation's trade. Some overseas firms come to look at the city, are fed with the false image and decide to go instead to Portugal.'

Confronted by the challenge we brought them from the Prime Minister about the possibility of restoring central government's reasonable confidence in the city, the members of the Michaelmas Group shied away from the notion of an extended Urban Development Corporation to run large parts of the city: impatience with local democracy does not destroy the importance of the democratic principle involved in local government. The group went to work to produce an outline of a common programme which councillors, who were prepared to put the good of Liverpool first, might jointly support without having to abandon their long-term party political preferences. The challenge was how to manage a reduced but renewed city, and within the law. Our group was clear that there was need for help from central government; but on the other hand the Government might reasonably demand to see a more stable and co-operative local government in office before any such help might be forthcoming. With some of the most senior business members, we went as a delegation from the Michaelmas Group to meet political and trade union leaders in London. We shared with them some notes we had produced, suggesting possible common policies in important issues like employment, housing, education, social services, etc. It was not our task to work out a detailed programme of recovery, but to support in any way we could a more co-operative approach.

THE CHURCHES' WITNESS

This account of how Liverpool is often perceived by Westminster and *vice versa* has provided one rather extreme example of the deep divisions running through our society. What is the task of the Christian Churches in such a divided nation? The best of efforts are often treated with great suspicion by politicians, and the media are always ready to set up Church v. State as an issue. The 'Hands across Britain' project of May 1987, when an attempt was made to achieve a human chain from Hope Street in Liverpool to Downing Street in London, in order to focus attention on unemployment, was a good example of this. Some inevitable gaps in the chain were made to appear of greater significance than the fact that more than a quarter of a million people turned out on a dreadfully wet Sunday afternoon to register their commitment to try to tackle the problem of the vast number of unemployed. Even though politicians were willing, at least when challenged, to admit the relevance of the Church's concern to play its part in trying to ease the problems of unemployment, media questioning was all on the subject of party-political involvement.

The Churches are able to provide bridges on which their members from Comfortable Britain and the Other Britain can meet. Linking parishes or local groups of churches one with another can help to remove some of the unknowing, provided that the relationship is carefully negotiated with a clear expectation that there can be mutual giving and receiving without being patronising. Out of that can come respect for one another's knowledge and qualities in light of experience, and a better understanding of scales of values, weaknesses and strengths. As one example of many links, we put a group of Churches in Hampshire in touch with an ecumenical grouping in one of Liverpool's outer estates. Another bridge has been half a dozen people, mostly unemployed, organised by Merseyside Church Action on Poverty, going to spend a study weekend with the Salisbury Diocesan Board for Social Responsibility. The Merseyside Churches Unemployment Committee has been organising a series of two-day visits to the area by two or three Members of Parliament at a time, from southern constituencies. Quite simply, the invitation to friends to 'come on up' and stay for a couple of nights has been to mutual advantage, has changed attitudes and has helped to close the 'divide'.

When the House of Lords came to debate the report *Faith in the City* just over a year after its publication, Archbishop Robert Runcie said,

> We have substantial evidence from opinion polls that many people would be prepared to pay more taxes and forgo tax cuts in order to help divert resources to the poor . . . If we are to have faith in the city, we must also have some faith in Comfortable Britain. I do not regard it as axiomatic that such a Britain is basically selfish, uncaring, greedy and vindictive.

DAVID SHEPPARD: Speaking in the same debate in the House of Lords, I related how at the time of the launch of the report I was confronted on television with a costing of all the recommendations the Commission had made. The figure had been revealed as if no sensible person could contemplate such expenditure. I added:

> *It turned out to be an increase of 4p in the pound on income tax. Of course no account was taken of the increased earnings resulting from a healthier, more productive, back-at-work, and more united nation. But never mind that. My response is that, if the running sore in the side of the nation of massive unemployment and urban deprivation could begin to be healed for only 4p in the pound on income tax, we should thank God and get on with it.*
>
> *I know that it is argued by some that a cut in the standard rate of income tax would help those of comparatively modest means and that they criticise an increase in taxation for hitting them. For over twenty*

years we have been moving away from a progressive tax system, in which those with larger incomes pay a larger proportion in tax. Another very recent report, Not Just for the Poor (1987), spelt out carefully how tax rates on the highest incomes have been reduced to 60p in the pound. The more prosperous taxpayers benefit more than the less well off from the wide range of tax reliefs and allowances, which have been rightly called the tax allowance welfare state. This has enabled the more prosperous so to reduce their tax liability that only 3.5% of taxpayers in Britain pay tax above the standard rate.

Again, the Churches have a continuing calling to serve as the conscience of the nation. Christians should not withdraw as a race apart, nor should they see today's world as enemy territory. We should recognise British society as *our* society and seek to understand our responsibilities as members of it. We have already pointed out that ecumenism is not only about Churches but about the whole earth. It is a Christian responsibility to insist on a concern for this 'whole', and not to be put off from making a Christian contribution to the public debate on the score that we live in a pluralist society. That concern for the whole should lead to a priority interest in those who are excluded from the better opportunities, which should be available to the whole.

For Christians the idea of the body is a natural way to think of society, as well as of the Church. When St Paul wrote of the Church as the body of Christ, he was using an analogy which had already been widely used of the body politic by Roman writers. Had he been writing today of the divided nation, he could well have used the words he wrote to the Christians in Corinth:

God has put all the separate parts into the body as he chose. If they were all the same part, how could it be a body? As it is, the parts are many but the body is one. The eye cannot say to the hand, 'I have no need of you,' and nor can the head say to the feet, 'I have no need of you.'

What is more, it is precisely the parts of the body that seem to be the weakest which are the indispensable ones . . . God has composed the body so that greater dignity is given to the parts which were without it, and so that there may not be disagreements inside the body but each part may be equally concerned for all the others. If one part is hurt, all the parts share its pain. And if one part is honoured, all the parts share its joy.

(1 Cor 12:18–22, 24–26 NJB)

11 'NOT ONLY INTELLECT, ALSO THE AFFECTIONS'

Pentecost Sunday 1982 was an unforgettable day in Liverpool's history. No one who was there that evening will challenge the police estimate of one million people on the streets of the city to welcome, or at least take a look at, Pope John Paul II, as he drove from Speke Airport to visit the two cathedrals and later to spend the night at Archbishop's House. The visit itself, which was the result of an invitation issued after the Roman Catholic National Pastoral Congress held in Liverpool in 1980, had been planned for nearly two years. The months of preparation had been filled with problems and anxieties. Some were of general concern, like the attempt on the Pope's life in Rome in May 1981 and the Falkland Islands conflict, which had almost led to a last-minute cancellation of the visit. Others were related specifically to Liverpool, like the Toxteth Riots – in spite of warnings from his security advisers, the Pope insisted on driving through Toxteth so as not to by-pass the black community – and some sectarian stirrings, orchestrated from outside Merseyside. There are many personal memories of these anxious months, when much of the spirit for which we stood was being put to the test. The moment which provided the sharpest and most significant recollection for both of us was when, after an address at Speke Airport and a six-mile journey into the city, along streets lined with great crowds, Pope John Paul in his Pope-mobile finally arrived outside the Anglican Cathedral.

As the Pope alighted from his vehicle, attended by, among others, the celebrated Archbishop Marcinkus, at that time still virtually 'tour manager' and self-appointed bodyguard, he was greeted by the Dean, Edward Patey, who had pioneered much of Liverpool's ecumenical partnership. The Cathedral was filled to capacity with a congregation drawn from all the non-Roman Catholic Churches in Merseyside. As we entered with the Pope, perhaps a little uncertainly, there was an explosion of sound, of cheering and clapping and singing, which was also the explosion of pent-up emotions, released at that moment in a great roar of joy, relief and thanksgiving that such an event had proved possible. In the sanctuary the Pope was formally welcomed, exchanged the sign of peace with all the assembled Church leaders, recited the Lord's prayer and then, at the Dean's invitation, gave the blessing. Amidst scenes of continuing enthusiasm, he moved slowly down the length of the Cathedral and out again into the sunshine and the vast crowds awaiting his progress along Hope Street to the Roman Catholic Cathedral, where he celebrated Mass.

As he remounted the Pope-mobile, casting a further look at the cheering, waving crowds, we thanked him for having made such a significant gesture, which was a clear affirmation of what we had attempted in religious reconciliation. He too was obviously deeply affected by the warmth of the feelings which had been expressed. Choosing his words carefully, Pope John Paul said: 'It is very important. Ecumenism is not only of the intellect; it is also of the affections.'

THE QUEEN IN LIVERPOOL

'Affections' may not be a particularly *English* way of expressing the 'gut feelings' of which we had often had evidence in the months leading up to the papal visit. We have in an earlier chapter referred to the importance which, on our coming to Liverpool, we both attached to 'imaginative events' as a means of drawing more and more people into the improving inter-Church relationships known by our immediate predecessors. The papal visit, and the visit of the Queen for the Service of Thanksgiving and Dedication to mark the completion of the building of the Anglican Cathedral, provided landmarks which imprinted on many Liverpudlian memories pictures of how church life might be.

We were of course fortunate to inherit two modern cathedrals, which for their size, architecture and position in the city, had captured the imagination both nationally and internationally. The first occasion when they were used together was for a celebration of the Queen's Jubilee by all the Merseyside Churches in June 1977. Between two parts of one single act of worship there was a 'walk' along Hope Street, from one mighty building to the other. We used the word 'walk' deliberately for fear lest there be association with the more aggressive 'processions' of the past. The Salvation Army provided a band for the first occasion. Subsequently the walks have been even more informal, with youth groups supplying guitar songs at appropriate places on the route. Not surprisingly there has also often been a cluster of twenty or so protesters near the Anglican Cathedral, alleging treachery and handing out leaflets. But the numbers involved have been few. It is always sad, even if understandable, that they have provided suitable sights and sounds to achieve quite disproportionate space in the local press and radio reports.

A few weeks later the city and county authorities arranged a celebration for the school-children, who were gathered in large numbers in both cathedrals and their precincts, to sing and dance for the Queen's visit to Merseyside. Some verses had been prepared by the Poet Laureate, Sir John Betjeman, and music for the occasion had been composed by Malcolm Williamson, the Master of the Queen's Music. The fact that the Royal party had been delayed by great crowds resulted in both poet and composer becoming ill, while standing outside waiting in the sun. The amplifiers in Hope Street proved at best spasmodic in their function. This left the children slightly disorganised in their miming, and the Royal entourage slightly on edge at what might be required of their principals, especially inside the Metropolitan Cathedral. But the Queen's relaxed participation in the children's occasion made the whole celebration an excellent opportunity for dedication afresh to the life of one nation. In the evening we were invited along with many others to a reception on the Royal Yacht *Britannia*, tied up at Liverpool's Pier Head. We were reminded of the earlier occasion at the Jubilee in 1935. The story is told that the Bishop and Archbishop of that day had never met, though each was anxious to make a tentative first move. But what about protocol? Where were they to meet? Would one have to cede seniority if he met on the other's territory? The then Earl of Derby skilfully arranged that they both be invited to the *Britannia*. The honour of all was satisfied aboard the Royal Yacht in the River Mersey.

There was another great church occasion the following year when the Queen attended the service to mark the completion of the Anglican Cathedral which had been building continuously for seventy-four years. This provided an opportunity for a further example of ecumenical sharing.

DEREK WORLOCK: We have already spoken of our belief that shared events have also to be planned together. I remember well David's phone-call to tell me that the date for the Queen's visit to his Cathedral had been settled. Could I be there? Was there any part in the celebration which I could fulfil? In the event, I presented a specially bound and inscribed copy of the Jerusalem Bible to the Dean and Chapter, as a symbol of our common proclamation of God's Word at either end of Hope Street. But of great importance was the fact that the Queen, after the Cathedral ceremony in the morning, was offering the afternoon to the Church in case there was anything the Bishop wanted to show her. 'I wondered whether you would like to come in on it and whether we and the Free Church leaders might mount something together.' Not merely did I agree but two years later I was able to repay the call by seeking his collaboration in arranging the Pope's visit to Liverpool.

The Queen's ecumenical walkabout in Liverpool in October 1978 was at that stage probably without precedent. After the Thanksgiving in the Anglican Cathedral and lunch with the Lord Mayor, the Queen walked through the streets of the city to the nearby Roman Catholic church of St Mary, in Highfield Street. In this church, which was part of the base of the City Centre Ecumenical Team, the Churches had gathered a group of people from the inner-city churches active in serving the wider community. While the Queen sat in the sanctuary, Donald Gray, then rector of the Anglican Parish Church, told her of the work of the team in the shops and offices of the city. Then Mary McAleese, a nun active in social work, explained the interests and concerns of the women of the neighbourhood; and finally, Peter Brain, a Free Church minister, much involved in world development, told her of the commitment of the poor and deprived towards Third World relief projects. The Queen then made a slow tour of the church, talking to one group after another about their work together: to young clergy about their ministry in the big stores; to mothers about the problems of trying to bring up children in high-rise flats; to those whose efforts exemplify commitment to needs far greater than those experienced on the home front. After that she went out to Kirkby and met a similar group from the Churches in the outer council estates.

THE PAPAL VISIT

Our shared experience made it natural that the invitation to Pope John Paul to place Liverpool on the itinerary for his visit to Britain should be shared with the Merseyside Church leaders before any announcement was made. In the nearly two years which followed, when many detailed arrangements had to be made, there were several uncertainties about the visit itself. We were concerned chiefly to be on the alert for any obvious signs of a return to sectarianism. We were often reminded of how difficult it was to tell how near beneath the surface of ecumenical tolerance were the hatreds of old; and the security arrangements demanded by the police were not solely due to the assassination attempt in St Peter's Square. We did not fail to take note of some of the disruptive threats which came from across the water or north of the border. The Lenten lunchtime sermons which are now traditional at the Anglican Liverpool Parish Church provided the protesters with the occasion, and set a challenge to Christian Liverpudlians.

DEREK WORLOCK: In the middle of March 1982, I got no further in my annual sermon at the Parish Church than 'My dear brothers and sisters in Jesus Christ', when two or three protesters stood up and began to shout and wave banners. I paused and signalled to the organist to begin a hymn to prevent the attempt to shout me down. The tactic was that while one protester was being taken out of church, another stood up to take over. With a fair selection of hymns and by my repeating the last words from the cross, the service was somehow completed, though not without obvious distress to the congregation. But this proved to be a 'dummy run' for the interruption of the service two days later when the Archbishop of Canterbury was the preacher.

DAVID SHEPPARD: After some three minutes Archbishop Runcie mentioned Pope Gregory's sending St Augustine to England. At that point a member of the Orange Lodge, wearing his sash, stepped out and began to argue. That was quickly followed by waving of banners, shouting and singing. A coach-load had come from Glasgow to support a smaller number of local protesters. The Archbishop was not able to say another word. He went and knelt silently at the altar, while the protesters shouted, rather than sang 'Dare to be a Daniel', with words adjusted to invoke curses on the Bishop of Rome. I felt that I needed to be some kind of bodyguard to help the Archbishop withdraw from the Church. A woman was standing on a pew, screaming at him. He turned and said to her, 'Don't be afraid. There's nothing to be afraid of.'

The following day the Grand Master of the Orange Lodge came to see me, very disturbed that some of his members had taken part in this demonstration wearing their sashes and regalia against his instructions. I asked if he would like to bring some senior colleagues to meet me and one or two others. Julian Charley, team rector of Everton and a member of the Anglican/Roman Catholic International Commission joined me, and six senior Orange Lodge officers came to Bishop's Lodge. I asked them what they were afraid of. 'We're afraid that the Pope will become the Head of the Church of England, the Queen will have to move over and our constitution and liberties will be lost.' I said, 'If I believed you were right in your fears, I would join you at the barricades.' Julian Charley and I tried to explain what our hopes for ecumenism were really about, but we were up against a deep-rooted ignorance, fed by the propaganda they regularly taught to their children.

The evening after the Archbishop of Canterbury was shouted down, I visited one of our clergy in a public ward in a Liverpool hospital. He told me that everyone had watched the scenes at the Parish Church on television and that everyone was furious. It became very clear that day that the great majority in Liverpool no longer supported the sectarian extremists.

I was the next bishop in line to preach in those lunch-hour services. I have never been so well prepared for a sermon in my life. There was a three-minute version, if I was only allowed to preach for so long; a seven-minute version and a seventeen-minute version. In the event all passed peacefully and I was able to deliver my whole address.

In many ways those incidents in mid-March proved the turning point in what might have developed into a most unpleasant sectarian campaign. In the weeks which followed there were one or two minor incidents when a fruitless attempt was made to start a fire in a city church, and two presbyteries suffered broken windows. It was interesting to see the efforts of those at the receiving end, not only to avoid retaliation but to make sure that what had happened was not reported in the media, lest it cause further tension or promote additional anxiety about the visit. There were those who seized these opportunities to say that we had been pushing matters forward too fast. They believed that, rather than risk trouble, we should have left matters in a state of peaceful and separate coexistence.

The fact that the proposed route for the Pope-mobile lay through Toxteth led a few Vatican advisers to question the wisdom of such a journey; but about this the Pope was eager to accept local advice, which of course was positive. A further tender spot for some was the proposed visit to the Anglican Cathedral before going on to the Roman Catholic Cathedral. There were those who were opposed to such a visit altogether and others who questioned the order of events. Both categories were to be found among Protestants and Roman Catholics, not excluding a certain number of Vatican officials. In the event it was the clear determination of the Pope and the patience of Dean Edward Patey which carried the day, and led to the remark which we have used as the title for this chapter.

DEREK WORLOCK: Originally it had been planned that, as the Pope was due to celebrate Mass at Coventry that morning and at Manchester the following morning, the visit to Liverpool on Whitsunday evening should take the form of a non-Eucharistic Service of Reconciliation in the Metropolitan Cathedral, following a short 'call' at the Anglican Cathedral, where the sign of peace might be exchanged. However, some months before the visit took place, I received a telephone call from Rome to say that the Pope wished to celebrate Mass in the Metropolitan Cathedral, preaching on the theme of reconciliation. This would be in addition to the Mass celebrated earlier that day at Coventry. To my amazement I was asked if this proposal would be acceptable. To my greater amazement I found myself replying that we should be delighted, provided I could consult Bishop Sheppard and that there was no question of pulling out of the prior visit to the Anglican Cathedral. Happily this was agreed.

My suspicions were shown to be not altogether unfounded when on Easter Sunday, just a few weeks before the visit, Archbishop Marcinkus arrived by air to check the route and other arrangements. I alerted Dean Patey to be in readiness at the Anglican Cathedral, but Archbishop Marcinkus delayed so long at Speke Airport that Edward Patey was about to leave when at last we reached him. Carefully he walked the course with the big American, describing in some detail all that would be expected of the Pope in the relatively simple ceremony which was proposed. I stood close at hand to help if any crisis should arise. When at last we reached the sanctuary, it was evident that an 'eyeball to eyeball' confrontation was about to take place. 'What would you do, Dean,' said Archbishop Marcinkus, 'if I were to tell you that the Pope might not be willing to carry out all your proposals?' The Dean smiled and replied: 'We have faced and overcome greater difficulties in the past four hundred years. I am sure that we could find an alternative arrangement.' 'And what would you do, Dean,' persisted Marcinkus, 'if I were to tell you that the Pope would not visit your Cathedral at all?' Edward Patey blinked and said stoutly, 'Quite frankly, we should not believe you.' That was the end of the conversation.

GREAT OCCASIONS

In retrospect 1984 is remembered as one of the great years in Liverpool's history. The International Garden Festival in the summer months produced attendance figures of nearly three and a half million. On the first Sunday after the official opening by the Queen, an ecumenical service was held in the arena and had to be repeated because the congregation of nearly ten thousand could not be accommodated at one session. Merseyside was full of hope at the time and it was not a far stretch of the imagination to speak of our 'Easter Garden', with the renewal for the new life given to parts of the riverside which had been an offensive dumping-ground. When at last the closure came in the autumn, a similar service of thanksgiving and dedication was held. Our preacher was able to speak of the variety of growth which had taken place and of the beauty of a different kind which can come to the land in winter, with all the promise of another spring ahead.

In the course of those summer months the restoration of the old Albert Dock buildings on the riverside had been completed. New life had come back to a great area of dereliction and decay. The silted-up docks had themselves been dredged and water filled them again as the Tall Ships came up the Mersey for their annual race and review. On the day of the sail past, more than one million persons crowded both sides of the river Mersey. Some of Liverpool's history and heritage had become alive again. Lights burnt once more in wharf buildings which in the past had been busy with trade. Now new businesses, often connected with tourism and the leisure industry, had begun to appear.

The key-word was renewal, and the gut-feelings (or 'affections') of the people reflected qualified hope and the desire of young people to stay and try to find a future in the place of their upbringing. Sadly the abolition of the Merseyside County Council, which had played so big a part in the achievements of 1984, was at hand; and with it the mounting crisis of confrontation between the City Council and central government. But the events we have recorded all showed the general feeling of unity, which helped to hold together a people threatened in so many ways but who could on occasions come together to celebrate, whether they called it 'life' or their 'faith'. The closing of the gap between life and faith has been a central part of the Churches' task.

THE BRUSSELS DISASTER

That gap was again closed in May 1985 with the great tragedy of the deaths in the Heysel Stadium in Brussels. The occasion was the European Football Cup Final when Liverpool FC were to play the Juventus team from Turin. Before the eyes of millions watching on television, a fierce confrontation between supporters, and pre-match hooliganism of the worst kind, erupted in part of the stadium. A wall collapsed and a number of spectators, most of them Italians, were crushed to death. Many of those present were even unaware of what had happened. Supporters from both clubs were certainly involved, though the culprits, when identified and charged, were by no means all from Liverpool. But the sense of shame throughout the city was enormous. The team's supporters enjoyed an excellent record from former encounters and clearly the players themselves were in no way to blame. But the whole of Liverpool had to bear the brunt of reasonable and widespread condemnation, and there was no attempt to evade responsibility.

Football and religion matter more in Liverpool than in many other places. In the days immediately following the Brussels disaster the two interests stood closely together. We had ourselves to meet extensive demands from radio and television: one of us in London, the other in Liverpool and Manchester. The city's pride in its two football teams was so great that it felt to some as though the one great achievement we still possessed had been shattered. We expressed deep sorrow for anything for which our citizens might be responsible, and endeavoured to show practical sympathy with the families of the victims of the disaster. At the same time we needed to help our fellow citizens to pick themselves up from the fall which had brought them low.

On the day after the disaster we both had to voice the sorrow of the city, without assuming its total guilt. That evening, as the team and supporters arrived back from Belgium, a Mass for the dead and the injured was celebrated in the Metropolitan Cathedral and was attended by great crowds. It is hard to judge which was the more moving; a representative group of the Liverpool players who, choked with emotion, brought a wreath to the altar in the offertory procession, or the number of quite young children, clad in their Liverpool 'strip', who attended with their parents. This Mass, arranged at very short notice, clearly met a real need of a sorrowing city. It was duly filmed by television cameras and was shown throughout the country the following Sunday.

It was agreed that ten days later a more formal service of sorrow and penitence would be held in the Anglican Cathedral. This was attended by Patrick Jenkin, then Minister with responsibility for Merseyside, the Italian and Belgian Ambassadors, and Liverpool's civic leaders. Large numbers attended the service, before which a book of condolence was placed in the Cathedral, and for hours that day ordinary people queued to sign the book to associate themselves with sorrow for what had occurred. Subsequently it was presented to the Italian Ambassador in London who stated publicly on the radio that he felt that the people of Liverpool had done more than might reasonably have been expected of them.

Only a few days after the tragedy, Derek Hatton, the Militant councillor who was deputy leader of the City Council, made the proposal that a delegation from the city should go out to Turin, formally to express regret in the name of the citizens. The message was transmitted to the Mayor of Turin, with an enquiry as to whether the timing of such a visit would be suitable. The reply was affirmative, and shortly afterwards we were both invited to join the official delegation from the city. We insisted that we would go only if all parties were represented, but when that condition was met, we gladly made ourselves available.

With a party comprising the leading Labour councillors, Liberal and Conservative representatives, representatives of Liverpool and Everton Football Clubs, and civic officials, we flew to Turin a few days later. There was considerable media interest in this country and in Turin itself, and it was not altogether surprising that at frequent press conferences some members of the delegation did not hesitate to try to make political capital out of the situation in Liverpool. Nevertheless, through the clear leadership of the Chairman of the City Council, Hugh Dalton, and the skill of the Chief Executive, Alfred Stocks, a very difficult act of reconciliation was carried through remarkably well. One wonders when last the official representatives of a city attempted a comparable corporate act of penitence and reconciliation of this kind.

Generally the delegation was well received. We were all housed together in one hotel and a police guard was supplied throughout our stay. As it happened, it proved quite unnecessary. There was considerable interest, especially among the press, in the presence of two bishops in what was recognised as primarily a political or sporting delegation. Yet as the visit took shape the role of the Church leaders and the reason for our presence became steadily clearer. There was an atmosphere of respectful formality when we were all received in the City Council chamber for the exchange of messages. After our Chairman and the Mayor of Turin had delivered their speeches, we were both invited to speak in the name of the community of Liverpool, and were followed by a spokesman for the two football clubs. We were also able to offer condolences to the widow of the Turin supporter who had been killed, though it should be said that it was Derek Hatton who first located her and went to her with his sympathy. But the subsequent press conference, at which the City Council leaders were most anxious that we should be present, produced a series of speeches, with Tony

Mulhearn insisting on being heard as 'the Chairman of the ruling political party'. The Italian sports correspondents did not fail to notice this, though it was the *Sunday Telegraph* correspondent who subsequently suggested that perhaps we were being 'used'.

There is always the danger of this, but significantly that correspondent was not present when we were all welcomed at the Juventus Football Club headquarters that afternoon. That was when the waving and smiles started from a small crowd in the street. Nor was he in evidence at the Mass of Reconciliation which was celebrated that evening in the presence of the Cardinal Archbishop of Turin at the town's principal shrine, *La Consolata*. There were more than two thousand enthusiastic Italians packed into the shrine as a congregation. When the Mass had been suggested, there was no great enthusiasm for the idea among the politicians in our delegation, but in the end all were present in the front rows, the leading Militants among them. By this time the delegation was being applauded by the people of Turin wherever we went. We both preached at the Mass, for which we had the skilled services as interpreter of Monsignor Peter Coughlan, an English priest serving in the Vatican. At the end Cardinal Anastasio Ballestrero added his own words of reconciliation and invited us to join him in blessing the congregation. Then with the other members of the delegation we made our way to the sacristy, where gifts were exchanged.

By the end the whole congregation seemed to be waving or applauding. Even the most reluctant of the Militants, recovering from his shock at being firmly clasped and embraced by several Italian ladies during the exchange of the sign of peace, entered into the spirit of things and remarked on how the Roman Church had changed since last he had known it. For the Turin supporters, and especially the officials of Juventus, it was a totally new experience of ecumenical sharing. For Liverpool, football and religion came closer together that night than ever before. The city retains the sense of the tragic disaster at the Heysel Stadium; but with the services in the two Cathedrals and the penitential visit to Turin completed, the two teams set to work once more to prepare for the next season, but, like all English clubs after Brussels, banned from Europe.

RED AND BLUE

In recent years it has been our custom to go together to a match or two each season, being careful to bestow our favours on both clubs and at both grounds. With John Williamson, the Moderator of the Free Churches, we were present at Wembley in May 1986 when Liverpool and Everton met in the FA Cup Final. Grace Sheppard and Mary Williamson were mindful to wear carefully blended silk scarves of both red and blue. Unexpected significance can be attached to the possession of any object of either colour. Some Evertonians, with their predilection for blue, had been put to the test when for his Pentecost visit Pope John Paul wore vestments of the liturgical season, coloured red.

We have to admit a near-disaster when we responded to an invitation, given in the enthusiasm of the moment, by the Liverpool Chairman, John Smith, that we should 'hold a short service' on the turf at Anfield before the new season started, following the Brussels disaster. We should have known better. Close as the relationship between football and religion may be, the two do not mix. With the Moderator, we carefully prepared a short announcement, to be followed by some verses of 'Abide with me' and a final prayer. The words were printed in the front of the programme, which however is not bought by many in the Kop end of the ground, where the younger Liverpool supporters are packed together and where they have their own songs – a kind of liturgical rite in itself.

Shortly before being led out on to the centre of the pitch, where a battery-operated hand-microphone awaited us, we were informed that unfortunately the battery-switch had been left on overnight, after being tested the previous evening, and was now flat. A search had been made for a replacement but in vain. We would have to use the police 'dug-out' at the side, with a built-in microphone for announcements. It proved disastrous. Though stilled by our first announcement, the crowd could not see us and many were puzzled by what was happening. When valiantly we sang our way into 'Abide with me', the visiting supporters started a chant of their own, which was promptly drowned by the Kop singing 'You'll never walk alone'. In one sense this was their own hymn. We completed the prayer quite unheard and emerged from the 'dug-out' to the evident embarrassment of the more devout of the spectators. Next day the Sunday newspapers made much of what they regarded as the latest outrage of 'football hooligans'. We did our best to exonerate all concerned on grounds of reasonable confusion. To humorous enquiries made nowadays as to whether we have any good prayers ready, we are at least able to point out that by the end of that season Liverpool FC had completed the 'double', finishing top of the League and winning the FA Cup Final. But we had all learnt a lesson.

THE DOUBLE ACT

We have described some of the most public events, when feelings were deeply touched. But the affections can also be stirred by the steady round of engagements in which we are seen together. For example, on one occasion we jointly opened some sheltered housing for the elderly. For once the chosen name, Bishopscourt (without an apostrophe), did not signify that it was run by one particular part of the community. On that occasion, and indeed on others where we have separately visited old people, our partnership was the point repeatedly mentioned. Often the opening remark would be: 'Of course, I am not of your faith but . . .' People of that generation, who have known the bitter divisions of the past, often go on to say, 'Thank you for what you do together for Liverpool.'

After a few years we began to understand that our friendship and partnership had wider consequences than we had anticipated. Now we were being asked to go further afield to give witness together to our commitment to work for Christian unity and indeed to the Church's concern for social justice. Someone invented the term 'the Mersey Miracle'. *The Times* followed up with 'the Dynamic Duo'. We tried not to take it too seriously and referred to the 'ecumenical pantomime horse': whoever was to speak first became the front legs. On one occasion, one of us was suffering exhaustion and pleaded to be the hind legs so that, in the best pantomime tradition, he might deliver his part of the joint address sitting down.

Inevitably these appearances together soon became known as 'the double act', and we developed the technique of preparing speeches and sermons in four parts, taking it more or less in turns as to who did parts one and three, and who parts two and four. Not merely does this require a considerable degree of consultation in advance. It makes clear to the audience or congregation that the preparation as well as the delivery is shared. One year we were both invited to preach in the University Church at Cambridge, one following the other on succeeding Sundays. Two years later we were back there again, but this time to preach the one sermon from the same pulpit. It appears to be a popular technique in universities and has an obvious appeal during the Week of Prayer for Christian Unity. In January 1987 we spoke together in different parts of the country on three successive nights: one of them at the University Church of St Mary the Virgin in Oxford, where Thomas Cranmer made his defence and where John Henry Newman was vicar in his Anglican days.

However, the invitation is not always from a university chaplaincy, nor are we always required to speak on an expressly religious subject. It may be about the North/South divide, inner-city matters, unemployment, housing, or racial discrimination. Experience indicates that whatever title is suggested, in the end what is wanted is some personalised account of 'what you two are up to in Liverpool'. We have spoken in Glasgow about whether a bias to the poor can create a Church of the Poor; and on one occasion we addressed a seminar in London organised by a body called SOLACE (which turned out to be the Society of Local Authority Chief Executives). There have been conferences for those engaged in fighting drug abuse, for Chief Probation Officers and for those engaged in urban planning.

We would not claim expertise in all these subjects. Perhaps it is felt that we are well-placed to set particular subjects in their context, or at least within a wider picture. We live in an age of specialist knowledge. Our experience is that many specialists are very grateful when someone tries to understand their particular field but insists on placing it in the context of the whole. Indeed there are times when speaking of the whole is as near as secular-minded people can come to speaking of God. There are also moments when it is understood that, in setting out such contexts, we can only explain our motivation and values if we spell out their Christian basis. But, as a rule, what is being sought from us is a combined approach to a problem affecting the community and made in light of experience gained through working together. There are also occasions when we are invited to address a day conference for diocesan clergy of our own two Churches. But probably the most challenging invitations have been those requiring us to speak or preach together in Northern Ireland, where sharing a pulpit carries implications of far greater significance than in this country.

NORTHERN IRELAND

It was in July 1983 that we were invited to speak together on reconciliation at the summer festival organised by the Corrymeela community in Co. Antrim. We were intensely conscious of the difference of our experience from that of most of the five hundred or more persons who had come to hear us. It was soon evident that our appearing together and our ease of relationship was of far greater importance to our audience than our words. The questions after we had spoken indicated the same basic problems as exist in any inter-Church situation, but to a degree and against a historical background where fear played a crippling part. But private conversations and group discussions that day also revealed many instances of quite remarkable Christian charity and forgiveness among those who had suffered tragic personal loss as a result of the violence of the last twenty years. We met some of the mothers who made up prayer-groups in Belfast and other Northern Ireland areas of conflict. Their common ground was that all of them had lost a son, murdered in the troubles. They brought together the divided communities as no one else could.

It was a visit which brought us both inspiration and a deep anxiety at the hopelessness which seemed to fill the hearts of so many. It also made us aware of the harsh reality of security measures. It was an eerie sensation when we first became aware of a car following us at a respectful distance, on the road from the airport to Ballycastle. Speaking from the platform later that morning we spotted one of the car's occupants standing purposefully at a strategic vantage point. Afterwards we deliberately went in opposite directions to separate rooms. Emerging at much the same time we duly identified the two guards on duty outside, who acknowledged that they had been assigned to us. They stayed within reach until we said goodbye to them at the airport that evening.

We were both invited back to Northern Ireland by Cardinal O'Fiaich and Dr Armstrong, the Church of Ireland Archbishop of Armagh, for the Christian Unity week in January of the following year, 1984. One of the difficulties facing a visitor to Northern Ireland is the demand of pressmen for statements or impressions within minutes of arrival at Aldergrove Airport outside Belfast. It was a particularly sensitive time, soon after the shooting by the IRA of several Pentecostal worshippers in their chapel at Darkley, near the border. By arrangement with our hosts we decided to hire a small plane to take us privately from Liverpool Airport to the airport in Belfast Harbour. In this way we avoided all direct encounter with the media until the following day, by which time we had had ample opportunity to consult with the two Primates, who clearly enjoyed a good personal relationship. Each of us stayed with his respective archbishop on the hills which face each other across the town of Armagh. That night we promised each other a telephone conversation at 9 a.m. next morning to discuss the day's programme. This accounted for the message brought to the Cardinal's breakfast table: 'The other hill is on the phone, Your Eminence.'

That evening, following the four-part form of sermon we have already described, we preached to about fifteen hundred persons gathered in St Patrick's Roman Catholic Cathedral in Armagh. Afterwards we spoke with members of the congregation who had moved across to the adjoining college for refreshments. Some had come from a considerable distance. The measure of their commitment to reconciliation within the community was a great inspiration. We felt that we received from them more in terms of love and courage than we could bring them. The next morning it was the turn of the Church of Ireland Cathedral in Armagh, where we were due to address many of the clergy of the Province. When we arrived we noticed a number of ministers coming out of the cathedral and making off at a fairly brisk rate. For a moment we were puzzled as to what had caused this last-minute boycott. Enquiry showed that, despite our hosts' insistence that this should be a private occasion, the BBC had gained entry to the building and were busy setting up their cameras in full view of the visiting clergy. Concern for their families rather than for their own safety led a number of them, principally Presbyterians, to move out lest their appearance be identified subsequently on Northern Ireland TV. A quick word with the presenter, and an undertaking to meet his team in Belfast that afternoon, led to the withdrawal of the cameras and the return of most of the clergy.

After the 'double act' in the cathedral, we moved to the Dean's house, where there was the necessary privacy and freedom for a 'question and answer' session. It was evident that fear of intimidatory tactics was a real issue for many of those present. We asked one Presbyterian minister if it was difficult for him to be present at this ecumenical occasion. 'Not for me,' he said. 'My people are wonderfully supportive.' He then pointed to a Methodist minister and told us how 'they' had got at him through his family. When he was away from home, telephone calls would immediately start, threatening his wife, alone with their child, that their house would be burnt down.

That afternoon we drove into Belfast for the second leg of our visit. We were due to preach that evening in St Anne's Cathedral, where some time earlier the redoubtable Cardinal Willebrands had encountered opposition, just as a few years before he had been interrupted in the Anglican Cathedral in Liverpool. There was some sharp questioning at the press conference, the sharpest being reserved for Cardinal O'Fiaich, present to show moral support. For some days he had been encountering opposition due to the selective reporting of an answer he had given in Dublin to a question about Sinn Fein. The same issue followed us to the Cathedral, where the road outside had been closed by the police because of a gathering of about fifty protesters. We were assured that the opposition was due not so much to our presence as to the alleged views and presence of the Cardinal. We saw something then both of the bitterness and tragedy of the differences and also of the courage of Cardinal O'Fiaich and Bishop McCappin of Connor, who quietly continued with their programme despite the protesters' singing what had sadly become known as the 'Darkley hymn' – that being sung in the chapel at Darkley at the time of the shooting a few weeks earlier. Though some persons may have been deterred by the closed street, there were a good thousand in St Anne's Cathedral; and after we had spoken, we stood at the cathedral doors to see them all away. Afterwards we bade farewell to our hosts who had to return to Armagh and we spent the night in a hotel, again under the watchful care of an armed guard.

As we flew home in a blizzard early the next morning, our feelings were a mixture of deep sorrow at the fear and even hatreds which persisted, and great admiration for many of those we had met. Their courage, faith and friendship amidst continuing appalling circumstances of stress and violence are seldom reported but very real. Our subsequent visits to Belfast have reinforced these impressions. On the one hand it was deeply disheartening to be shown the 'Peace Line', as the Northern Ireland Housing Executive took us with Church leaders from Belfast, Glasgow and Liverpool – the 'North-West Triangle' – in and out of terraced streets all along the Falls Road and the Shankhill Road. We got out of our small bus to see an excellent housing development of forty Protestant houses, in the middle of three hundred Catholic houses, in a mainly Protestant district. We asked what the new brick wall was for, built alongside the houses. Four metres high and with a metal shield on top, it was the 'Peace Line', apparently the only way in which people could feel safe, a permanent dividing wall into the future. On the other hand, we saw the developing friendship and trust among many of Northern Ireland's Church leaders which, though seldom reported in the press, is one of the few rays of hope in this most desperate and heart-rending situation.

MARRIAGE AND CELIBACY: UNDERSTANDING THE DIFFERENCE

To have shared these and some of our other experiences in the public expression of our partnership has undoubtedly led to the strengthening of the bond of friendship between us. In writing this book, we have been anxious that people should understand that our collaboration reflects the relationship which should be ours because of our beliefs. At the same time we gladly acknowledge that in all this, personal friendship, even if not the cause of what we have attempted together, has been a very considerable bonus. Yet in the same way as we have said that ecumenism is between Churches, and not just between individuals, so we gratefully recognise the understanding and support of those close to us. The demands upon us, and the pressures, have inevitably been shared with them. This applies to colleagues and especially to chaplains, to friends and family, and in some ways most of all to Grace Sheppard, who has helped to sustain both of us.

Those who know us well will recognise that we share many interests, especially in the realm of social justice. We believe that our commitment to Christ and to the service of his people brings us steadily closer together. To have attempted to write this book together is an indication of an already close understanding of each other's mind, methods and priorities. But we also know each other well enough to share the view of our friends that we are in fact very different persons. It is easy to claim that our characteristics are complementary. In truth, friendship and partnership both call for sensitivity about those areas of concern and character which we do not share, as well as about those things we have in common. Fundamental to this is the recognition that one of us has received a vocation to be married, while the other is called to celibacy.

Both Christian marriage and a celibate life can bring increased vitality to a personal union with God. But they are not the same way to spiritual growth, nor the same way of offering service to others. We recognise and accept this in our partnership, in the individual following of our personal vocation, and in our responsibilities. Married love is an interdependent way of life for husband and wife, and daily living of a common destiny in all its details. Celibacy, which is not the same thing as being a bachelor, is a particular response of an individual, even if living in community with other individuals, to the love of Christ and to the demands of the Church in the service of the people of God.

This emphasis on the individual should not suggest isolation, which sometimes can lead to selfishness and eccentricity. The celibate priest is not denied the support of all human relationships. There is a place in his life for the free and generous interdependence of charity, for mutual prayer and inspiration, for deeply enriching friendships. In the living sign which he is called to give, he can be greatly supported by close friendship with married people. Equally in the marital bond between them, husband and wife can be strengthened by the practical witness and fidelity of one consecrated to celibacy. One way of responding to God's love is not a challenge, let alone a rebuke, to the other. They exist together to help build up the Kingdom. But the true friendship which can result demands the recognition of both bonds and to some extent barriers: certainly there are differences in lifestyle and in the manner of commitment. Just as marriage demands a particular form of selfless sharing so that in interdependence husband and wife become 'two in one flesh', loving one another 'as Christ loved the Church' (Eph. 5:25 NJB), so celibacy – if it is properly lived – demands a lifestyle reflecting a relationship of pure self-giving for God. Both marriage and celibacy can be an important witness to chastity, especially in these present days. But the witness, even though given together, is in different ways. Both are put under strain if they are seen merely as a legal requirement, unrelated to God's love and the love of others.

DAVID SHEPPARD: Several years ago I caught myself comparing my workload with Derek Worlock's. I suppose I wanted to prove to myself that I gave as much time to Christian service as he did. That made me stop and recognise the spirit of competitiveness. It was important too to understand that in celibacy he had a different calling from mine. I would be unfaithful to my calling to be married if I tried to outwork him. St Paul says that single and married persons are each given their special gift. I would be rejecting the gift God has given me if I did not set aside quality time to be with my wife, rather than just collapse in an exhausted heap at the end of each day and week. I urge our clergy to take six weeks' holiday in the year, a day off every week and two hours for themselves and their home every day. Though it was concern for marriage which led me to insist on time like that, I have come to believe that of course single clergy also need to make space to cherish their home, family, friendships and interests. The commandment to love your neighbour as yourself includes caring for yourself, whether married or celibate. It is important to me to make space to reflect on the personal experiences and feelings which make up my own inward journey. Married partnership has been likened to two trees growing side by side. Each partner needs enough space to grow, as well as the interlocking of roots which gives each greater strength. That growing is enriched for me by taking time to paint, to read, to garden, to follow cricket from afar.

Strengthening the marriage relationship needs not only time but love in action, which brings the will, the energy, the trust and the courage to communicate and receive what is deepest and most important to each partner. I wrote earlier about how being married to Grace has enabled me to learn to acknowledge my own deep feelings. That has helped me to recognise that in Jesus, the model for all Christians, we see much vulnerability and not always cast-iron success. Through taking time with Grace to know and be known at every level, I believe I bring a deeper and more loving understanding to my whole ministry. I know much more about 'feminine' gifts, such as cherishing people who may not seem to be very successful, or repairing relationships which could easily be left in ruins.

I grew up with a strong drive to 'get on with the work'. That drive is still strong. The call to be a married priest and bishop includes sacrificial giving of myself and ourselves; I respond best to those parts of my calling if I include Grace as an equal partner in major decisions about them. She has been wonderfully ready to support me in such situations, though she stands her ground about our need of quality time for each other. I believe there are times when we can offer more as a couple, sometimes to other married couples, than either of us can alone, and certainly to many groups and individuals who come to our home. Writing as I have done about our growth may give an impression of turning inwards more than we do. The mutual strengthening, which comes from our common faith and our companionship, makes us want to turn outwards, to be fully involved in the world God made. In our Liverpool years Grace has become more deeply involved in the wider community, as she has developed her own particular calling and gifts. The danger to stable marriage, which is sometimes ascribed to women pursuing their own gifts, only grows when communication is neglected or taken for granted. Our experience is that, provided we keep closely in touch, and share the different directions in which we are growing, trusting partnership becomes stronger and more full of rich surprises.

We have greatly appreciated Derek's sensitivity to us both. His interest in Grace's own doings and the particular pressures which sometimes fall on her has meant much to her. Our decision to go into Toxteth and walk through the streets on the night of disturbances there was made in our kitchen. Grace saw us off, and then rang each of the vicarages in the area to ask the wives of clergy how they were feeling. She was glad to see us safely back and to stay with us while we debriefed. She was at Speke Airport to see us off to Turin and to Belfast, and again to *welcome us back. On our return from Turin she had a meal ready for us in the garden so that we were able to share our experience of that trip together, and to begin to unwind in the brilliant Liverpool sunshine. The many occasions when Derek rings to speak with me often lead also to trusting conversations between him and Grace. He has taken an unfailing interest in our family life and in our daughter's comings and goings. In 1985 he invited us both to go on holiday to Italy for a fortnight with him and his chaplain, John Furnival. There was a certain risk for all of us, for many friendships have not survived joint holidays. Part of the risk for him was to share with us places which had been very special to him in his personal life – all of twenty years ago. We allowed each other space to be on our own: we shared meals and travelling. We also shared feelings quite deeply about family, hobbies and interests. We worshipped together informally in an olive grove and in hotel rooms. The holiday had an element of joint pilgrimage when we went together to Assisi, as we shall describe in the final chapter.*

DEREK WORLOCK: In the years when I have been a priest, I have seen a great development in the approach of the Church to celibacy. Clearly it was a highly significant and important issue in my years of training. Yet it was very much presented as an act of self-denial, and seen almost as part of the whole package one had to accept if one was to be ordained to the priesthood. It is impossible to say precisely what proportion of my fellow students, who gave up in the course of the customary six years of training, did so because they felt unable to accept celibacy. Many left saying quite openly that they wanted marriage and family life. In our training the segregation, of which I have written earlier, applied most rigidly to female company. Numquam solus cum sola *was the maxim set before us – 'never be alone with a woman' – so that it is not altogether surprising if, in the 'liberation' of the 1960s, many of my generation felt ill-prepared for the contacts which the greater involvement in the community now demanded of them.*

The fact that it was seen as all part of the package – our parents used to have to endure sympathy about the lack of grandchildren and were expected to reply about the joy which our spiritual children would bring them – led us none the less to the realisation of our real need to know God's love. Activity would not be enough. We were given perhaps a more inflexible programme for our spiritual life than would be regarded as practical today. We used to talk about having a 'positive' approach to celibacy, but in the eyes of others at least it was often seen as self-abnegation, doubtless admirable in motive but sufficiently unnatural as to render the celibate out of touch with the realities of life.

The fact that in the years following the Second Vatican Council a number of priests felt it desirable to seek a dispensation from their active ministry and from their vow of celibacy, at least emphasised that the great majority who remained made a 'positive' decision to retain their celibacy. Nowadays those preparing for priesthood would seem in most cases to have a more open approach to the vow they take at the time when they are ordained to the diaconate. They do not seem to regard it as just an inescapable part of the package of holy orders. They see it and discuss it as something of great importance in itself. In this they are undoubtedly helped by the insight offered by Pope John Paul II, who always speaks of celibacy as a special gift from God. It is not so much giving up something, as receiving from the Lord the gift of a special relationship with him. 'And', adds the Pope, 'you never give back a gift you have accepted.' In speaking to those approaching the priesthood, I always emphasise that the gift of celibacy also involves a special relationship with their future brother priests and with the people they have been called to serve.

In each of these three respects the gift can be an enrichment. Of course if it is undertaken for the wrong motives or is in any way dishonoured, it can become a cause of embitterment and loneliness. If recognised as a gift, it can enhance the recipient's relationship with the Christ whose priesthood he is called to share; it can be the building up of a unique bond of brotherhood with his fellow priests; and it can lead to a beautiful relationship of trust with his parishioners. This trust and even sense of responsibility for the priest is not unconnected with his celibacy, which is recognised as a sign to his people. Their response is often revealed when they speak with remarkable possessiveness of 'our' priest. Celibacy has a great deal to do with that word 'our'.

To write in this manner is in no way to play down the loving, generous and self-sacrificing response which, in accordance with the traditions and disciplines of other Christian Churches, can be involved in a married vocation. There the interdependence of husband and wife has to be nurtured amidst the multitudinous duties and responsibilities of an ordained ministry. It is sometimes said that we celibate priests are inclined to be starry-eyed about the marriage of others. The hoary old joke about their having the better halves and our having the better quarters no longer amuses or applies, if it ever did. In most parts of the country nowadays presbytery housekeepers have become a rarity; many priests have to manage on their own, with occasional part-time domestic help from a lady parishioner. If at any time the priest is taken ill, he has to call for outside assistance, should this be needed. This is a sign of changing times. We recognise that there are also signs of changing times within the married state.

For myself, fortunately with a household well looked-after by two *religious Sisters, I must gratefully acknowledge the help and support I have received by being admitted regularly to the home and family life of David and Grace Sheppard. Our contact has to be frequent, as we have already explained. But through the exchange each week of details of each other's engagements, I try at least to leave him in peace for his regular times for prayer and reading, and — for the benefit of the family man — to stay clear personally or on the telephone on his much-cherished day off each week. In this Grace has often to be my ally as well as his.*

BETTER TOGETHER

In a chapter which began with emphasis on the importance of 'the affections' and continued with the development of friendship between partners, we have concluded by stressing the need for the recognition of differences and for sensitivity in light of them. The lesson must surely be that true collaboration does not mean merely working alongside one another but genuine sharing. Even where there is a difference in calling and some quite profound differences in belief, there may still be sharing. Christian partners do not have to be identical. Sharing can itself add a dimension to combined activity. That is why we mentioned earlier the criterion we follow in responding to a call for joint action, or for 'the double act' at a meeting or religious service: 'Where one plus one can add up to more than two.' To achieve that sort of sharing, it often happens that other things may be shared as well. Perhaps most important of all is shared prayer. Sharing does not always mean possession in common. The sharing of minds is at least as important as the sharing of resources. That will come only through knowledge and trust, which result from habitual sharing.

We do not for a moment pretend that we are always original or engaged in breaking new ground. Our predecessors have in their own way tackled many of the problems which now claim our attention. In other parts of the country our contemporaries, men and women, seek in their own way to bring the light of the gospel to bear on the same issues which confront society at this time. We do believe that, despite differences in character and calling, we best approach the demands made of us in that way which we have borrowed from the slogan used by the Eldonian Housing Co-operative: 'we do it better together'.

12 THE JOURNEY FORWARD

Journalists visiting Liverpool to write up a city seldom out of the news often rely for local colour on the chorus from Peter McGovern's song, 'In my Liverpool Home':

> We speak with an accent exceedingly rare,
> Meet under a statue exceedingly bare;
> And if you want a Cathedral we've got one to spare
> In my Liverpool home.

The Liverpool accent speaks for itself. Peter Moloney, a member of the Polytechnic staff and one of the city's long-term comedians, diagnoses it as the flat, harsh tones of Belfast, given Merseyside catarrh. The 'exceedingly bare' statue outside Lewis's store in the city centre no longer seems to arouse a blush: like most outside statuary, it has weathered to become part of the local scene. As for the two cathedrals, of which we have already written much, by the time the visiting journalists reach us, they have usually stumbled on reports of the 'Mersey Miracle'. Not infrequently they invite our opinion as to which of the two buildings will have to give way to the other if the Churches 'get their act together' and Christian unity is achieved. The more percipient then apply the same question to ourselves: 'Which of you will go spare?' The easy answer is that, if or when that blessed day comes and the fullness of unity is attained, personal position would be a small price to pay.

The fullness of Christian unity is not a matter of victor and vanquished, of triumph and defeat, of take-over and being absorbed. As we work and pray to meet in him who is the supreme reconciler, our common life becomes a living expression of that bond of fellowship in Christ which the theologians call *koinonia*, or communion. Increasingly it becomes a trusting relationship which reflects, however imperfectly, the relationship within the Trinity. Indeed this is a concept which helps us to understand unity and diversity in the one Church of God. We need this objective, even if we cannot foresee precisely how it is to be achieved. The necessary steps towards the full visible unity of the Church cannot easily be determined without some vision of the goal of unity itself. The ultimate vision is not the same for everyone, but it is clear that total uniformity is not necessarily implied. For centuries there has been the example of the Western Church and the Eastern Churches of the Oriental Rites, with their different traditions and disciplines, existing side by side but in communion with one another. Indeed, the very fact of the multi-cultural society in which the Church is set today seems to exclude uniformity and to point to the richness of diversity.

Concentrating our vision, and looking from one end of Hope Street to the other, are we not justified in praying that, when the fullness of unity is achieved, the two communities will be judged to have done so much that there will be determination to preserve both Cathedrals as a sign of the joint commitment which helped to restore unity of belief? Meantime there is unfinished business to be resolved. We are not yet at the end of our pilgrimage.

YOUNG PEOPLE, THE HOPE OF TOMORROW

We have been very conscious that as we have tried to move forward together it has been necessary to put down certain markers so that, if God wills, others may follow. But it is not just a question of handing over the torch of unity to another generation. The company of young people has been a great help and encouragement in looking to the future. Three times, together with Free Church leaders, we have led ecumenical youth pilgrimages to Taizé, Iona, and Holy Island, Lindisfarne. On each occasion we travelled in one large coach with some forty-five young people between the ages of seventeen and twenty-five. A certain pattern has emerged from the days we have spent together. The stages we have seen our young pilgrims go through seem to us very similar to the stages in ecumenical partnership which all of us have to face. There may be seven ages of man. We have detected eight stages in ecumenical pilgrimages with young people.

1. *Preliminary enthusiasm*

Before each pilgrimage there has been an evening's preparatory gathering, when there has been carefully prepared but informal worship and music, and the opportunity for members of the group to meet and begin to get to know one another. At first the young pilgrims, who up to that time will have had little ecumenical experience of any consequence, tend to hang together in their own denominational groups. There they can feel some security from the recollection of previous acquaintance in youth weekends, rallies and excursions of various kinds. To extend those encounters, which may merely have reached across parish boundaries, to going on a pilgrimage with members of other Churches, may have seemed, when first suggested, to be the natural next step. There are some initial hesitations. Yet when the young people gather at the coach for departure, there is still preliminary enthusiasm, even though it can be tinged with uncertainty at an adventure into the unknown.

2. *Early unease*

On the outward journey, despite the confident assurance evident among the old hands in the early hours of the trip, it is soon plain that the size of the commitment begins to weigh heavily. Our first youth pilgrimage was to Taizé in Eastern France. On that occasion the coach drive took the best part of two days. Just before we arrived at our destination, the coach stopped, and Norwyn Denny and the two of us were asked to get out and stand by the road sign at the entrance to the village so that a photograph might be taken for the record. Norwyn had been sitting at the back of the coach. He reported to us the anxious, even edgy conversation taking place. The cheery first exchanges among the young pilgrims had led on to questioning about the practices and beliefs of other Churches. Unfamiliar language and ideas seemed to threaten what had until then appeared to be the boundaries of the Christian family. What was being said and heard now seemed a further outreach, well beyond those limits. Were these others, with their strange ways, really brothers and sisters in Christ? In another part of the coach there had even been an attempt to rediscover the loyalties and antipathies of former generations, distinguished by their wearing of the orange or the green.

3. *Discovery in friendship*

It has been important to choose as the place of pilgrimage what may be seen as neutral, if not common, ground, where no denominational group need feel at a disadvantage. This is especially significant in the hours after arrival, when personal contact must give way to friendship through shared experience. Generally, barriers start to be crossed in shared interests; these can be music (the youngsters frequently bring their own cassettes), daily chores, primitive toilets, football, beautiful landscapes, the discussion of human issues, and daily worship. With a group drawn from a variety of backgrounds, it was a surprise to discover that cultural and class divisions seem to prove deeper than denominational differences. This was especially true at Taizé, where we were part of the international youth camp. Students found it easier to cross the barriers posed by language. Working-class young people found this and differences of nationality more difficult to manage. The former were prepared for a lifestyle akin to camping. The latter found meals of mushy peas and of pudding spooned into the hand hard to take. Yet the group hung together increasingly well. Moments of coming together as 'Liverpool' were important to keep our identity and enjoyment alive. One afternoon we felt that we might release some of the group's defensive feelings by offering a coach trip to a nearby town. We asked the Brother, assigned to us by the Taizé community, how far it was to Cluny. 'There is nothing worth seeing at Cluny,' was the reply. The Brother evidently regarded the ruin of the great monastery at Cluny as a symbol of the worst days of wealthy, decadent monasticism. What he did not understand was that the interest in this historic place was purely the hope that a familiar steak and chips could be found there as a relief from mushy peas. For young Liverpudlians, of whatever faith, 'foreign' food is a problem, though it can sometimes help more than theological insight to unite against the common foe.

4. *Awareness of shared roots*

The language and cultural differences experienced at Taizé, together with the desire for common ground, led us first to Iona, off the west coast of Scotland, and two years later to Lindisfarne or Holy Island, off the Northumbrian coast. In both places of pilgrimage our denominationally divided group of Christians was enveloped in the powerful atmosphere of a holy place, where long ago in the undivided Church people had managed to keep the faith in an extremely dangerous world. In both these small islands we saw the place where marauding Vikings had massacred the unarmed monks who had come to the beach to greet them. We were fortunate in being taken on pilgrimage around both these islands by persons able to share with us the history and worship of the locality. The stillness of a beautiful day on Iona helped to provide the perspective of God's presence through all ages. The rough wind of Lindisfarne reminded us what rugged heroes were Aidan, Cuthbert and their friends. As our group of pilgrims made its way around the island – Methodists, United Reformed Church, Salvation Army, Anglicans and Roman Catholics – there was a strange but profound feeling that we were all far more distant in understanding and common experience from those Christians of 1200 years ago than we were from one another. Amidst the variety of experience and practice of Christians today, it was a reminder of the shared roots we all possessed in the one Church of Jesus Christ.

5. *Placed in the context of mission*

While Iona and Lindisfarne inspired us all with the spirit of Cuthbert and Aidan, the worship of Taizé and the rule of life of its ecumenical community consistently challenged us as to how we were to serve the poor of the world. Not that Iona and Lindisfarne could be regarded as places of escape from the hurt and dangers of today's society. Before we went on to the remote islands, we were given on the first night of our pilgrimages welcoming hospitality by the Iona Community in Glasgow and by the Christian Churches in Newcastle. They showed us examples of the Church's commitment and work in their cities. This provided an important context within which we were able to assess our pilgrimage to the holy places of the past. A vivid mental picture remains of the Pilgrim's Way to Holy Island: stakes in the sand and water, marking the route which Aidan and Cuthbert took at low tide as they went out from their firm base of worship and community into the dangerous forests of pagan England. Our experience of a deep living faith in Iona and Lindisfarne helped to show us how faith is to be lived today in Glasgow, Newcastle – and Liverpool.

6. *Impatience at the rules of the Church*

As the pilgrims on these occasions gradually grow together and increasingly want to be together and do everything together, it is inevitably part of the learning process that they should discover both the opportunities to share their beliefs and their prayer, and also the barriers within joint worship which reflect differences in belief. We will have explained at the preliminary session that we do not believe that there is anything to be gained by breaking the rules or disciplines of our Churches. But until the consequences of points of different teaching are experienced, the separation of disunity is not appreciated. The first reaction of the young people is to break down the barrier on the score that it should not be there. There is need for patience all round as they slowly find their way to the point when they question why it *is* there – which often leads to frustrated anger. If, then, they can come through this stage, they may learn how to handle such situations and how to be understanding and sensitive to the beliefs of others. Ideally, this leads to a commitment to work for the fullness of Christian unity, based on present reconciliation and the faith that is already shared.

During these pilgrimages a whole variety of questions is raised for discussion. By the third day it is usually necessary for us to have a long session at which we open ourselves to questioning and often to impatient criticism of the Church. The young people themselves can be torn between their desire to break through the difficulty and their own sense of loyalty to their Church, if it is criticised by someone else. For many it is quite a new experience and a very important part of the whole exercise. Invariably we are both pressed about sharing in Holy Communion. Some of the pilgrims come from Free Church traditions in which Church authority rests in the local congregation, or where all who love the Lord Jesus are welcomed. Others belong to the Salvation Army, which does not have sacraments but believes that every meal is to be kept as a reminder of the Lord.

When these distinctions emerge in the discussions, whether personally in private, or at an open session with ourselves, all the impatience against institutional religion overflows. Voices are raised, and sometimes tears are shed, as we argue that nothing is to be achieved by responding to our natural longing in the middle of a short-term experience, especially if the price is to create a rift within the Church to which we belong. We explain that the Anglican position is that those who are full members of other Christian Churches are welcome to receive Holy Communion at an Anglican celebration of the Eucharist, but that Roman Catholics offer Holy Communion only to members of their own faith. This is invariably a cause of confusion and indignation. We endeavour to explain that the Roman Catholic Church teaches that to receive Holy Communion is a sign not only of communion with Christ, but also of a community of faith, based on unity of belief. Sadly, despite the growing spirit of reconciliation between the Christian Churches today, that full unity of belief has not yet been achieved. We try to restore the balance by reference to the agenda of ARCIC II, where the subject of the mutual recognition of ministries is included. But it has to be said that for most of the young people, in the stress of their first ecumenical encounter, such explanations are not easy to accept. Facing the issue together is for them, as for us, an important part of the pilgrimage.

7. *Joy and pain in worship*

Prayer together as the days go by has a certain healing effect. We try to talk with the young people and the youth chaplains who are with us about how all can be drawn into the principal act of joint worship before we start for home. It usually helps when on succeeding days we all attend each other's celebrations of the Eucharist, according to Roman Catholic, Anglican and Free Church rites. The young people begin to note what we all possess in common, notably the Word of God, so that the task of preparing the final act of worship, where as much as possible is to be shared, becomes easier than might be expected. But even where the liturgy of the Word is concerned, there are different underlying approaches. What the young people prepare is often a rather lengthy amalgam of rites they have known in their own churches.

DAVID SHEPPARD: I have a vivid memory of our last evening in Iona. The young people had prepared and led a liturgy of the Word and the prayers of the people of God in one of the huts of the youth camp where we had all gathered. Then we processed, singing as we went, into the ancient and restored Abbey. Anglicans and Free Church members went into the chapel on one side of the sanctuary, Roman Catholics (accompanied for that occasion by the Salvation Army) to the other, for the great thanksgiving prayer of the Eucharist. After we had received Holy Communion separately, we all came together in the sanctuary before the high altar to share the Peace – a highly emotional moment – and to sing our last hymns together, led by the Salvation Army. The final blessing was given jointly. For many it was an overwhelming experience, reflecting starkly what we share and where we are separated.

DEREK WORLOCK: As we walked away from the Abbey afterwards, I said to David, 'We really must find a way forward together. I found it almost unbearable when, from the other side of the church, I could hear you saying almost exactly the same words as I was.'

8. *Enduring commitment*

The kind of joint, yet separated, celebration we have described is possible only on such an 'enclosed' occasion, when those taking part have been through preliminary experiences such as we have described, understand what is happening, and appreciate the 'so near and yet so far' character of the situation. What they experience in worship reflects much of the relationship between many of the Christian Churches today. On the journey home the talk is all of future contacts and of the desire to persevere in working and praying for Christian unity. In fact the joy and the pain of these pilgrimages has often led to enduring commitment to ecumenical partnership. It is now nine years since the first of these pilgrimages, and both of us still see a number of those ecumenical pilgrims as we move around the area.

On the journey home from each of these pilgrimages we have tried to share with the young people our feelings after what we have experienced together. After Taizé, the first ecumenical pilgrimage, we prepared a joint Declaration, which emphasised the context of mission and included these words:

> The simplicity of life at Taizé has helped us to identify the true priorities of life in our homes, in Merseyside and beyond. Our work together, our discussions and sharing of life and experience with those visiting Taizé from other countries, have enabled us to avoid self-pity in our own problems and to see our commitment within the context of world needs. Above all, our frequent meetings with the Prior of Taizé, Brother Roger Schutz, and with the Brothers of his Community, have increased our understanding of the importance of prayer and Christian witness in daily life.

The demand for copies of this Declaration by the young pilgrims led us, after the visits to Iona and Lindisfarne, to try to put into words on each occasion a rather long pilgrims' prayer, which might remind us all in the future of the feelings which we had experienced together during those days. Extracts now reveal those feelings of those days. The Iona Pilgrims' Prayer includes these lines:

> Lord, we came to Iona committed to the truth:
> a truth expressed in our faith
> which gave us little knowledge, and less understanding
> of the beliefs and traditions of others.
> But, Lord, we found that people like us,
> who do not share our beliefs,
> share our love of you;
> and they also share our impatience
> at some of the obstacles to Christian unity.

We found that we could respect differences,
must respect consciences,
and cannot force the truth by short-cuts
to satisfy our determination and our pride.
Lord, we found that as we acknowledge your way
and humbly meet beneath your cross,
we grow closer to one another in your broken body.
Lord, we know that you are the Way.

The same mood was picked up in only slightly different form
after the pilgrimage to Lindisfarne:

Dear Lord, we made our third ecumenical pilgrimage
as your Christian people kept festival
in honour of the most Blessed Trinity.
We came to the land of Aidan, Cuthbert and Bede –
three saints who had shown us
how to walk in the light of your holy Word.
But, Lord, we had to accept
that we represent at least three different traditions.
In our desire to share so much
we suffered the pain of separation
in that which is most precious to us.
Lord, heal the wounds of our division
in the way that you know best.
As we strive to reflect the perfection of the Trinity,
grant us your gift of Unity.

YOUNG PEOPLE, THE CHURCH OF TODAY

We are very much aware that young people, in addition to being
the hope of tomorrow, are already the Church of today. It is good
that their insights should be taken seriously in their parishes and
local congregations. We are happy that such committed young
people should be the recipients of the experiences we have shared.
They are the bearers of our hopes for the future. We see their
enthusiasm released when they are given the opportunity to serve
the sick and needy, or to take their proper and important place in
worship. There can be no doubt that the uncertainties in life today
gravely affect their willingness to enter into long-term or even
lifetime commitment. Their uncertainties may be related to 'the

bomb', to grave difficulty experienced with regard to employment, or to the frequent breakdowns of human relationships which they observe. This results in a shortage of persons willing to enter a lifetime commitment, whether it be in marriage, the priesthood and religious life, or a life-work of any kind. On the other hand there is nearly always generous willingness to undertake a difficult task, provided that it is for a fixed period, or at least not indefinitely.

Young people expect the Church to be a place where strong convictions are combined with a certain openness. They wish to find in the Church a strong conviction that Christ is risen and is present with the pilgrim in life's journey. They also want to find among Christians an openness to continuing questioning from people of different social, racial or religious positions. They need to feel that, if they are to join life's pilgrimage, their insights and experiences will at least be wanted by the Church. Their fear is lest the Church is living in the past, or is stationary and not on a pilgrimage at all. Personal contact is perhaps the best way of dispelling such fears. The generation gap does not always have to do with age. We believe that we can with a good heart invite young people from the different Christian Churches to come on board for the joint Christian journey of the ecumenical movement. They have their authentic contribution and responsibilities. These must be seen within the context of the life and mission of the whole Church, without being stifled by its long-established ways of doing things. They will ask their own questions and we must be open enough to help them produce the answers which have meaning for their own generation.

DAVID SHEPPARD: Bishops know at least as well as anyone else the bad parts of church life, for when a disaster happens, they send for the bishop! Sometimes the truth about our Churches includes such features as a fearful defensiveness, or rigid assumptions, or preoccupation with 'in-house' religious experience. But that is not the whole picture. The 'poor in spirit', those who 'hunger and thirst after righteousness', the gentle and merciful, and the peacemakers of the Beatitudes are as much in the Church today as they were among the Lord's disciples. My testimony must be that my eighteen years as a bishop have given me a greater experience of the body of Christ than I ever knew before. That experience has been given additional depth as I have come to know and to join hands with Christians from other Churches, who bring the love of Christ into needy parts of the world through the networks of which they are part.

DEREK WORLOCK: Perhaps there is significance in the fact that the Inter-Church Process 1986/7, in which some thirty-three Churches agreed to sit down and discuss their beliefs concerning the nature of the Church, was called Not Strangers but Pilgrims. *Here was a realisation that Christian unity was not to be achieved by the mere reorganisation of the structures of the British Council of Churches, but that first we must all make plain our vision of the Church and of Christianity. In the light of that we would have a better understanding of our relationship with one another, and we would be in a position to see what kind of ecumenical instrument might be needed in the future to service the Churches in their continuing pilgrimage towards unity. On a very large scale it was not altogether unlike the inter-church youth pilgrimages we had made to Taizé, Iona and Lindisfarne.*

In the course of *Not Strangers but Pilgrims* many meetings and discussions took place. It was not a case of talk for talk's sake, but a genuine attempt, in light of a very free exchange, to assess what point had been reached on the Churches' ecumenical journey, and to try to make sure that we were on course. It was evident that some would find it difficult to press on, because they wanted to know not only where they all stood at that moment of assessment, but also with whom they stood, and what would be the ultimate relationship. It is not easy to journey on with unresolved questions still unresolved, and open-ended situations still open-ended. That is a difficult but not altogether unexpected, let alone unauthentic, part of walking by faith. Pope John XXIII is reported to have said to the Vatican astronomer, as he walked in the Vatican gardens beneath the starry sky, 'I am content, like Abraham, to walk ahead in the darkness, one step at a time, but with my hand in the hand of God.' Sometimes that will seem to our young fellow pilgrims slow progress; but it will be important that, as part of the Church of today, they try to ensure that we all go forward together. The uncertainties of our common journey we must entrust to the Holy Spirit. When we look back at how far he has brought us in the last twenty-five years, there is little ground for gloomy suggestions that 'the steam has gone out of ecumenism' and that we can make no more progress.

Some years ago now, Doctor Robert McAfee Brown, a Presbyterian professor of theology in the United States, set out some 'Ground-rules for Dialogue'. His sixth and final ground-rule was that 'each partner must recognise that all that can be done with dialogue is to offer it up to God'. While unity is the ultimate goal for which Christians are striving, they must not be too set in their ideas as to the form it will take. 'If we are immediately impatient for results,' wrote Doctor Brown, 'we will simply have to learn something about the patience of God – or we will try his patience further . . . No Christian is entitled to believe only what is humanly possible. We have to affirm that "With man it is impossible, but with God all things are possible"' (*The Commonweal*, 1960).

THE INWARD JOURNEY

It would be quite wrong for us to write of 'The Journey Forward' without our stressing the importance of prayer. There can be no real hope of meeting in Christ without our seeking to recognise Christ's presence within ourselves and in the circumstances of those we endeavour to serve. In this book we have linked the approach to Christian unity with the need for Christian partnership in trying to bring healing and justice to those who suffer in society today, especially in situations of urban deprivation. For us, the unity and renewal of the Church and the unity and renewal of the human community are inextricably bound together. Religion can be a sham unless we are seeking a deeper knowledge of God, and striving to bring about a greater degree of justice in the whole nation. Nowadays we speak of the inward journey and the outward journey. The late Father John Dalrymple, the much sought-after spiritual director in Edinburgh, once wrote:

> The journey inwards is the journey from the issues of this world towards God. It is a journey towards the mind of Christ, beyond feelings of expediency or fear of what people will say, to truth itself. It is followed by the journey outwards, back from the depths where we meet God, to the issues facing us in our everyday life, a journey which we now undertake with a new sensitivity to the will of God in all things.
>
> (John Dalrymple, *The Longest Journey*, DLT, 1979)

This distinction well fits our double theme.

The inward journey to the knowledge of God, towards the mind of Christ, includes a deepening knowledge of ourselves. This is beautifully described in Psalm 139:

> Yahweh, you examine me and know me,
> you know when I sit, when I rise,
> you understand my thoughts from afar.
> You have traced *my journey* and my resting places,
> you know every detail of my conduct.

A word is not yet on my tongue
before you, Yahweh, know all about it.

You knew me through and through,
my being held no secrets from you
when I was being formed in secret,
textured in the depths of the earth.
(vv. 1–4, 14b–15; adapted from NJB and NEB)

This psalm reveals the depth of God's knowledge as we journey to him to confess our feelings, to share our thoughts so that we may know his mind. We do not have to tell him the facts themselves. All our experience, alone or together, all our moods, our 'highs', our 'lows', all our personal journeyings, are known to God. They matter to God and can be the raw material of our spiritual life. Often it is in prayer together that we reveal ourselves and our yearnings. Increasingly, leaders of the Churches are devoting more and more of their time together to prayer and spiritual reflection. There can be certain inhibitions. Many of us have been brought up in a particularly English form of Christianity in which we have learnt to keep our innermost feelings to ourselves. It was sturdy Christian manliness to stand on one's own two feet. More than that, the suppression of our deepest feelings from the notice of others often led to our failure to admit our own feelings even to ourselves. But this spiritual stoicism does not accord with the New Testament, which speaks about bearing one another's burdens in the body of Christ.

We have already spoken of the strength which comes from mutual support and spiritual sharing. Prayer itself is sometimes described nowadays as sharing one's thoughts with Christ. Even this process can in certain circumstances be carried out by persons together. The stress in recent years on community prayer has often been criticised as being detrimental to private or personal prayer. The two are not exclusive. Personal prayer can prepare an individual to take part in community prayer, just as the latter can set minds and hearts in the right disposition in which to engage in personal prayer. Shared prayer, whether shared by two persons or a prayer group, lies somewhere between community prayer and private prayer. For two individuals it will as a rule mean spontaneous prayer aloud, a sharing with another person of those thoughts and aspirations we are encouraged to share with Christ: trying to see with his eyes, so that we may be drawn into the closest union of all, in him. In one sense it is spiritual communion, the perfect sharing which adds a spiritual dimension to common purpose.

Over the years we have prayed together in shared moments of adoration and informal worship. We have prayed together before entering the office of a government minister, or in a studio before a difficult radio or television interview, or before going out into church or hall in response to a demand for the 'double act'. As we shall record at the end of this chapter, we have on one memorable occasion prayed together by the wayside on life's pilgrimage, sharing a search for guidance as to the way forward.

Prayer which the two of us share, even on the inward journey, is almost always in the context of the needs of the wider community we are called to serve. During these years there have been times when it has felt as though Liverpool were under siege. The level of stress on many sides has been very high, and we have felt its pressure. The content of our prayers has sometimes included the threatened closure of factories, with the kind of death which redundancy means for so many men and women; at others, brittle relationships between police and communities; at others again, people's sheer sense that they have been deserted. As bishops, we have often felt ourselves in between two fires. Trying to stand close to those who are constantly bearing stress of this kind has led us back to our meeting-point at the cross. Here we have learnt again that the Suffering Servant is very close to all of us in the hurt city.

As on our inward journey we try to thread our daily lives with prayer, we discover the comfort and encouragement that come from this openness with God. The psalms, which were the prayers of Jesus, enable us to pour out to the Lord our very human feelings. The psalmist lets out all his deepest emotions, good and bad. These include fear, grief and anger, deep desire and physical happiness. The prayer which Jesus taught his disciples tells us that on our inward journey we can face our Father, with thoughts and words uncensored, not afraid to disclose the dark side of our inner selves, nor to admit moments of failure. We know that we are accepted as we are by a loving Father. This gives us confidence in our search for the unity for which his Son prayed. Despite the deep hatreds and suspicions of the past, new hope is born on the inward journey, because the love and forgiveness of the Lord surmount the hesitant yet impatient gropings of uncertain hearts.

THE COMMUNION OF SAINTS

On the journey inward, as in our ecumenical pilgrimages with young people, we discover the heroes and heroines of the past who have helped to lay the trail we seek to follow. This was evident with the young people who learnt much of St Columba in Iona, and of St Aidan, St Cuthbert and St Bede in the North-East. These chosen ones of God ceased to be shadowy figures from the pages of ecclesiastical history and assumed the role of guides in whose footsteps we were now enabled to tread. Lifted above our differences, they became part of our common heritage, and in the lands where they lived and prayed we were all equally at home. In choosing the destination of these pilgrimages, it has been important – as we suggested earlier – to avoid those places where some members of the group might feel at a disadvantage, or not so much at home as others.

For the Roman Catholic young people, many of whom may perhaps be used to making an annual visit to Lourdes with the archdiocesan pilgrimage from Liverpool, this careful choice of somewhere else has needed some explanation. A young person usually finds it much easier to be active than just to 'be there'. At Lourdes 'Les Rouges', as the Liverpool youth are known from the colour of their T-shirts, are renowned for the long hours of strenuous and cheerful service they give to the many sick pilgrims. Quite understandably they would love to share that experience with their new-found friends. But if a place can be identified with one particular denomination, so can devotion to the saints. Until recently this applied more sharply to Mary, the Mother of Jesus, than to any other whose memory we may encounter on the inward journey of life's pilgrimage. Hopefully, as we may see today from the membership of the Ecumenical Society of the Blessed Virgin Mary, even this centuries-old misunderstanding is closer to being resolved.

DAVID SHEPPARD: Our chapel at Bishop's Lodge is furnished simply, the holy table in polished wood reflects the panelling of the lower part of the room's walls. We have two aids to worship on those walls. Centrally there is a plain wooden cross, and on the side wall there is an icon painting of the Virgin Mary and her child. I was given the painting by colleagues several years ago, and am glad at its presence in our daily worship. It helps the reality of the Communion of Saints to come alive, with a strong awareness of belonging to the Church of all the ages.

I have long enjoyed the picture of an athletics stadium, inspired by the letter to the Hebrews. We are on the running track, with the 'great cloud of witnesses' in the stands, cheering us on. We are to 'run with resolution the race for which we are entered, our eyes fixed on Jesus, on whom faith depends from start to finish' (Heb. 12:1, 2, NEB). The Protestant part of me has always wanted to keep Jesus absolutely without rival, at the centre of my faith, as the one mediator who brings us to the Father. The first account of the Church in the Acts of the Apostles includes Mary, the Mother of Jesus, present with the eleven apostles. In the same way, Mary's presence in the cloud of witnesses brings a particular kind of support to people in a hurt city like Liverpool. She knew what it meant to stand by, apparently helpless, while crucifixion slowly and cruelly drained away the life of her son. Her continuing faith and obedience in the face of such suffering is a witness which helps when attempt after attempt to bring about simple justice is brushed aside. As was the case with Mary, sometimes there is nothing we can do but continue to be there.

The picture in our chapel stands also for the high calling God has for women. The greatest task ever entrusted to a member of the Church was given to a young woman. Her sensitivity to the Holy Spirit, her obedience to God's call, her keeping faith with her Son all the way to his death – like so many mothers – provide a model to which I find myself repeatedly returning. Faced with a future that was mysterious and unknown, she responded, 'Here am I. I am the Lord's servant; as you have spoken, so be it' (Luke 1:38 NEB). The words of the Magnificat are not only based on Hannah's song before Samuel's birth. They are full of the insights of the great prophets, whose writings were to mean so much to Jesus, with the confidence that the humble and the hungry are lifted up and satisfied with good things. We are one with the communion of all the saints from the very beginning, and we are to be open to the callings which the Holy Spirit may have for us in the neediest parts of Liverpool.

DEREK WORLOCK: The traditional devotion of Catholics to the Blessed Virgin Mary is rooted in Christ's gift of his own mother from the cross to St John and through him to all Christians. It is impossible to think of the incarnate Son of God except with a mother, and in fact we know nothing of her save in the context of our Saviour. This is not extravagant theology, nor indeed extravagant language. In the summer of 1987 I heard Pope John Paul describe Mary as 'the humble woman of the people of Israel and Christ's first disciple . . .' Although, because of the words from the cross, some theologians like to speak of her as 'Mother of the Church', I prefer to think of her as a member of the Church. Indeed during the Second Vatican Council there was at first a proposal that there should be a special document or decree devoted to Our Lady. The English bishops led the move to abandon treating her in this way, separately from the document on the Church, and were successful in ensuring that the special document was dropped, and the subject of her relationship with Christ and with Christians dealt with as a chapter in Lumen Gentium, *the Constitution on the Church. This was no easy task, as I discovered when trying to talk about our proposal to bishops from Latin countries. Emotions are rightly strong where Mary is concerned; but in the end our argument won the day.*

Early in 1987, Pope John Paul II wrote an encyclical letter, Redemptoris Mater, *on 'The Blessed Virgin Mother in the life of the pilgrim Church'. Suitably enough for this chapter, the Pope dealt with 'The Church's journey and the unity of all Christians'. He wrote: 'By a more profound study of both Mary and the Church, clarifying each by the light of the other, Christians who are eager to do what Jesus tells them will be able to go forward together on "this pilgrimage of faith".'*

'Pope John Paul also deals squarely with the question of the one Mediator, which in essence is as important to Roman Catholics as it is to others. 'The Church knows and teaches with St Paul that there is only one mediator,' writes the Pope, quoting from the first letter to Timothy: 'For there is one God, and there is one mediator between God and men, the man Christ Jesus, who gave himself as a ransom for all' (1 Tim. 2:5, 6 RSV). 'The maternal role of Mary towards people in no way obscures or diminishes the unique mediation of Christ, but rather shows its power; it is mediation in Christ.' A clear distinction is made between the mediation of Christ, and the intercession of his mother, as we see in the account of her pleading with Jesus on behalf of the young couple in trouble at Cana when the wine ran out.

THE OUTWARD JOURNEY

All the efforts to achieve Christian unity will add up to no more than a busy, highly-organised, institutional amalgam of Christian communities and Churches unless there is at the same time an inward journey towards the mind and mystery of Christ through prayer and the Christian life. On the other hand, the result will be inward-looking, preoccupied with our own 'churchy' experiences, unless there is also an outward journey into God's world. The journey Christians are to make together must continue in the context of mission, with a consciousness of God sending us out into the world.

There is of course real sadness and pain in the fact that, although we make the inward journey together, we are separated in the Eucharist which is central to the reconciliation and healing which we find in Christ. We pray together that here too, in the years that are left to us, we may yet be united. At the present time certain outstanding differences of doctrine and discipline are under examination by ARCIC II. But our vision of unity must include a common baptism, a shared Eucharist, shared ministry and shared mission. In the meantime, apart in this matter of great consequence to us, together we take the world's needs and hopes for unity with us in our straining to find the way forward. Built up by prayer and by eucharistic living, we trace the outward journey together in the spirit of the Risen Lord.

The two-way journey is to be recognised in the twin theme of the Old Testament prophets, who spoke of the knowledge of God and of his concern that justice should reign in his whole Kingdom. Both inward and outward journeys may be pressing, but they are not always equally attractive, nor easily understood. Part of the mission of the Church is, by the evidence of its priorities, to be a reminder of different values. We are often praised for the step forward we may be taking in bringing our Churches closer. We are much less popular, and are accused of being disturbers of the peace, when we question the basis of our nation's pursuit of prosperity for the majority at the price, as we see it, of the exclusion of a sizeable minority of the people.

It was put to us in plain terms by a senior Roman Catholic layman in a discussion following dinner in a London club with a group of his colleagues: 'We like what you two do in leading the Churches closer together. But we think that you are both rather "lefty"!' The point was challenged by an equally distinguished Roman Catholic layman, who said that he was sure that Jesus Christ would probably also have been classified as 'lefty' in that company. When he was Executive Officer of the Anglican Communion in the 1960s, Bishop John Howe travelled widely and said at that time that he believed that the Church in our day would be judged on whether or not it was seen to stand up for justice. It is hard for anyone to take exception to great Christian words like justice, peace, reconciliation. Yet to try to bring reconciliation to a polarised society risks being attacked from both sides. That does not mean that conflict can always be avoided. All points of view are not equally valid. Standing for justice can mean on occasion taking sides. It can mean supporting one side or the other in particular political arguments, though without endorsing any one party's political programme.

If, as is often the case, we are accused of being political, we like to respond with the words used at Puebla in 1979 by a South American bishop, Mgr Schmitz Sauerborn. On that occasion some persons claimed that they were scandalised by the possible adoption by bishops of certain aspects of Marxism. He replied: 'Let him who is without an ideology cast the first stone.' If a Christian claims to be non-political, it seems fair to interpret that as meaning either that the status quo is acceptable, or that the way the nation is ordered is of no concern to God. It is necessary to test certain ideologies against the gospels. For example, the creation of wealth is good, but Jesus gave a sharp warning against that becoming the prime purpose of life: 'You cannot serve God and money' (Matt. 6:24 NEB).

Those who derive most benefit from our competitive, consumerist society often expect the Church to be a defender of standards which they see as making for success. For such people the crucial values of Christianity are self-reliance, discipline, responsibility, high standards of excellence. Sadly their attitudes towards those whom they regard as unsuccessful misfits are inclined to be punitive and fearful. We too wish to affirm self-discipline, excellence, responsibility, but we come by a different route, a long way round, which is often costly. The gospel of Jesus Christ begins with valuing all people. It is about acceptance, forgiveness, hope, new life, love. As hurt people feel themselves valued, they begin to experience the challenge to responsibility and excellence. Many successful people are impatient of that long way round. They even see it as a threat to the established order or their sectional interest. They accuse us of encouraging the poor and disadvantaged to expect further state help rather than stressing self-reliance. Nevertheless we find hope in the fact that many more parts of the Church seem ready to stand in the firing line on issues of justice. The more united the witness, the greater will be the pressure on governments to change their priorities. But we have to remember that the Servant of the Lord, who is our model for the Church, became the Suffering Servant, despised and rejected.

SIGNS OF HOPE AMIDST HURT

What signs of hope can we detect on this outward journey to everyday life in a hurt city? We must never romanticise about poverty, nor even about its victims, the poor themselves. The mystery of evil persists in urban priority areas as much as in unacceptable attitudes in the world of big business. Christians must not fall for the temptation of identifying evil and injustice with one group, be it social class, profession, trade or political party. Bitter rivalry between one community group and another can be a distinctive feature in an area of deprivation, especially where there is competition for limited resources. Any community development can be narrowly partisan unless its goals are clearly defined and of broad benefit. Amidst such pressures and dangers, where do we look for hope? Must such pitfalls and snares reduce our outward journeyings to inertia or pessimism? Desperation is not the same thing as despair, nor suffering the same as defeat. The hurt is very great and we would not be true to ourselves if we did not try to share it.

The mystery of evil continues, but another mystery can overcome it: the mystery of Christ's presence at the very heart of the hurt itself. Just as we try on the journey inward to increase our knowledge and understanding of Christ's suffering, so on the outward journey we become aware that he is beckoning us to join him in compassion and to stay present with his enduring love where the hurt is keenest. Compassion which adds the perspective of the cross does not deny the need for practical relief. Nor yet does it obscure the hope which flickers again at the rediscovery of hidden or unconscious faith.

The whole scene becomes more poignant and yet more hopeful when presented in personal terms. One of our clergy wrote recently:

The pain comes from the efforts being made by friends, those I love, to move but one pace forward in asserting human dignity. Why should this child have to suffer so much to gain one small measure of respect? Why should the members of this family endure such acute stress from causes which are beyond their control? Why should my black brother or sister have to fight for equal acceptance in a world which boasts equality for all?

We have often to answer questions about the balancing signs of hope, to provide examples matching the catalogue of distress which may otherwise seem to threaten the future of Merseyside and its people. Just as it is the repeated, small but personal blows which knock away present supports and the opportunities for future initiative, so our answer has to rest upon frequent, if small instances of personal example. Hopefully, in time the signs of hope engendered by such example can be brought to increase by major industrial or commercial projects in which they may grow to fulfilment and stability. Small as they are, in one sense, we would wish to record some of them against the day when their present significance may be lost in the light of more spectacular events:

- The love and self-sacrifice of a mother, insisting on values for her children after other parents have given up.
- Clergy faithfully visiting and caring for families, the disadvantaged, the elderly, and handicapped, whether thanks or acknowledgment are forthcoming or not.
- Lay Christians accepting responsibility in their parish or community.
- Spontaneous moments of real celebration in a community festival.
- The indignation and persistent representation by community leaders when the real needs of those they represent are ignored.
- The willingness of some MPs, councillors and local representatives to listen to angry criticism and to respond even when a successful outcome is most unlikely.
- The determination of those bearing the burden of management to preserve their involvement in Merseyside.
- The refusal of teachers and youth leaders to accept failure or to lessen their faith in young people.
- The fair-mindedness of many police officers under extreme pressures.
- The generosity with time and cash of the relatively poor to give help to their neighbours who may be facing tragedy.
- The concern of the disadvantaged for the poor in Third World countries.
- The resilience and wit of Merseysiders who refuse to allow repeated disappointments to sour their spirits.
- The trusting partnership between Christians of different traditions and communities, who would once have seen each other only as rivals or enemies.

Even though we cannot speak with easy optimism of the future of Merseyside – there would have to be a great shift in national priorities to enable us to do that – we are able to recognise in these small examples real signs of hope. As may be seen, they rest with people. To encourage such people is central to our task.

DAVID SHEPPARD: Some time ago I gave a series of lectures in Liverpool on 'The Divine Bias for the Losers'. Subsequently I was taken to task by a post-graduate student at the university. He admitted that I had described the realities of life in the city quite truthfully; but he claimed that all I had to offer was 'flickers of hope'. If I had really believed in the power of God, he said, I 'ought to have been talking about great streams of light'. I understood his challenge very well. But on Good Friday there were no obvious streams of light. Many parts of Merseyside today are facing Good Friday situations. If we can notice and share even flickers of hope, it may help to encourage others not to give up.

OUR PARABLE OF ASSISI

We have written of both the inward journey and the outward journey. Each needs the other if commitment is to be sustained and life itself is to take on the character of pilgrimage. One journey we undertook had this character, but it also bore the lessons of a parable.

It must be said that our pilgrimage together to Assisi in 1985 was a long time in the making. It began with a postcard in October 1983, sent en route to a synod in Rome. It read: 'We need to share the spirit of St Francis, still very much alive here. Derek.' This produced the reply: 'If you are serious, perhaps in two or three years' time. David.' Then as now, diaries held a dominant place in our lives. But the seed was sown and planning began. It is never easy for us both to be away from Liverpool for any considerable length of time, but we marked down a carefully chosen fortnight towards the end of September 1985. The precise choice of date was made twelve months in advance, at a time when so many things that were good for Merseyside were taking place. But there followed a period of grave reversal in the fortunes of the area. The abolition of the Merseyside County Council was enacted, the football tragedy took place in Brussels, and the Militant Tendency embarked on its course of confrontation with central government. The summer months passed, with their spate of engagements. Increasingly we looked forward to what was becoming in anticipation a pilgrimage in search of unity and peace, and a renewal of the spirit likely to be needed in the future.

As the date of departure drew near, Liverpool's problems came to a head. The District Auditor served notice on most of the Labour councillors, alleging that their delay in making the rate had deprived the city of funds and amounted to wilful misconduct. We were not to know that the long-anticipated legal process was to take some twenty months. The crash, which the Council's collision course made inevitable, seemed at hand. Against such a background, could we reasonably undertake our pilgrimage to Assisi? We consulted our advisers and were told that it was unlikely that the city would grind to a halt through bankruptcy before October. By then we should be back. Pilgrimage was to be combined with some days of holiday, with Grace Sheppard and John Furnival. So we left a series of telephone numbers with our immediate aides and set out for Assisi, by way of Siena, and a small coastal resort for some days of sunshine, swimming and rest.

The sun shone. Liverpool faded into the distance. Late one September evening we drove across the Umbrian plain to the hillside town of St Francis, the world's most famous advocate of simple poverty and peace. That night the four of us made our way up to the great basilica, and then down into the crypt and the simple tomb of *Il Poverello*. There large crowds of Italians, men, women and children, claimed their national patron saint as their own.

We stood well back and tried to pray. What had we come for? Why especially Assisi? Like most men and women we desired peace in the world. We wanted to understand better the implications of the famous prayer of St Francis, for ourselves and perhaps especially for the people of Liverpool. We wanted time to pray together for unity among all Christians. Most of all, we sought in these hallowed surroundings to know God's will for us and the path we should follow together in the future, in order to build upon the covenanted friendship and relationship existing between us. We needed this opportunity to 'come apart awhile' and to reflect on a possible way forward.

Next morning we set aside three hours to explore the basilica. We found the Cimabue portrait of Francis, humble, small, simple and strong, almost tucked away on a side wall in the lower church. Then we climbed to the upper church, with its great Giotto frescoes, telling the story of this Umbrian merchant's son who had shown the world a new way of life in poverty and simplicity. Perhaps a little self-consciously, each of the four of us wandered off alone to discover and wallow for a while in some treasure which spoke to our devotion as well as to artistic choice.

DEREK WORLOCK: David went in search of Old Testament scenes, disturbed a little by his difficulty in finding the prophets. Grace was enchanted to discover, hidden away in the monastic cloister, the majestic features of a thirteenth-century portrait of God the Creator. I spotted John Furnival lost in wonder before the fresco of Francis preaching to the birds. Not for the first time I chuckled at another fresco nearby, showing Pope Innocent III asleep in bed, dreaming of Francis, who is shown holding up with his shoulder the toppling basilica of St John Lateran. 'It is surely this one', said the Pope, 'who will bolster up the Church, and sustain her with his work and doctrine.'

When we met at the doors of the basilica at lunch time we were full of our personal discoveries, which had been more of a spiritual experience than a visit to an art gallery. We made our way to a restaurant in search of pasta, peaches, figs and cheese. Liverpool and its problems seemed miles away. Was this the disengagement from the affairs of the city which we needed?

When in mid-afternoon we returned to our hotel we found a telephone message from Paul Thompson, the Roman Catholic Information Officer at Liverpool. Matters civic and political were deteriorating. The media were seeking comments and our absence had been noted. Our advisers had met that morning and decided that we ought to try get home by the end of that week. It would take three hard days of driving to reach Liverpool. We agreed to be back by Sunday night. That would give us just one more day to complete our pilgrimage to Assisi.

There is no end of basilicas to be seen in the little town, and places especially associated with Francis. We decided to give most of the next day to the small church of San Damiano, set in the hillside between Assisi and the plain stretched out below. Here it was that, before the now famous crucifix, St Francis heard the words: 'Go, Francis, and rebuild my house which, as you see, is falling into ruin.' It seems that at first he took the words literally and, with some of his early followers, tried to restore materially the chapel which is at the heart of the buildings today. Now it is looked after by a community of Francisan monks, who also care for the monastery with its very picturesque cloister.

There it was that the next morning we sat and rested a while after some moments of prayer before the crucifix. We needed to collect our thoughts before the journey home. The contrast of our idyllic surroundings with the Liverpool scene to which we must return was obvious. Was the message entrusted to Francis irrelevant to the Servant Church in the hurt city? How far was it possible or desirable to separate the spiritual thrust of our ministry from the need to seek an answer to the material problems blighting the lives of many we must serve in the inner city? As we meditated in the cloister garden, our peace was shattered by a hammer used to repair a blocked drainpipe, and by the excited laughter of youthful pilgrims in search of Franciscan joy.

After a time we abandoned our vantage point and made our way up a rough track through the olive-groves behind and above the monastery. The view was spectacular, the solitude and the silence were apparently complete. The four of us sat down beside the track, unaware at first that we were but a few feet away from a wayside Calvary. The significance of the olive-trees on the hillside was not lost on us. One by one, and then as a group, we prayed that we might be faithful, hopefully together, wherever the Lord might be leading us.

It was when Grace persuaded us to sing some verses of a hymn that we noticed that our seclusion was over. A group of about twenty pilgrims approached, following our path up the side of the hill. They seemed oblivious to us, or at least uninterested in us, as they passed uphill and out of sight. As we resumed our prayer, another group appeared. And then another. It was as if the whole panorama of life's pilgrimage was passing before us: a parable of a busy world hurrying past a Church preoccupied with its own prayers.

At last a young boy straggler at the back of a group stopped to look at us, four strangers sitting by the side of the track. He called out a question but in a tongue we could not understand. John Furnival tried him in Italian, French and Spanish, but to no avail. Try as we might, we could neither understand nor make ourselves understood. Eventually the young boy ran off after the others, evidently perplexed and perhaps a little angry. What *was* the Lord saying to us?

It was time to return. We took one last look at the Calvary. But the figure on the crucifix did not need to speak to us. We knew quite plainly that we must go back together to face the challenge of our hurt city, now in crisis.

Or, like the disciples, were we being called to go with him 'up to Jerusalem'?

INDEX